1950

TELEVISION PROGRAMMING ACROSS NATIONAL BOUNDARIES:

The EBU and OIRT Experience

TELEVISION PROGRAMMING ACROSS NATIONAL BOUNDARIES:

The EBU and OIRT Experience

Ernest Eugster

The Poynter Institute
For Media Studies

Copyright© 1983.
ARTECH HOUSE, INC.
610 Washington St.
Dedham, MA 02026

All rights reserved. Printed and bound in the United States of America. No part of this book may be reproduced or utilized in any form or by any means, electronic or mechanical, including photocopying, recording, or by any information storage and retrieval system, without permission in writing from the publisher.

International Standard Book Number: 0-89006-128-9
Library of Congress Catalog Card Number: 83-071835

To Suzanne

CONTENTS

Foreword	*xi*
Acknowledgements	*xvii*
Introduction	*xix*

1 PROGRAM EXCHANGES AND THE STATE — 1
1.1 International Television Exchanges — 1
1.2 Aims of Exchanges — 3
1.3 Variations in Controlling National Television Broadcasting — 5
1.4 International Control of Television — 17
1.5 Conclusion — 18
    Endnotes — 19

2 THE IBU EXPERIMENT — 29
2.1 Establishment and Structure — 29
2.2 The Years of Growth: 1925-38 — 32
2.3 The Years of Conflict: 1939-45 — 37
2.4 The Years of Defeat and Rebirth: 1946-50 — 39
2.5 Conclusion — 46
    Endnotes — 47

3 INSIDE THE EBU AND OIRT — 57
3.1 Purposes — 57
3.2 Membership — 59
3.3 General Assemblies — 61
3.4 Administrative Councils — 62
3.5 EBU and OIRT Secretariats — 64
3.6 Specialized Committees — 67
3.7 EBU and OIRT Finances — 80
3.8 Relations with Other International Organizations — 82
3.9 Conclusion — 83
    Endnotes

4 EUROVISION AND INTERVISION OPERATIONS — 95
4.1 Eurovision — 95
4.2 Intervision — 104
4.3 Eurovision-Intervision Links — 106
4.4 Administrative and Technical Coordination — 109
4.5 Eurovision and Intervision Finances — 117
4.6 Conclusion — 121
    Endnotes — 122

5	**EUROVISION PROGRAMMING**	**133**
5.1	Eurovision Traffic	133
5.2	Eurovision Program Exchange	142
5.3	Eurovision News Exchange	150
5.4	Conclusion	156
	Endnotes	157
6	**INTERVISION PROGRAMMING**	**165**
6.1	Intervision Traffic	165
6.2	Intervision Program Exchange	171
6.3	Intervision News Exchange	174
6.4	Conclusion	178
	Endnotes	178
7	**EUROVISION — INTERVISION PROGRAMMING**	**183**
7.1	Eurovision-Intervision Traffic	181
7.2	Eurovision-Intervision Program Exchange	187
7.3	Eurovision-Intervision News Exchange	190
7.4	Conclusion	196
	Endnotes	197
8	**PROBLEMS AND PROSPECTS**	**201**
8.1	Problems	201
8.2	Prospects for the Future	204
	APPENDICES	**209**
	Appendix A Members of the IBU	209
	Appendix B Members of the EBU	214
	Appendix C Members of the OIRT	219
	Appendix D Members of Eurovision	221
	Appendix E Members of Intervision	223
	Appendix F Growth of the Eurovision Program Exchange 1954-1982	224
	Appendix G Growth of the Eurovision News Exchange 1960-1982	225
	Appendix H Type of Eurovision Programs	226
	Appendix I Growth of the Intervision Program Exchange 1960-1982	227
	Appendix J Growth of the Intervision News Exchange 1964-1982	228
	Appendix K Type of Intervision Programs	229
	Appendix L Growth of the Eurovision-Intervision Program Exchange 1960-1982	230

Appendix M	Growth of the Eurovision-Intervision News Exchange 1966-1982	231
Appendix N	Type of Eurovision-Intervision Programs 1972-1982	232
Appendix O	Origins of Intervision Programs 1960-1982	233

LIST OF ACRONYMS   **235**

BIBLIOGRAPHY   **239**

FOREWORD

For two decades after the Second World War, mankind was devoted, at least in principle, to the concept of a free flow of information across national boundaries. If people had sufficient knowledge of other nations and their cultures, so the argument went, the result would be mutual understanding and ultimately the substitution of peace for war among nations. The concept was written into the UNESCO Constitution when it was created in 1945 and in the 1948 Universal Declaration of Human Rights, which established the right of everyone to "see, receive, and impart information and ideas through any media regardless of frontiers."

Mass communications were considered to play a primary role in this process. Program exchanges were initiated and studies were commissioned by organizations such as UNESCO to find out how radio and television could best be used to promote the free flow of information. Technical agencies, including the International Telecommunication Union (ITU), labored valiantly to eliminate problems that stood in the way of achieving the overall goal.

In the past two decades, however, there has been a retreat from the free flow of information concept, primarily because of the revolutionary change that has occurred in the international political system. Approximately 60 nations were responsible for initiating the free flow concept in the 1940s. Today, there are about 160 nations eager to participate. The vast majority of the newer nations are in the process of development, and their objectives and needs are drastically different from those of the older group of nations. With regard to the free flow of information, the newer members of the international community feel that the existing flow of information is weighted heavily on the side of the developed countries. The developing nations are mainly recipients of information from the richer nations; that situation is likely to continue into the forseeable future because of the lack of telecommunications facilities and the funds to maintain them. Many of the developing countries are actually convinced that if the old principle of a free flow of information is perpetuated, it could lead to what has been called electronic colonialism.

As a result, the concept of a free flow of information has received a series of setbacks. These include demands by developing countries for the substitution of a "balanced" flow of information between the developed and the developing nations of the world for the older concept of "free" flow in UNESCO. The balanced flow concept, it is argued, would allow restrictions on incoming information to achieve the equilibrium in question. Another manifestation of the same principle is the demand in the United Nations Commission for the Peaceful Uses of Outer Space for the adoption of a rule that would make it necessary to obtain a country's "prior consent" before sending a program directly to its viewers by satellite. One could also include the proposal that was made at the ITU's 1982 Plenipotentiary Conference to condone the use of jamming techniques to stop unwanted shortwave broadcasts. Fortunately, this proposal was not passed, but interest in the measure was shown by a number of delegations.

The one bright spot in this darkening picture is the European radio and television program exchange system so ably portrayed in this book by Ernest Eugster. For over half a century that system has enabled a large, heterogeneous group of states to exchange television news and entertainment programs across national borders on a regular basis. Not only has the system continued to grow over the years, but the benefits have been such as to permit it to survive the schism that occurred between West European and East European states after World War II. Although at that time two organizations were formed in place of the previous one, arrangements were made almost immediately for the exchange of programs between them.

I submit that, with some minor modifications, the European program exchange experiment could have universal application. It could provide an efficient and reliable system for the exchange of programs between all of the nations of the world and, at the same time, put a stop to the present drift toward electronic isolationism.

The European experiment in program exchange has a number of characteristics that make it eminently attractive for this purpose. In the first place, it involves a series of pay-offs for all those who are associated. As the main supplier of programs for exchange, the larger countries gain both prestige and profit from having their programs used by the other members. Since television audiences have a voracious and insatiable appetite for programs, it is almost impossible for the smaller nations to produce enough to take care of their most minimal needs. The exchange, therefore, gives them access to programs that they would be unable to produce themselves. In addition, both large and small members benefit from being a part of a larger segment that can present a common front in contract negotiations with artist and musician groups.

The European system also provides an efficient and effective method of facilitating program exchange. The administrative headquarters of the European Broadcasting Union (EBU) in Geneva is a model of efficiency where offers and acceptances of programming are made known in the shortest possible time. Members are speedily informed which of their programs are being requested and which programs of other members are available for them to use. For news programs, the efficiency of the process is especially important.

The EBU's technical headquarters in Brussels is also a model of efficiency. The most practical routes for program exchange are worked out quickly and effectively, and the attendant technical problems are solved with dispatch. As the technology of telecommunications continues to advance, there is an excellent possibility that the process will become even more efficient.

The one aspect of the European experiment that seems to have contributed the most to its success is its organizational structure. In the first place, the membership criteria are such to permit the participation of any national broadcasting entity as long as it has official sanction. In the case of the EBU, this means that private operating agencies can participate in its work on the same basis as those that are government-controlled. Although there is some flexibility in the membership criteria of the International Radio and Television Organization (OIRT), most of its members are agencies of a central government. The important point is, of course, that membership in each of these organizations tends to reflect the political systems of the countries involved.

Another important aspect of the European experiment that has contributed a great deal to its success, and one that is related to the above, is the semisecretive nature of the whole process. Although there are certain events (such as championship soccer matches) that the viewers come to expect, the vast majority of the programs that are available for exchange are known only to the broadcasting entities involved. As a result, members retain firm control over the number and types of foreign programs that are shown over networks.

As we can see, the European program exchange offers a great many advantages with few, if any, attendant risks.

The first step in applying the European system to the rest of the world would be to create viable regional broadcasting unions for other regions. The existing ones mentioned in this book could be reorganized and strengthened and new ones established. There would be no maximum or minimum number of such unions; the exact number would be determined solely on the basis of compatibility of interests of the nations involved. A union could be formed on the basis of a common political ideology, a geographical affinity, a similar stage of economic development, or any other consideration that a particular group of countries may feel is appropriate.

Each regional union would have its own administrative center. The principal tasks of the center would be receiving program offers from members of the regional organization and bringing those offers to the attention of the other members. The staff would be held to the minimum necessary to process offers and acceptances in a rapid and efficient manner.

Each regional union would also establish a technical center, which would occupy itself with all details concerning routing of transmissions, including the determination of how costs should be shared. The regional technical center could be located in the same city where the administrative center is located to keep down costs; it could be in a different country if the politics of the situation should dictate.

The actual structure of the regional unions should be as simple or elaborate as the membership wishes. It could consist of only administrative and technical centers or it could also include technical, legal, and program study committees as in the case of the EBU and the OIRT. The entire membership could meet on an annual basis or even once every four years to discuss the progress of the organization as interest and finances dictate.

Of utmost importance would be to give the governments involved complete discretion in the designation of the actual broadcasting entity that will participate in the work of the union. It would also be essential to keep the program offer and acceptance procedure non-public. For countries that have had little experience in such endeavors, these two conditions are necessary in order to inspire the confidence to make the scheme successful.

The centerpiece of a new worldwide system would be a new organization, which could be named the Universal Broadcasting Union (UBU), to facilitate the exchange of programs between regional unions. The UBU's sole tasks, at least in the beginning, would be to serve as a reception point for program offers from regional unions and to disseminate information about them throughout the system. The regional units would be left completely free to decide on the number and types of programs to be offered and accepted based on the requests of its membership. Additional tasks could be given to the central organization in time, but only after the confidence of the members of each of the regional unions has been attained.

At one time, the technical aspects of an exchange program between the various regions of the world would have provided the most difficult of the barriers to be overcome in a plan of this kind. Modern technologies, however, have reduced this barrier to little more than a serious nuisance. It has become so insignificant that it would be possible to devise a single system that could provide for the exchange of programs between regional broadcasting unions, and between the countries within each of the regional unions. This should be considered a long-term goal, however, to be actively pursued only after the basic system has worked long enough to win the confidence of the new members. In the meantime, the technical details of program exchange between individual nations should be left to the regional unions and the exchange between regions to the UBU's technical center.

While the creation of a universal radio and television program exchange such as the one envisaged here could not be expected to convert all or even a major portion of the nations of the world to the ranks of advocates of free flow of information, it could have some important advantages over the present situation. It would permit a variety of responses to the changing technology of communications. It would allow those nations that wish to proceed with experiments in direct broadcasting by satellite to indulge in such activities without bothering others. It would permit other nations (probably the majority as it now appears) to move into the new information era at their own speed, depending on interest and availability of finances. Above all, it would guarantee at least a minimum of program exchange which would be an effective counterforce to what presently seems to be a serious trend towards electronic isolationism.

George A. Codding, Jr.

Department of Political Science
University of Colorado

ACKNOWLEDGEMENTS

I would like to acknowledge the help of the European Broadcasting Union. I am especially indebted to Miro Vilcek for his perceptive comments and suggestions on the manuscript and for taking part in my doctoral examination. Because of the nature of the work, great demands have been made on EBU library facilities and resources. My thanks to Jean Cerantola for his help.

I am also grateful to the International Radio and Television Organization for interviews and documents.

The library and staff of the International Telecommunication Union have also been helpful.

I would also like to thank Marcel Bezençon, Jerzy Rutkowski, and Léo Wallenborn for reading the manuscript and making valuable comments.

I am especially indebted to George A. Codding, Jr., Professor of Political Science at the University of Colorado and friend, whose help throughout the years has made this book possible. Also I thank my advisors Professors Jean Siotis and Marlis G. Steinert of the Institut Universitaire de Hautes Etudes Internationales for their guidance.

I would like to thank Marlene Kuster for helping type the manuscript.

Finally, I would like to express both appreciation and indebtedness to my wife, Suzanne. In addition to typing the manuscript, I want to thank her for giving the greatest gifts that could be received, the encouragement, sympathy, and patience necessary to complete this book.

INTRODUCTION

Television is the most powerful mass medium yet created by man. It can forge links between people and make the best of man's culture available to all. But the benefits anticipated from international television programming are restricted by many factors. Sharp differences in transmitting and receiving equipment, television rights, and languages as well as viewer tastes and interests may render program exchanges impossible. Most important, the number and kinds of exchanges may be limited by the desire of many governments to prevent the transmission of propaganda to their citizens. In today's world, each government strictly controls the programs that may be telecast, and each regards it as essential that the integrity of these decisions be protected. Any international program system has to take into consideration the limits imposed by the importance of television to national sovereignty.

Perhaps no other international arrangement so dramatically shows the benefits and difficulties of international television than the networks of the European Broadcasting Union (EBU) and the International Radio and Television Organization (OIRT). These two organizations provide the means by which the Western and Socialist broadcasters of Europe can exchange programs. In the engineering field, the EBU and OIRT maintain technical centers which primarily route television transmissions over Europe's two networks — Eurovision and Intervision respectively. In addition to linking national television stations, both organizations negotiate legal agreements to protect broadcasters against high television rights costs. In the program field, the EBU and OIRT provide mechanisms for broadcasters to offer and request programs from another. Moreover, they offer a way of controlling the reception of foreign programs so as not to violate national programming rules and expose viewers to programs deemed harmful. Without the EBU and OIRT, the transmission of television programs to stations in Europe and the rest of the world would be impossible.

While offering a wealth of information in understanding international television exchanges, particularly between the Western and Socialist countries of

Europe, the literature comparing the EBU and OIRT is very limited. This lack of research seems surprising in view of the fact that much of the entertainment and news shown on European and world screens would not be possible without the EBU and OIRT. Furthermore, the transmission of programs between Eurovision and Intervision is one of the few permanent communications channels between Eastern and Western Europe.

As this is the first book devoted exclusively to Europe's television networks, a serious attempt will be made to examine the history, operations, problems, and prospects of international television programming. This study will identify the elements within the EBU and OIRT as well as Eurovision and Intervision which have contributed to their success. Most important of all, it will examine the kinds of programs exchanged, the existing limits to freer communications, and the predominant role which governments play in the organizations. This study should be of value to broadcasters, policymakers, and students interested in international communications.

The first chapter analyzes the importance of international television program exchanges to states. It contains a brief look at television in the USSR, the Federal Republic of Germany, Italy, and Luxembourg to show the wide diversity in national control which, taken together, also shows the difficulties of transmitting programs across national borders. Chapter Two takes a closer look at how programs were exchanged through the world's first international association of broadcasting organizations — the International Broadcasting Union (IBU). The EBU and OIRT evolved directly from the IBU. Chapter Three compares the structure and functions of the EBU and OIRT. Chapter Four explains the origins and inner workings of Eurovision and Intervision.

Chapter Five through Seven examine the use, limitations, and prospects of Eurovision and Intervision. This shall be done by analyzing "who takes what and why?" Answers to this question will be based on official program information sheets such as the Eurovision Program Summaries of the EBU and a look at a day's news exchange within and between Eurovision and Intervision.

The final chapter takes a closing look at the problems of international television networks and which direction European broadcasting collaboration may take in the future.

CHAPTER 1
PROGRAM EXCHANGES AND THE STATE

Technologies which sounded exotic only yesterday—multi-channel cable television, home video, satellites—have forged an era where today a large share of the world's population can be found watching the same television program. For years, governments have strictly regulated the bulk of the entertainment, news, and advertising that may be telecast. The increasing ability of new technology to transmit programs across national borders troubles many governments. At the very least, programs transmitted directly from abroad can dilute government control. European nations have found that they can maintain control over the reception of foreign programs while reaping the benefits of international television by exchanging programs through two regional broadcasting organizations — the European Broadcasting Union (EBU) in the West and the International Radio and Television Organization (OIRT) in the East.

This chapter analyzes the importance of international television program exchanges to states. First, we will look briefly at the extent of program exchanges and their aims. Then we will turn to some of the policies that influence the control of television in the Soviet Union, the Federal Republic of Germany, Italy, and Luxembourg. These countries were chosen largely because they provide diverse examples in television regulation — examples which, taken together, also show the difficulties of transmitting programs across national borders.

1.1 International Television Exchanges

It will be of some value to look briefly at the sources and size of international program exchanges. The BBC, for example, reported that on July 29, 1981, 109 television services in 74 countries transmitted live coverage of the Royal Wedding.[1] In Italy, private television stations imported over 4,000 programs, including feature films, totaling more than $26 million in 1980, while RAI, the national network, imported about 2,800 television programs for over $10 million.[2] Members of the daily Eurovision and Intervision news exchange report similar findings. France took 90 percent of the 7,636 news items exchanged over Eurovision in 1982 and sent out 480 items.[3] The same year, the USSR took 49 percent of the 5,205 items relayed over Intervision and originated 862 news items.[4] As one can see, television programs cross national borders daily.

Even exchanges between countries of different political outlooks are significant, although a heavy imbalance can develop. In Europe, for example, more than 3,000 hours of programs a year flow from the Western countries to the Eastern countries, while the flow in the opposite direction is only 1,000 hours a year.[5] In 1982, for instance, the USSR took 197 programs (436 hours 18) from Eurovision, while Eurovision members only accepted 14 Soviet programs (29 h 59).[6] Viewers in the Socialist countries of Europe see far more of the West than vice versa.

Government agreements contribute to the international flow of television programs. Cultural agreements between governments often allow program exchanges. An example of such agreements was concluded in 1971 between Austria and Rumania. This agreement holds that both countries shall:

> facilitate the exchange of documentary films and of other audio-visual materials of cultural content on a non-commercial basis...
>
> encourage the continuation of direct cooperation between the Austrian broadcasting company (ORF) and the Rumanian radio and television services (TVR).[7]

Another agreement which provides for the exchange and coproduction of radio and television programs is the Final Acts of the Helsinki Conference on Security and Cooperation which was signed in 1975 by thirty-three European states, plus Canada and the United States.[8]

Broadcasters organize most exchanges through bilateral and multilateral arrangements. Commercial production and distribution companies are a major source of foreign programs. Worldvision Enterprises, a U.S. television distributor, for example, sold "Dallas" to 90 countries in 1983.[9] Programs also change hands at international film festivals. In 1981, the Cannes television festival drew 1,044 exhibitors, 288 of them television stations and 756 production and television companies; promoting sales of $50 million.[10] Moreover, broadcasters of different countries coproduce programs. In 1982, for example, Teleclip (France) finished a nine-hour series entitled "Mozart," coproduced with TF1 (France), Galaxy Films (W. Germany), MTV (Hungary), RAI (Italy), SSR (Switzerland), RTBF (Belgium), and Société Radio-Canada.[11]

Finally, an important source of foreign television material are the program exchanges coordinated by regional broadcasting unions. Europe has two such agencies: the European Broadcasting Union (EBU) and the International Radio and Television Organization (OIRT). These agencies are responsible for Eurovision and Intervision, respectively. As we shall see in Chapter Four, coordinating, planning, and supervising live international television transmissions is the largest single activity of the EBU and OIRT.

In addition to the EBU and OIRT, other regional broadcasting unions also promote program exchanges. They are:

> Arab States Broadcasting Union (ASBU)
> Asia-Pacific Broadcasting Union (ABU)
> Asociación Inter-Americana de Radiodifusión (AIR)
> Caribbean Broadcasting Union (CBU)
> Commonwealth Broadcasting Association (CBA)
> North American National Broadcasters Association (NANBA)
> Organización de la Televisión Iberoamericana (OTI)
> Union of National Radio and Television Organizations of Africa (URTNA)

When compared with the rest of the world, however, Europeans have the most developed international program exchange networks. In Latin America, for example, the OTI's news exchange system, called Servicio Iberoamericano de Noticias (SIN), transmitted 2,684 items in 1981.[12] But in the same year, Eurovision transmitted 6,820 news items.[13] One reason for OTI's smaller exchange is that only edited news segments are transmitted in order to lower satellite costs.[14] Eurovision, with its own permanently-leased network, can transmit longer takes, thus allowing members to edit items themselves.

1.2 Aims of Exchanges

There are at least three reasons why countries organize program exchanges: 1) the desire to understand other peoples, 2) the need for program variety, and 3) the desire to maintain control over the reception of foreign programs.

The international community has generally agreed that one of the major potential benefits of television is that the large-scale program exchanges can play an important role in improving international understanding. At its second session, the U.N. Working Group on Direct Broadcast Satellites recognized

> ...that the medium of television is especially suited to increasing contacts between peoples of the world and to advancing the principles and purposes of the United Nations. Among the potential...benefits from satellites would be improved education and greater flow of news and information of general interest, including cultural programs and the development of closer ties between peoples of countries and within countries.[15]

The second reason why broadcasters engage in exchanges is to satisfy the need for program variety. Generally speaking, broadcasters around the world aim to vary their programming. But few, if any, have the resources — money, talent and equipment — to satisfy their audiences' insatiable appetite for programs. One way of overcoming these limits is to import programs. Importing gives broadcasters a broad selection of programs at a price which is often lower than the cost of a similar homemade production.

In fact, most countries rely heavily on foreign programs to supplement their own output. In Latin America, half of the television programs are foreign with Guatemala importing up to 84 percent of its shows. A similar situation exists in Asia. Countries like Singapore, Malaysia, and New Zealand import more than 70 percent of their programs, as do Zambia and Nigeria in Africa. A third to a fourth of the programs in Europe are imported, with figures rising as high as 67 percent in Iceland and 45 percent in Bulgaria.[16] But, while many countries import programs, only a handful of producer-exporter nations exist. The leading exporter is the United States which sends 100,000 to 200,000 program hours abroad each year. The United Kingdom holds second place with 30,000 hours, followed by France with 15,000 to 20,000.[17]

Finally, states are happy with program exchanges because it permits them to control the reception of foreign programs for political purposes. Program exchanges have an important advantage over direct international broadcasts in controlling program content. With direct broadcasts, states can prevent listeners from receiving programs by jamming the foreign signal.[18] With program exchanges, however, control is institutionalized. Foreign programs reach audiences only through national broadcasting organizations. Thus, any offensive material can be suppressed before it reaches the viewers.

In Eurovision and Intervision, for example, the decision to see a foreign program rests with each member organization, not the viewers. Of course, Europe's viewers have come to expect the networks to relay the top international events. But, since program offerings are not publicly circulated, viewers can only suspect subtle manipulation by government bureaucrats when major events are not telecast. Every station connected to the networks is able to reject any material it deems objectionable which the networks send out.

Much of the desire for controlling program content comes from the widely held fear that the media will spread propaganda. Admittedly, the definition of propaganda and to what degree it is subversive to governments varies from one country to another. Still, history suggests that a society will always attempt to suppress information which is deemed harmful to the authorities in power.[19] Indeed, information control is one of the oldest temptations of governments.[20] No society has found it beneficial to allow the unrestricted flow of information. Even countries with long traditions of free speech have deemed it necessary to impose controls in times of crisis.

The international debate on direct satellite broadcasting is a prime example of the concern states have for harmful propaganda. Since 1969, the U.N. Working Group on Direct Broadcast Satellites has been discussing whether or not to establish an internationally agreed upon detailed code of program content to which all satellite broadcasting would have to conform. Because many countries, chief of which is the USSR, worry that unregulated satellites could become vehicles of propaganda, proposals have been submitted making satellite broadcasts illegal if they were transmitted without the consent of the recipient country.

The United States, however, has opposed proposals for controlling satellite broadcasts for fear that the free flow of information would be curtailed. That fear has not been widely shared. Even countries which highly value free speech objected to the United States's view partly because of fears that their own territory would be flooded with American television programs.[21]

As the international satellite debate shows, controlling the reception of foreign programs is an important element of national sovereignty. Each state determines who may broadcast what programs. Each state has decided how much entertainment, advertising, and violence viewers will see. But because airwaves freely cross national borders, the decision about programming may be reversed by programs transmitted from other countries. Thus, controlling incoming programs becomes an essential element in protecting national sovereignty from foreign control.

1.3 Variations In Controlling National Television Broadcasting

Any international program exchange network will have to take into consideration the different decisions which governments have made as to who may telecast what programs.[22] These varied decisions not only make international coordination difficult, but can limit the number and kinds of exchanges. Let's look at four countries to show the degrees of national broadcasting control.

1.3.1 USSR

Since the introduction of broadcasting, the government and the party have kept a firm hand on control room dials. Television and radio function under the direct tutelage of the Council of Ministers — the top government decision-making body — while the party provides the guiding principles.

The birth of broadcasting in the USSR was a paradox. The nation that produced a ship-to-shore radio system in 1895[23] lagged behind most West European countries in developing broadcasting. In 1928, four years after the first public broadcast, only 92,000 radio sets existed in the USSR.[24] One factor for radio's slow growth was the general economic backwardness of the new Soviet state. Also the geographical vastness of the USSR and its dispersed population made building of a radio network costly.

Another factor explaining radio's laggard growth was that Soviet leaders were slow to recognize the potential power of the new medium. Bolshevik leaders viewed radio's social duties as no different from that of the press: to educate and organize the masses under the leadership of the party in order to achieve clearly set goals.[25]

Although Lenin cast the mold for a Soviet centralized media system, Stalin integrated radio into the state machinery, building direct day-to-day control over its operations. In 1928, one year after Stalin gained full power, the Commissariat for Posts and Telegraph was given full management of Radio-peredatcha, a joint-stock company created in 1924 by the Council of People's Commissars.[26] Broadcasting was brought closer to government with the creation of the Committee for Radiofication and Radio Broadcasting in 1933.[27] It functioned under the direct tutelage of the Council of People's Commissars and remained in existence until 1949 when Soviet broadcasting had to deal with the growth of television.[28]

Radio's editorial control mirrored the control over the press. Glavit censors were assigned to radio stations, and Agitprop directives provided radio's ideological directions. The rules which emerged to control radio duplicated those previously issued for the press.[29] To safeguard against receiving foreign broadcasts, Stalin's regime set about covering every part of the USSR with wired radio sets. The number of wired sets grew from 1.4 million in 1932 to 5.9 million in 1940, while wireless sets grew from 97,000 to 1.1 million over the same period.[30]

Like radio, television also had a low priority in Soviet planning. Although regular transmissions began in 1948, years before most European countries,[31] television grew slowly. The number of sets increased from 200 in 1945 to only 15,000 in 1951.[32] Television's growth was partly hindered by the low political priority which television received against the needs of industry, the military, and agriculture. In addition, the fact of having an established press and a growing radio system weighed against making large investments in television.[33] Moreover, television's social responsibility was still equated with that of the press. Wilson P. Dizard, in his study of Soviet television, wrote that even "if television had been an important medium of communication in Stalin's day, he would have confined its activities to reproducing daily editorials and articles from Pravda."[34]

After Stalin's death in 1953, however, broadcasting was no longer neglected.

The Kremlin decided that broadcasting could be one of the most effective tools available in its efforts to unify a nation that encompasses 10 major ethnic groups and sprawls across 11 time zones. In light of this new interest, the total number of wireless radio sets soared from 1.7 million in 1950 to 130 million in 1981.[35] The importance of wired receivers remained paramount. From 1950 to 1974, the number of sets increased from 9.7 to 59 million.[36]

Television also saw rapid growth. The number of sets grew from 10.4 million in 1963 to over 70 million in 1981, penetrating 85 percent of Soviet homes.[37] Color television was inaugurated in 1967. Also, the USSR traditionally has transmitted more satellite programs than any other country.[38]

Broadcasting's comprehensive and ambitious development was accompanied by changes in government control. In 1949, the Committee for Radiofication and Radio Broadcasting gave way to the Committee on Radio Information attached to the Council of Ministers. Another reorganization took place in March 1953, shortly after Stalin's death, when control of Soviet broadcasting was given to the Ministry of Culture.[39] This move was largely prompted by the desire to shed Khrushchev's government of any images of Stalinist totalitarianism. While the Ministry of Culture controlled program making, the PTT provided the transmission equipment.

In 1957, as Khrushchev consolidated his power, the Council of Ministers reassumed control of broadcasting and set up the present-day State Committee of Radio and Television. The Committee consists of seventeen members appointed permanently by the Council. The transmission network and studios are supervised by the PTT.[40] Soviet broadcasting is financed by government subvention, advertising, and sales taxes on new television sets.[41]

While the Committee manages national and international broadcasting activities, a system of geographical decentralization has attempted to bring broadcasting closer to the regions. Numerous broadcasting committees, largely patterned after the State Committee, have been set up in the republics, regions, oblasts, and cities. Also many public councils and editorial staffs are involved in planning and evaluating broadcasting.[42]

Although the government is responsible for Soviet broadcasting, the party is always involved. The party issues the guiding principles for the operation and development of the media. At its twenty-sixth Congress in 1982, the late Communist Party leader Leonid Brezhnev called for television to play a fuller role in the country's "moral and esthetic education."[43] It is the government's primary duty to see that the party's decisions are carried out.

The monopoly which the government and party have over broadcasting has been supplemented by measures to control foreign propaganda. The Soviets commit considerable resources to jamming signals from stations such as

Voice of America, Radio Liberty, and the BBC Overseas Service, particularly during times of East-West tension. After seven years of undisturbed service, for example, Soviet authorities resumed jamming BBC programs to the USSR in August 1980 largely for fear that news of the Polish labor crisis might cause worker unrest at home.[44]

After six decades of experience with their carefully controlled broadcasting system, the Soviets are in the midst of a debate about dullness and effectiveness of programming. Government and party officials regard television as a useful propaganda tool, devoting about 25 percent of the air time to political messages.[45] But they have also recognized that television's effectiveness is limited by the poor quality of most political programs, plus the availability in most cities of only one channel.[46] Moreover, Soviet viewers tend to turn their sets off if the program is laden with propaganda. A 1971 opinion survey in Leningrad, for example, showed that viewers preferred to watch fewer political telecasts and more films, variety shows, and drama.[47] Attempts are under way to make Soviet programming more appealing to viewers.[48] However, any major change to the broadcasting system will still hinge on the course of Soviet politics.

1.3.2 The Federal Republic of Germany

When the Soviets were integrating the control of television into their centralized political system, the West Germans decided to entrust the operation of their broadcasting to the German provincial states, the Länder. The Länder formed broadcasting administrations, each of which set up a separate and independent station. While the federal government assigns frequencies, collects license fees and maintains the actual transmission system, the nine regional stations are free to set their own policies. Because it was impossible for each small independent station to run television, two centralized networks were set up. (West German television can be received in roughly 80 percent of East Germany's territory.) Nevertheless, the West German broadcasting system is dictated by a desire to decentralize and to increase pluralism. In most Land stations, various interest groups are allowed to place representatives on the Broadcasting Council, the supreme decision-making organ, where they outnumber politicians.

The decision to decentralize broadcasting control owes much to the desire to avoid the tight government controls of the Third Reich. Germany was one of the first European countries to introduce radio.[49] As early as 1917, radio programs were transmitted to German troops on the western front. At the end of World War I, the Weimar Republic decreed that the state held overall control of radio. By 1924, the government granted concessions to eight private regional stations, although the technical facilities remained state property.

State control over private broadcasting, however, grew with the creation of the Reichsrundfunkgesellschaft (RRG) in 1925. Although the RRG's primary objective was to provide broadcasting to all of Germany, its creation also reflected the view of politicians that broadcasting was too important to be left to private interests.[50] The RRG gained financial control over the private stations. In 1932, the state gained control of newscasts.[51] Still, the private stations managed to evade total nationalization until Hitler's rise to power.

After Hitler seized power, radio was fully nationalized and became part of the Nazi propaganda machinery. In March 1933, two months after Hitler became Chancellor, the RRG was placed under the direct control of the National Ministry of Public Enlightenment and Propaganda, headed by Joseph Goebbels.[52] Private stations were quickly banned. With the RRG fully under Nazi control, radio became an important tool for reinforcing the official propaganda line. Hitler and other Nazi spokesmen, described radio's role as "the shock troop of the National Socialist World outlook" and as "the most modern, the strongest and most revolutionary weapon which (the Nazi Party has) in the battle against an extinct world."[53]

The Reich placed importance on extending radio's national and worldwide coverage. At home, the number of radio sets grew from over four million in 1933 to over 15 million in 1941.[54] Abroad, Germany greatly expanded its shortwave services and foreign language broadcasts. Also, as countries were incorporated into the Reich, radio stations were annexed and began relaying programs originating from the "Funkhaus" in Berlin. In fact, before the war ended, the Third Reich controlled much of the mass media in Europe.

While seeking to ensure that the RRG's programs were heard nearly around the world, the Nazis had their official mechanisms for preventing the reception of foreign programs. Every German, for example, was encouraged to buy or was given a "Volksempfänger" ("People's Receiver") which made it technically impossible for listeners to receive foreign programs. In addition, Hitler ordered strict punishments for listening to foreign stations.[55]

Following the war, the Western occupation powers were determined to make sure that broadcasting would never again be taken over by the state. The Allies all agreed that the defeated nation should have a publicly accountable system where major decisions would be made by "socially relevant" groups such as political parties, the churches and trade unions. The constitution and the three-tier administrative structure of most of today's nine regional stations can be directly traced to the stations the Allies set up.[56] Moreover, the decentralized broadcasting structure was reinforced by the federal political system set forth in the Basic Law of the Federal Republic of Germany.

The most basic endorsement of the present broadcasting system came in 1961 when the Länder's right to broadcast was upheld by the Federal Constitutional Court. In 1950, the nine stations formed the Arbeitsgemeinschaft der öffentlich rechtlichen Rundfunkanstalten der Bundesrepublik Deutschland (ARD), West Germany's first television channel. Ten years later, however, Chancellor Adenauer, feeling that ARD's programs were too liberal and biased against him,[57] proceeded to set up a second television channel called Deutschland Fernsehen GmbH. Although the company got as far as recording programs, the Länder refused to participate on grounds that national broadcasting was a Land, not a Federal, responsibility. In 1961, the Federal Constitutional Court ruled that Deutschland Fernsehen was unconstitutional. The judges held that the Federal Government's broadcasting duties were limited to granting station licenses, to assigning frequencies, to collecting user license fees, to maintaining the telecommunications network, and to broadcasting to foreign countries via Deutsche Welle and Deutschlandfunk.[58] Otherwise, individual stations have the right to set their own policies.[59]

The Länder, armed with this victory, created West Germany's second television channel, Zweites Deutsches Fernsehen (ZDF) in 1963 to rival ARD. One reason why the Länder did not choose to give ARD control of the second channel was to prevent a monopoly. But to prevent cutthroat competition, ZDF was formed as a public corporation — not a commercial firm.[60] ZDF was obliged to provide the widest possible coverage, geographically and culturally, in its programming. Furthermore, as ZDF's charter states, program-making must serve the entire Federal Republic, as opposed to regions, and, in so doing, promote independent opinion.[61]

A third channel, provided by ARD, offers mainly educational programs regionally. The use of the five ARD-3 channels varies. But with all of them the emphasis is mainly on providing minority audiences with informative and educational programs. In addition, ARD-3 may broadcast programs which ARD-1 deems too controversial to show to the entire nation. Such was the case with the American series "Holocaust," a story on the Nazi extermination of the Jews.[62]

It is generally agreed that the business of broadcasting should be kept out of the hands of the federal government. But West German society has yet to find a way of keeping it out of the hands of Land politicians. The problem came to a head over the Norddeutscher Rundfunk (NDR), the country's second largest Land station. In 1980, the conservative Christian Democrat (CDU) states of Lower Saxony and Schleswig-Holstein passed a law to reorganize

NDR primarily in an attempt to exclude the liberal Social Democrat (SPD) city state of Hamburg — one of the three partner Länder running NDR since 1955. The two CDU Länder hoped that the exclusion of Hamburg from NDR's management would stop what they deemed to be slanted left-wing programming by Hamburg. In addition, the CDU Länder called for the start of private commercial broadcasting.

The Federal Constitutional Court barred the CDU Länder from carrying out their plan. But the present broadcasting system seems to have won only a reprieve. A subsequent compromise agreement was reached between the CDU Länder which called for the abolition of NDR's radio monopoly in Northern Germany and the start of private commercial broadcasting stations. SPD politicians favor the plan because NDR will remain intact. But North German newspaper publishers are less than eager about the new media plan because of fears that commercial broadcasting will result in a loss of advertising revenue.[63]

In short, the West German government has no right to broadcast to its own citizens. Broadcasting was deliberately decentralized after the war and placed in the hands of individual Land administrations, each of which created a separate and independent public broadcasting body. Although television required the creation of a centralized network (ARD), a second channel was created to prevent a monopoly. But ZDF was set up as a public organization in order to prevent harsh competition and concentrations of profit and program control in private hands.

1.3.3 Italy

Italy presents an utterly contrasting picture of a system where the state broadcasting monopoly has been supplemented with local programming and private ownership. Today Europe has the unprecedented spectacle of a country with over 2,000 private commercial radio and about 1,200 television stations competing with one another and with the government-controlled organization Radiotelevisione Italiana (RAI).[64] The government has little say over the private stations' program-making.

Historically, Italian broadcasting has been a state monopoly conceded to a private company. The state's monopoly traces its origins to a 1924 royal decree which stipulated that radio belonged to the state. But rather than carry out broadcasting itself, Mussolini's government chose to grant a concession to a private company, Unione Radiofonica Italiana (URI), so that broadcasting operations would be autonomous and free of bureaucratic delays.[65] The first official broadcast occurred on October 6, 1924.[66]

The state's grip on the new medium, however, tightened. In 1926, the government prohibited the broadcast of any public performance without the government's prior approval.[67] A year later, URI was replaced by Ente Italiano per le Audizioni Radiofoniche (EIAR). Apart from lengthening the concession from seven to twenty-five years, the government had the power to appoint EIAR's president and other top officials. Moreover, programs were scrutinized by national and local surveillance councils as well as by the PTT.[68] Finally, Mussolini nationalized EIAR in 1944.[69]

After the war, the Italian Republic accorded an exclusive concession to Radio Audizioni Italia (RAI). A 1947 decree granted RAI a five-year concession and placed it under the control of the PTT and a parliamentary committee.[70] In 1952, RAI's charter was renewed, and its formal functions were expanded to account for television's arrival.[71] Regular television started in January 1954, and three years later, "television" was added to RAI's official title.

The 1952 concession gave RAI considerable financial and operative autonomy. But the government still maintained considerable control over RAI's administration and programs. RAI's budget, financed mainly from fees and advertising, was subject to review by the Treasury and the PTT. In addition, the government owned the majority of the stock and designated seats on RAI's Board of Managers and Board of Auditors. In the field of program-making, RAI was required to submit its proposed program schedule every three months to a PTT advisory committee charged with setting artistic, cultural, and educational policies.[72]

Although the validity of the government's monopoly over the airwaves was upheld in a 1960 Constitutional Court decision,[73] it did little to silence growing complaints about RAI's biased programming. Traditionally, many of RAI's executives backed the ruling Christian Democrats and thus would often spare the party any embarrassment by ignoring or downplaying touchy subjects. During the 1974 civil divorce referendum, for example, RAI often censored government criticism.[74] In fact, many viewers in Northern Italy turned to Swiss television, rather than RAI, for information on the divorce issue.[75] Calls for reform also reflected the larger political struggle in Italy, especially as a result of the increased strength of the Italian Communist Party.[76] In 1972, RAI's concession expired without any agreement on the future of Italian broadcasting. The government extended RAI's license several times to permit a ministerial commission to report on how broadcasting should be institutionalized.[77]

While the government was studying RAI's reform, local businessmen, among others, started their own stations to protest against the state monopoly. The first assault on the monopoly came in 1972 when a businessman in Biella bought two portapacks and, with cables strung from telephone poles, started local cablecasting.[78] To the government's dislike, the idea of cable television (CATV) spread rapidly. In 1973, CATV was outlawed on the grounds that the state monopoly included all audio-video programs distributed by cable. The law, however, was repealed by the Constitutional Court. While reaffirming its 1960 decision that RAI owes its existence to the scarcity of frequencies, the Court ruled that RAI's monopoly did not include retransmitting foreign television or CATV. In addition, the Court declared that RAI's monopoly was not guaranteeing public access and objective programming. Thus, the government's monopoly was illegal.[79]

Private broadcasters were elated over the Court's ruling that the government's monopoly was illegal. The number of CATV stations increased from twenty-two in 1973 to ninety in 1974.[80] Also, small, privately operated repeater stations started relaying programs mainly from France, Switzerland, and Yugoslavia down the peninsula, treating Italians to color television years before their own country introduced color in 1977.[81] Furthermore, taking advantage of a lack of regulation, pirate radio stations began broadcasting music, local news, advertisements, and political propaganda.[82] Moreover, some CATVs switched to over-the-air broadcasting in order to reach larger audiences.[83]

In an effort to protect the state monopoly from the onslaught of pirate broadcasting, the government approved RAI's long-awaited reform in 1975. Although the Act of April 14, 1975 upheld RAI's exclusive right to broadcast nationally, it shifted the control of broadcasting from the executive to the legislature. A forty-man Parliamentary Commission was now vested with supreme authority over RAI. Furthermore, the Act provided new measures for electing RAI's officials.[84]

RAI's program-making tasks were decentralized. The Act divided broadcasting among three nationwide radio stations and three television channels, each with independent news services. Political control of the two competing national RAI-TV channels was divided between the Christian Democrats and the Socialists, while the third channel provided regional telecasts. Furthermore, the relaying of foreign programs and local CATVs were permitted, though their establishment and operations were brought under tighter control. The Act limited CATVs to a single channel and forbade interconnections for live transmissions. CATVs were also subject to PTT licensing and to rules limiting the length of commercials.[85] Overall, the reforms aimed at eliminating a centralized and uncompetititve broadcasting system. The government also hoped the reform would accommodate public demands for greater access.

The new system, however, was shaken by a 1976 court ruling authorizing private local radio and television stations to compete with RAI's networks. In 1976, the Constitutional Court rejected the government's contention that the 1975 Act gave them the right to prosecute and close down pirate stations. The Court concluded that the 1975 law was unconstitutional on the grounds that the government did not allow for the installation and operation of local over-the-air radio and television stations and that the frequency spectrum could accommodate new stations.[86] The significance of the 1976 ruling was that local broadcasts were removed from the state monopoly, though RAI retained the monopoly on the national scale.

The private telecasters appear to be competing successfully with the RAI networks. The private channels are cashing in not only on the frustrations of advertisers with the limited commercial time allowed by RAI, but also on the irritation of Italian viewers with RAI programming. The offerings of private stations range from political talk shows to pornography. The private stations have lured away an estimated 20 to 40 percent of Italy's prime time viewers from the state run networks.[87]

Neighboring countries, however, have not shared the enthusiasm of Italian viewers for the private commercial stations. To protect its radio monopoly, Switzerland, for example, repeatedly pressured the Italian government to close down Radio 24 which was broadcasting German-language commercial radio from Italy into Switzerland.[88] In a similar move, RAI and Radio-Télé Monte-Carlo (controlled by the French government through SOFIRAD) concluded an agreement to prevent private Italian television interests from renting one of the five satellite channels which Monaco received in the 1977 World Administrative Radio Conference on Broadcasting-Satellites.[89]

Historically, broadcasting in Italy was a state monopoly conceded to a private company. But the courts in the 1970s declared the government's monopoly illegal because it failed to guarantee public access and objective programming. The decision resulted in the advent of hundreds of private local radio and television stations which not only compete with each other, but also with the government-controlled network. The Italian Parliament has little power over the programming policies of the private stations.

1.3.4 Luxembourg

Preventing the concentration of profit and program control in private hands is an important policy objective for many European governments. For Luxembourg, however, commercially based private broadcasting is a way to finance a public service which is heard throughout most of Europe. Undoubtedly, Radio-Télé-Luxembourg (RTL) is Europe's largest commercial broadcaster. An estimated audience of 40 million tunes in weekly to its five radio and two television channels. RTL also is one of Europe's richest stations.

Because the Luxembourgers do not pay license fees, RTL's survival entirely depends upon the high profits of advertising. In 1981, the Compagnie Luxembourgeoise de Télédiffusion (CLT) — RTL's corporate owner — took in 7.3 billion Lux. Frs. ($162 million) in gross advertising sales.[90] But many of Luxembourg's neighboring countries look at RTL's commercials as a direct threat to their own broadcasting systems.

RTL has been broadcasting commercial radio since 1932.[91] Although the government had long operated the posts and telecommunications, many politicians realized that a radio station without advertising that was run by the state would be beyond the government's financial means.[92] Thus, the government gave a broadcasting monopoly to a company of businessmen and radio amateurs which set up CLT to build and operate a commercial service.[93] In addition to realizing that the government could not finance a radio service, politicians also were aware that advertising would be an important revenue source for the government.[94] In fact, in 1981, CLT paid about $40 million in taxes, making it the country's second largest taxpayer.[95]

The government granted private broadcasters a concession in return for numerous obligations, primarily designed to safeguard the national interest. The "cahier des charges," an agreement drawn up between the government and CLT, provides that the members on the company's board and stations staff include a majority of Luxembourg citizens. In addition, CLT must observe international agreements to which Luxembourg is party.[96] Furthermore, the government shares in CLT's profits,[97] though it has no stockholdings. Finally, RTL's programs must observe strict political neutrality and contribute to a higher cultural level.[98]

The Director of Internal Revenue is the government official who must ensure that the provisions of the "cahier des charges" are being observed by CLT. He is nominated by the Prime Minister and is advised by a technical committee, consisting of PTT officials, and a cultural affairs committee, composed of prominent people in the cultural life of Luxembourg. His primary duties include participating in the executive meetings of the CLT and receiving program complaints. The government is supposed to be excluded from all forms of editorial control, but he has the power to censor programs which breach the laws of security or social order. But to date, he has never had to decide a complaint.[99]

The ultimate responsibility for broadcasting rests on the management of CLT. The purpose of CLT, as set out in its statutes, is to construct, equip, and run the radio and television facilities in Luxembourg. The supreme decision organ of the CLT is the General Assembly that meets once a year and is composed of stockholders. In addition, a twenty-five member Board of

Directors oversees the administration of CLT and elects the president. A director-general regulates CLT's daily activities.[100]

RTL's powerful transmitters have offered advertisers an effective way of reaching all of the most heavily populated portions of Western Europe in several languages. The biggest audience — nine million a day — follows RTL French radio, which produces its programs in Paris and sends them by cable to Luxembourg, where they are broadcast from a 2,000 kw transmitter twenty-two hours a day. This program is heard in about two-thirds of France. On the shortwave, medium wave and FM bands, RTL broadcasts English and German radio shows. Radio transmissions also exist in Luxembourgish and Dutch. CLT began regular television in 1955 and introduced color in 1972. Today, RTL's French-language television programs reach four countries; Northeastern France, Belgium, the Rhineland provinces of West Germany, and Luxembourg itself. The second channel is given to Luxembourger shows.[101]

In addition to a large radio and television audience, RTL remains attractive to advertisers because commercials in neighboring countries are either forbidden or strictly limited. In fact, Luxembourg's neighbors have long regarded RTL's advertisements as a threat to their own broadcasting systems. The start of Radio Luxembourg, for example, angered the BBC and the British Post Office, partly because of the fear that Radio Luxembourg would set a dangerous precedent and partly because of the fear that the BBC would lose the monopoly over its own listeners. Between 1929 and 1932, for example, the BBC lobbied other broadcasting organizations and the International Broadcasting Union to move against Luxembourg receiving frequencies.[102]

Today, France and West Germany are fearful of CLT's plans to start a direct broadcasting satellite system, thereby endangering the control of their own broadcasting services. CLT's satellite would cover large areas of Belgium, France, the Netherlands, and West Germany. In 1979, France and West Germany declared that broadcasting from a Luxembourg satellite would damage their interests.[103] Historically, France has given high priority to limiting broadcast advertisements, especially those originating from stations existing outside its borders. To that end, the French government has gained financial control of "périphérique" stations such as Europe No. 1 and Radio-Télé Monte-Carlo.[104] The French government does not control CLT, although it has a minority interest through the state-owned Havas and Paribas, two important CLT stockholders.[105] The West German government, for its part, fears that if CLT's satellite is launched, German family life would be damaged by the flood of RTL commercials.[106] Today, advertising on West German television is limited to about twenty minutes a day and forbidden on Sunday.[107]

1.4 International Control of Television

One of the most serious problems of controlling television at the international level is the fear of propaganda. The world's broadcasting systems, as we have seen, differ greatly. At present, each country asserts that its sovereignty gives it the right to broadcast what it pleases. But because legitimate programs in one country may be considered propaganda in another, governments also want to be able to control the reception of foreign programs.

This fear of harmful propaganda seems greatest whenever a new technology permits a country to better transmit its programs to other countries. The arrival of radio saw a flurry of diplomatic activity to forbid harmful propaganda which might, for example, lead to war. Their efforts climaxed with the signing in 1936 of the International Convention Concerning the Use of Broadcasting in the Cause of Peace. As we shall see in Chapter Two, the agreement succeeded in defining prohibitive broadcasts, but it did little to deter the use of radio for propaganda purposes, particularly during the height of the cold war in the 1950s.

Television is several times more threatening than radio. Because it can carry into people's home the new dimension of pictures with sound, politicians feared that if any harmful program is telecast, its impact on viewers, and ultimately on society, would be relatively greater. Of course, television absorbed many of the national regulations of radio. But before the full development of television could go ahead, governments had to find ways of controlling the reception of harmful propaganda from abroad.

One remedy was to organize program exchanges. Program exchanges offer the benefit of program control. Foreign programs reach viewers only through the stations linked to a program exchange network. Thus, any offensive material can be suppressed before it reaches the viewers.

In addition, the organization of program exchanges allows states to take full advantage of television technology. Because of television's limited propagation range, about 80 km (50 miles) around the transmitter, local stations have to be linked by either terrestrial or space facilities if a national service is to be provided. Similarly, the transmission of programs across national borders requires the linking of national stations.

In Europe, the EBU and the OIRT were created to organize program exchanges. Today, the agencies preside over elaborate procedures for obtaining international circuits, for coordinating offers and requests as well as for buying programs. Without the EBU and OIRT, as we shall see, the electronic exchange of programs and news across European borders would be impossible.

The exchange of programs and news across European borders would also be impossible if members were not first assured that they have complete control over incoming programs. All members connected to the program exchange networks of the EBU and OIRT are free to accept or reject any foreign program offer or request. Program decisions are made by national television organizations — which in most countries are government agencies or licensees — and not by the viewers.

1.5 Conclusion

International transmissions of television programs can trouble many states. Most states regulate what its own viewers may or may not see in the name of national sovereignty. But programs received from abroad can dilute government control. Thus, governments have had to find ways of maintaining control of incoming programs before the full benefits of television could be realized. Although the world's television systems differ greatly, controlling the reception of harmful propaganda is an important policy objective of many states. In the USSR, the government and the party control all aspects of broadcasting. The Soviets devote considerable resources to jamming Western broadcasts which are deemed "anti-Socialist." Another tool for banning foreign broadcasts has been the massive installation of wired receivers. The Federal Republic of Germany presents a contrasting picture of a system where the control of broadcasting — its licensing and its content — is decentralized, residing largely in the hands of the German provincial states, the Länder. But West German broadcasting has also seen attempts at program control. Nazi Germany saw the use of "Volksempfängers" to limit foreign radio listening. Hitler also imposed strict punishments. Today, the West German government fears that its limits on television commercials will be harmed by commercial telecasts from a planned Luxembourg satellite.

Elements of program control can also be found in Italy and Luxembourg. Italian broadcasting control has been placed in the hands of hundreds of private radio and television stations which compete with one another and with the state-operated networks. Although the Italian Parliament has little control over the private stations, it has prohibited the private stations from broadcasting their programs nationally. National coverage remains a public service granted exclusively to RAI. In Luxembourg, broadcasting is privately owned and operated. Nevertheless, even this small country has placed jurisdictional limits on what may be telecast in order to protect the national interest. As we have seen, economic, political, and commercial interests control programs deemed harmful in many states. Any system for exchanging programs will have to take into consideration the different ways in which countries control broadcasting. This wide variety of control makes international coordination difficult and limits what can be exchanged.

One way to prevent the reception of harmful programs is to organize program exchanges. Indeed, program exchanges offer the benefit of institutionalized program control. In an exchange, foreign programs reach viewers only through national television stations. Thus, national bureaucrats can suppress any propaganda before it reaches viewers. The prevention of over-the-air broadcasts generally involves jamming which can be noticed by the audience. But in program exchanges control is subtle and is unnoticable to the general public.

European states created the EBU and the OIRT to coordinate the exchange of programs across national borders. But, as we will see in Chapters Five, Six, and Seven, members do not take all the material which Eurovision and Intervision send out. Some are inappropriate. In addition, this limitation results at least in part from the desire of states to prevent the reception of programs which may be considered propaganda. We turn now to a closer look at how programs were exchanged through the world's first international association of broadcasting organizations — the International Broadcasting Union (IBU).

Endnotes

Chapter 1

1. C.R.Longman, "The Royal Wedding. Some Aspects of the Television Operation," *EBU Review*, 32:5, (September 1981), p. 18.
2. Daniele Doglio, "The Imported Arms Race," *TV World*, 4:12, (October 1981), p. 38.
3. EBU, Doc. no. SPG 2279, June 1983.
4. OIRT, "Intervisionsstatistik des Aktualitätenaustausches zwischen den Intervisionländern und zwischen Intervision und Eurovision und Anderen FSO 1981 und 1982," (unpublished OIRT document).
5. Kaarle Nordenstreng and Tapio Varis, *Television Traffic – A One-Way Street? A Survey and Analysis of the International Flow of Television Program Material*, (Paris: UNESCO, 1974), p. 41.
6. EBU, Doc. no. SPG 2279, *op.cit.*
7. UN, "Austria and Rumania — Agreement on Cultural Cooperation. Signed at Vienna on September 17, 1971," *Treaty Series – Treaties and International Agreements Registered or Filed with the Secretariat of the United Nations, 1973*, (New York: UN, 1978), p. 258.
8. See James A. Joyce, "Helsinki Accords," *Human Rights: International Documents*, 3rd Vol., (Alphen aan den Rijn, the Netherlands: Sijthoff and Noordhoff Publishers, 1978), pp. 1416-17.
9. "Les Americains Expliquent Leur Succes," *Tribune de Genève*, August 18, 1983.
10. A. Ball, "Outlook for MIP-TV is Bullish Despite Recession; Some 4,000 Visitors From 107 Countries Expected," *Television/Radio Age*, 29:4, (April 1982), p. A-17.

11. John S. Roberts, "Mozart: the Demythologizing of Musical Genies," *BM/E's World Broadcast News*, 4:10, (June 1982), pp. 21-22, 24.
12. OTI, Doc. D.P. No. 760, January 7, 1982.
13. EBU, "Statistics of Eurovision Programs and News Exchanges, 1.1.1981-31.12.1981," *EBU Review*, 33:3, (May 1982), p. 38.
14. "OTI — Gets Things Done," *BM/E's World Broadcast News*, 1:3, (January-February 1979), p. 18.
15. UN Document, A/AC. 105/66, (1969).
16. Nordenstreng and Varis, *op. cit.*, pp. 13-15.
17. *Ibid.*
18. For a look at jamming and anti-jamming techniques, see Stanley Leinwoll, "New Developments in Jamming," *Radio-Electronics*, 52:3, (March 1981), pp. 15-20.
19. Paul L. Laskin and Abram Chayes, "International Satellite Controversy," *Society*, 12:6, (September-October 1975), p. 33.
20. A short bibliography on the history of information control would include the following works: Zechariah Chafee, Jr., *Free Speech in the United States*, (Cambridge: Harvard University Press, 1941); Fred S. Siebert, *Freedom of the Press in England 1476-1776*, (Urbana, Ill.: University of Illinois Press, 1952); John McCormick and Mairi MacInnes, eds., *Versions of Censorship: An Anthology*, (Chicago: Aldine Publishing Company, 1962); and Ben H. Bagdikian, *The Information Machines: Their Impact on Men and the Media*, (New York: Harper & Row Publishers, 1971).
21. For more about the international direct satellite broadcasting debate, see Benno Signitzer, *Regulation of Direct Broadcasting from Satellites. The UN Involvement*, (New York: Praeger Publishers, 1976); Josef C. Nichols, "Some Aspects of Direct Satellite Broadcasting,"*EBU Review*, 25:3, (May 1974), pp. 10-19; and EBU, "Memorandum on Direct Television Broadcasting by Satellite and the Legal Norms for its Use," *EBU Review*, 26:1, (January 1975), pp. 58-74.
22. A useful basic description of broadcasting systems around the world can be found in Walter B. Emery, *National and International Systems of Broadcasting: Their History, Operation and Control*, (East Lansing, MI.: Michigan State University Press, 1969). Other comparative works include Wilson Dizard, *Television – A World View*, (Syracuse, N.Y.: Syracuse University Press, 1966); Pierre Miquel, *Histoire de la radio et de la télévision*, (Paris: Edition Richelieu, 1972); Timothy Green, *The Universal Eye – World Television in the Seventies*, (London: The Bodley Head, 1972); Albert Namurois, *Structures and Organization of Broadcasting in the Framework of Radiocommunications*, (Geneva:

EBU, 1972); and Anthony Smith, *The Shadow in the Cave, A Study of the Relationship Between the Broadcaster, His Audience and the State*, (London: Quartet Books Ltd., 1976).
23. Burton Paulu, *Radio and Television Broadcasting in Eastern Europe*, (Minneapolis: University of Minnesota, 1974), p. 30.
24. Mark W. Hopkins, *Mass Media in the Soviet Union*, (New York: Western Publishing Company, 1970), p. 244.
25. *Ibid.*, p. 242.
26. Paulu, *op. cit.*, pp. 50-51.
27. The term "radiofication" refers to the construction and putting into service of stations. "Arrêté du 29 novembre 1933 du Conseil des Commissaires du peuple de l'USSR. Règlement concernant le comité de radiofication et de radiodiffusion de l'Union auprès du Conseil des Commissaires du peuple de l'USSR," *Journal des télécommunications*, 1:2, (February 1934), p. 50.
28. *Ibid.*, pp. 50-52.
29. Hopkins, *op. cit.*, p. 91.
30. These figures are from Gayle Durham Hollander, "Communications," in Ellen Mickiewicz, ed., *Handbook of Soviet Social Science Data*, (New York: The Free Press, 1973), p. 183.
31. UNESCO, *Statistics on Radio and Television 1950-1960*, (Paris: UNESCO, 1963).
32. Hollander, *op. cit.*, p. 183.
33. Hopkins, *op. cit.*, p. 251.
34. Dizard, *op. cit.*, p. 181.
35. Figures for 1950 from Hollander, *op. cit.*, p. 183. Figures for 1981 from OIRT, "Volume of Television Broadcasting in the Soviet Union," *OIRT Radio-Television*, 32:1, (1982), p. 10.
36. Figures for 1950 from Hollander, *op. cit.*, p. 183. Figures for 1974 from UNESCO, *Statistical Yearbook: 1976*, (Paris: UNESCO, 1977).
37. Figures for 1964 from Hollander, *op. cit.*, p. 183. Figures for 1981 from OIRT, "Volume of Television Broadcasting in the Soviet Union," *op. cit.*, p. 10. In 1981, of the four national television channels, 85 percent of the Soviet population received the first channel, about 65 percent received the second, and more than 20 percent received the third and fourth channels. Nearly 100 percent of the population may follow the first Central Program of the Soviet Radio, 80 percent can follow the second program and 70 percent the third. In addition, two union radio programs and one local program are broadcast to all Soviet republics. Television broadcasts are presented in 40 languages.
38. See S.V. Borodich, "Development of Satellite Communications and

Broadcasting in the Soviet Union," *Telecommunication Journal*, 45:9, (October 1978), pp. 547-552.
39. Paulu, *op. cit.*, p. 53.
40. *Ibid.*
41. *Ibid.*, pp. 56-68. Commercials do exist on Soviet television. What is being advertised are not products, but a particular set of economic policies. Commercials feature new state products and industrial achievements as a way of showing citizens that the current policies are making the USSR productive and that better times are coming. Advertising time is limited to about three percent of total air time.
42. *Ibid.*, pp. 54-55.
43. "Soviets Plan New Channel, More Open Programming," *BM/E's World Broadcast News*, 4:8, (April 1982), p. 6.
44. BBC, *Annual Report and Handbook – 1982*, (London: BBC, 1981), p. 48.
45. David E. Powell, "Television in the USSR," *The Public Opinion Quarterly*, 39:3, (Fall 1975), pp. 287-288. See also Hopkins, *op. cit.*, p. 239; M. Andreyev, "Television in the USSR," *Bulletin of the Institute for the Study of the USSR*, 7, (1960), p. 31; and Richard Tuber, "A Survey of Programming on the Central Studios of Television, Moscow, USSR," *Journal of Broadcasting*, 4, (1960), pp. 234-235.
46. *Ibid.*, p. 287.
47. *Ibid.*, p. 290-295.
48. "Soviets Plan New Channel, More Open Programming," *op. cit.*, p. 6.
49. In addition to radio, Germany was also one of the first countries to experiment with television. Television was publicly shown at a Berlin exposition in 1933 during which Goebbels expressed his interest in the new medium. In 1935, four television rooms were set up in Berlin. Although the BBC started the world's first regular television service in 1936, transmissions stopped with the outbreak of the war. But, in Germany television service continued until 1943. See "Les progrès de la télévision — Allemagne," *Journal des télécommunications*, 2:5,(May 1935), p. 152; and Asa Briggs, *The History of Broadcasting in the United Kingdom*. 2nd Vol.: *The Golden Age of Wireless*, (London: Oxford University Press, 1965), p. 583.
50. Jean Gantelme, "From Private Enterprise to the Idea of Public Service in Broadcasting," *EBU Documentation and Information Bulletin*, 1:1, (May 15, 1950), pp. 45-46.
51. Emery, *op. cit.*, p. 297.
52. Goebbels was the propaganda director for the Nazi Party. But, from March 1933 to the end of the Third Reich, he never had overall control of the propaganda machine. Jurisdictional disputes often arose with

Reich press secretary Otto Dietrich and with the radio services of the Foreign Ministry and those of the Wehrmacht.
53. Quoted in Asa Briggs, *The History of Broadcasting in the United Kingdom*. 3rd Vol.: *The War of Words*, (London: Oxford University Press, 1970), pp. 5-6. For more about Nazi mass media use, see Heinz Pohle, *Der Rundfunk als Instrument der Politik. Zur Geschicthe des deutschen Rundfunks von 1923-1938*, (Hamburg: Verlag Hans-Bredow-Institut, 1955); and Josef Wulf, *Presse und Funk im Dritten Reich: eine Dokumentation*, (Gütersloh, W. Germany: S. Mohn, 1964).
54. The figures for 1933 are from *Journal télégraphique*, 57:4, (April 1933), pp. 115-116. The figures for 1941 are from *Journal des télécommunications*, 8:8, (August 1941), p. 137.
55. "Ordonnance du 1er septembre 1939 concernant l'écoute des informations radiophoniques des stations étrangères," *Journal des télécommunications*, 6:10, (October 1939), p. 310. See also Briggs, *The War of Words, op. cit.*, p. 183.
56. See Alex Toogood, "The British Legacy in German Broadcasting," *Combroad*, 40, (July-September 1978), pp. 11-14; and Arthur Williams, *Broadcasting and Democracy in West Germany*, (London: Bradford University Press, 1976).
57. Smith, *op. cit.* p. 69.
58. Deutsche Welle and Deutschlandfunk are the Federal Government's two radio stations. Deutsche Welle, set up in 1953 although not becoming an autonomous body until 1960, produces and broadcasts foreign-language programs to overseas listeners. It has a network of shortwave relay stations that enables it to make itself heard in almost every corner of the world. Deutschlandfunk, created in 1960, broadcasts its programs on longwave to other European countries, especially East Germany. Both stations are directly financed from the federal budget, and their transmission systems are managed by the PTT. But, in the program-making field, the sole criterion imposed on the stations is to provide objective programming.
59. Williams, *op. cit.*, pp. 20-31.
60. Namurois, *op. cit.*, p. 123. For a recent look at the dualistic nature of German television, see Georg Kacher, "Protection from Competition," *TV World*, 2:5, (May 1979), pp. 14-18.
61. Williams, *op. cit.*, p. 33.
62. See John Abrams, "Holocaust: Mirroring Society's Conscience?" *TV World*, 1:6, (June 1978), pp. 23-26; "Change of Mind," *TV World*, 1:8, (August 1978), p. 5; and Peter Diem, "Holocaust and the Austrian Viewer," *EBU Review*, 31:1, (January 1980), pp. 35-40.

63. Elgin Schroeder, "Plans for Privately-Run TV Stir Strong Feelings," *Financial Times*, October 27, 1980. See also Georg Kacher, "Will There be a Commercial Revolution?" *TV World*, 3:4, (April 1980), p. 102; and Jonathan Carr, "North German Radio Reprieved," *Financial Times*, May 29, 1980. For more about ways in which Land politicians can exercise influence in broadcasting, see Williams, *op. cit.*, pp. 112-114; Smith, *op. cit.*, pp. 67-69; and John Sandford, *The Mass Media of the German-Speaking Countries*, (London: Oswald Wolff, Ltd., 1976), pp. 78-79.
64. Figures from Claude Collomb, "1,208 télévisions privées en Italie," *Le Monde*, November 14, 1982. See also, Guiseppe Richeri, "The Politics of Italian Broadcasting," *Intermedia*, 5:10, (October 1977), p. 16; and Daniele Doglio, "Shadow Boxing with the Law," *TV World*, 4:11, (November 1980), p. 14.
65. Bruno Vasari, *Financial Aspects of Broadcasting*, (Geneva: EBU, 1965), p. 41.
66. RAI, *Annuario RAI 1972-1975*, (Rome: RAI, 1976), p. 433.
67. Emery, *op. cit.*, p. 262.
68. G. Anema, "Organisation de la radiodiffusion en Italie," *Revue juridique internationale de la radioélectricité*, 9:1, (January-March 1933), pp. 12-22.
69. Emery, *op. cit.*, p. 265. Four months after the liberation of Rome, the name of the city's radio station was changed to Radio Audizioni Italiano (RAI) so as not to be confused with Mussolini's EIAR which was relocated to Turin.
70. RAI, *op. cit.*, p. 438.
71. Carlo Zini Lamberti, "Aspects juridiques de la télévision en Italie," *UER Bulletin de Documentation et d'Information*, 2:3, (May 15, 1951), pp. 241-251.
72. Namurois, *op. cit.*, pp. 127-129.
73. See P. Greco, "Monopoly in Television Broadcasting Services and Freedom of Expression," *EBU Review*, 64B, (November 1960), pp. 29-34. Italy has one of Europe's most complex systems for ensuring government control of telecommunications. See Geoffrey Thompson, "Communications Administration in Europe...Home of Monopoly," *Communications News*, 11:11, (November 1975), pp. 6-8; and James Buxton, "Italy Could Go Private with Illegal Data Networks," *Financial Times*, June 10, 1982.
74. Vincent Porter, "Italy Changes Direction Again," *Intermedia*, 4:10, (October 1976), p. 21.
75. *Ibid.*
76. See Filippo M. De Sanetis, *La."vidéo libre" en Italie*, (Strasbourg:

Council of Europe, 1976); and Roberto Faenza, *The Radio Phenomenon in Italy*, (Strasbourg: Council of Europe, 1977).
77. R. Esposito and A. Grassi, "The Monopoly Reformed, the New Italian Broadcasting Act (Part I)," *EBU Review*, 26:4, (July 1975), p. 41.
78. De Sanetis, *op. cit.*, pp. 15-17.
79. R. Esposito and A. Grassi, "The Monopoly Reformed, the New Italian Broadcasting Act (Part II),"*EBU Review*, 26:5, (September 1975), pp. 52-57.
80. De Sanetis, *op. cit.*, pp. 6-7.
81. EBU, "Official Inauguration of Color Television," *EBU Review*, 161, (February 1977), p. 43. For an account of the politics in Italy's color television choice, see William Tuohy, "Color TV Pirates Invade Italy, While Rome Dithers,"*International Herald Tribune*, July 16, 1975.
82. See Faenza, *op. cit.*, pp. 8-19.
83. See Francesco Cavalli-Sforza, A. Donati and Huw Evans, *Independent Television Networks in Italy at the Turning Point from Cable to Broadcasting*, (Strasbourg: Council of Europe, 1977).
84. The Commission ended the tradition of electing members to sit on the Administrative Council on the basis of party affiliation. The Commission's appointees are chosen from a list of administrators and educators. An understanding also exists that IRI shall elect its members on apolitical principles. "New RAI Governors,"*Intermedia*, 5:2, (February 1977), p. 3.
85. For an analysis of the 1975 Act, see Esposito and Grassi, "The Monopoly Reformed, the New Italian Broadcasting Act (Part II), *op. cit.*, pp. 52-57.
86. E. Santoro, "Judgement of the Italian Constitutional Court on the Monopoly of RAI — Radiotelevisione Italiana," *EBU Review*, 28:1, (January 1977), pp. 29-30.
87. "Porn Time, Black and White or Color, Italian TV's Increasingly Blue," *Time* (Europe), April 24, 1978. For a look into the operations of several private stations, see "Independent Broadcasters — A Guide to the Activities and Holdings of the Major Independents," *TV World*, 4:10, (October 1981), p. 42.
88. Bruce Vanervort, "Swiss Crack Down on International Pirates," *BM/E's World Broadcast News*, 4:7, (March 1982), pp. 14-16.
89. "Monaco," *BM/E's World Broadcast News*, 4:9, (May 1982), p. 19.
90. Interview with Jacques Neuen, Administrative Assistant, RTL, July 1982.
91. Gust Graas, "Petite...et grand histoire de Radio-Télé-Luxembourg," in R. Mehlen, ed., *30e Anniversaire au carrefour de l'Europe Radio-Télé-Luxembourg*, (Luxembourg: Imprimerie Bourg-Bourger, 1961), p. 30.

92. Jean Le Duc, "Adieu Vat!" in R. Mehlen, ed., *30e Anniversaire au carrefour de l'Europe Radio-Télé-Luxembourg*, op.cit., p. 20.
93. *Ibid.* The public service principles, justifying the private broadcasting monopoly, were reaffirmed in 1966 when the government refused to license any other company but CLT. See Gust Graas, "Refusal of Operating License for a Broadcasting Station," *EBU Review*, 100B, (November 1966), pp. 83-84.
94. Grass, "Petite...et grand histoire de Radio-Télé-Luxembourg," *op. cit.*, p. 31.
95. Neuen, *op. cit.* See Paul Zahn, "Europe's Airwaves Need a Real Prince Charming," *Advertising Age Europe*, 1:6, (June 30, 1979), p. 8.
96. *Cahier des Charges*, (August 20, 1930), Art. 7.
97. *Ibid.*, Art. 8.
98. *Ibid.*, Art. 7.
99. Interview with Daniel Schwall, Legal Affairs, RTL, Luxembourg, December 1982.
100. *Cahier des Charges*, *op. cit.*, Art. 11, and CLT, *Statuts*, (February 1964).
101. Neuen, *op. cit.* For an account of RTL's program-making, see "Europe's Superstation: RTL," *BM/E's World Broadcast News*, 2:6, (February 1980), pp. 10-11; and "Europe's Superstation: RTL (Part II): Télé-Luxembourg," *BM/E's World Broadcast News*, 2:7, (March 1980), pp. 10-11.
102. Briggs, *The Golden Age of Wireless, op. cit.*, pp. 352-356, and 359-369.
103. See Jean-C. Texier, "Le défi français," *La vie française*, (March 31, 1980); "Satellite TV Franco-Allemand: Confirmation d'un accord avant pâques," *Electronic actualités*, (March 21, 1980); and Dominique Simonnet, "TV: Satellite contre monopole," *L'Express*, April 26-May 2, 1980.
104. For more about the "périphérique" stations, see Jean-Emmanuel and Muriel Ray, *Corsaires des ondes: Europe 1, RTL, RMC et compagnie*, (Paris: Editions du Cerf, 1978); and Charles Debbasch, *Traité du droit de la radiodiffusion*, (Paris: R. Pichon et R. Durand-Auzias, 1967), pp. 63-73.
105. In 1982, the major CLT stockholder, with 54.6 percent, was Audiofina/Fratel group which includes the Compagnie Bruxelles Lambert, Havas, Régie Information et Publicité and Baron Empain. The remaining shares are divided among the following: Compagnie des Compteurs, with 12.8 percent; Hachette, with 16.2 percent; Paribas, with 10.3 percent; and the rest dispersed among the public. W. van Poucke, "Luxembourg: Fly in the Ointment," *BM/E's World Broadcast News*, 4:10, (June 1982), p. 32.

106. The idea of limited advertising is to avoid transmitting commercials when children are watching television. W. Long, "West Germany Pushing Cable Hard," *Advertising Age Europe*, 3:1, (January 1981), p. 2. See also "Schmidt Resisting Video," *Advertising Age*, 51, (December 15, 1980), pp. S1-S4; and "Luxembourg — With it Broadcasting Beams Far — and Brings in Healthy Taxes," *The Christian Science Monitor*, March 10, 1980.
107. *Ibid.*

CHAPTER 2
THE IBU EXPERIMENT

The International Broadcasting Union (IBU) was the world's first international association of broadcasting organizations.[1] During its twenty-five years of operation, it provided the means by which broadcasters from around the world could achieve many objectives including managing frequencies, preventing harmful radio propaganda, and organizing program exchanges. These objectives could be met only by international collaboration. Although its record was good, the IBU collapsed because of sharp political controversies between broadcasters of Western and Socialist Europe. The IBU experiment clearly signaled that it was impossible to unite Western and Socialist European broadcasters under one roof.

Because the EBU and OIRT trace their origins to the IBU, this chapter looks at the IBU's creation, functions, and structure. It then divides the years of the IBU's existence into three periods: 1925-38, 1939-45, and 1946-50. The first of these involved the growth of the IBU into a primary center for attacking technical, legal, and program problems. The second centered on the struggle to keep the IBU alive during World War II. The third was the postwar clash between Western and Socialist broadcasters which led to the creation and transfer of the OIRT's headquarters to Prague as well as the dissolution and transfer of the IBU's assets to the newly created EBU.

2.1 Establishment and Structure

The growth of large-scale broadcasting in the early 1920s found many European governments unprepared to meet new international obligations in this field. The news of America's radiophonic chaos prompted many European countries to carefully control the debut of national broadcasting.[2] Until 1927, no rules existed between countries for broadcasting frequencies, hours of broadcast, and limits of power.[3] In addition to an absence of international allocations, the spectrum was crowded by a growing number of stations. In 1925, for example, more than 200 stations were planned to go on the air, although only enough interference-free room existed for 99 stations.[4] The international chaos problem was further complicated by Europe's close borders and high population density. Unlike the United States, where one government agency handled interference problems, Europe's radio anarchy could only be solved by international collaboration.

Worn out by the radio anarchy and conscious that broadcasting's future depended upon international frequency regulations, European broadcasters reacted with enthusiasm and hope to the creation of the IBU in 1925. Discussion of the necessity of a world organization had begun a year earlier. At the Preliminary Conference for an International Agreement on Wireless Telephony, which met in Geneva from April 22-23, 1924,[5] there were 39 representatives of national telecommunications administrations, of radio stations, of international organizations, of radio clubs and of the radio industry. They took the first step toward establishing an international broadcasting union.[6] The conference, among other measures, decided to create a provisional executive committee to arrange a meeting to define the nature and purpose of the new organization. It was further agreed that one of the first tasks of the organization would be to establish international rules of governing broadcasting frequencies.[7]

Detailed planning began in London in March 1925. At the BBC's invitation, broadcasters from nine countries attended the two-day Informal International Conference on Broadcasting.[8] BBC Chairman, Lord Gainford, reminded the delegates of the conference's importance at the opening meeting:

> We realize that broadcasting is a new science, and it is necessary, if we are to preserve some system which is going to be satisfactory to all the nations of the world, that we must act together in a manner which will be satisfactory, efficient and not chaotic.[9]

The delegates were unanimously in favor of an international organization. The name chosen was the Union Internationale de Radiophonie — which was changed in 1929 to Union Internationale de Radiodiffusion.

Considerable wrangling arose over questions of authority and location of the secretariat. The BBC pushed for a secretariat headed by a strong director and furnished with executive powers, in order to effectively attack problems including harmful international interference.[10] The majority of delegates, however, were reluctant to create a strong, independent secretariat. They wanted the secretariat to be responsible to a watchdog committee.[11] The decisions finally embodied in the IBU's constitution specified that the secretariat would report to a council, and that it be headed by a secretary-general elected by a General Assembly. In addition, most of its tasks were aimed at facilitating contacts among member organizations.

The conference also had difficulty agreeing on the location for the secretariat.

The delegate of Radiojournal/Czechoslovakia advocated that the seat of the new organization be left to the BBC because of its expertise in broadcating.[12] But this proposal was rejected ultimately, and Geneva was chosen as the site for the Union's headquarters. The majority of the delegates felt that Geneva would give the IBU wider representation partly because of Switzerland's traditional neutrality and partly because the new organization would be close to other international organizations having allied interests, including the International Telecommunication Union (ITU) and the League of Nations.

Once agreement on all contested points was finally reached, the delegates agreed to hold the agency's first general assembly on April 3, 1925 in Geneva. The constitution of the IBU, called the Statutes, was drafted on April 3 and was unanimously adopted on April 4 at the Palais des Nations in Geneva. It was signed by representatives of eleven broadcasting organizations from ten European countries.[13]

The new organization was not intended to group representatives of national governments, for it was charged to promote and protect the interests of broadcasters. Its declared purposes were to develop good relations between broadcasters in Europe and around the world, to solve broadcasting problems, to foster the development of broadcasting, and to cooperate with national telecommunications administrations and with the ITU.

To achieve these purposes, the IBU was provided with several different representative, executive, and administrative bodies. It had an assembly in which all its members had equal rights of representation and a council with more restricted and preferential membership. The General Assembly met annually to determine the general policies of the IBU as well as to elect the secretary-general, and the members who served on the Council. The Council, which was composed of one delegate from every European country, was designed to give direction and leadership to the work of the organization as a whole. It met at least twice a year. The Council was assisted by four specialized consultative committees: the Budgetary Committee, the Legal Committee, the Program Committee, and the Technical Commmittee.

The secretariat of the IBU was divided into two separate parts, each headed by an elected official. The IBU's secretary-general was based in Geneva. His tasks were largely administrative, including publishing IBU's *Monthly Bulletin*, organizing meetings, and executing the decisions of the General Assembly and the Council.[14] The Checking Center in Brussels was the "technical arm" of the IBU. Its activities ranged from monitoring the uses of the frequency spectrum allocated to broadcasting, to providing secretarial services to the IBU Technical Committee. It was headed by a director who was appointed by the general assembly. The IBU's staff was traditionally small; increasing from six in 1925 to fourteen in 1937. With the outbreak of World War II, the number of staff fell to four.

Although it was mainly concerned with European broadcasting problems, the Union did invite broadcasting organizations from around the world to become members. IBU Statutes divided membership into active and associate members. Active membership was only open to national European broadcasting organizations, and those in countries bordering the Mediterranean Sea. Associate membership was granted to organizations outside this area. The major difference between the types of membership was that associates did not have the right to vote and hold office. From eleven founding organizations in 1925, IBU membership was at its height by 1938-39 with fifty-nine active and associate members.[15] Nearly all European countries were members with Luxembourg and the USSR as the only holdouts.[16]

The IBU's major source of income came from assessments on members. The fees of individual active members were determined on a complicated formula which took into account the number of receiving sets and the antenna powers and frequencies used.[17] Associate members shared in the costs by means of an annual contribution fixed by the Council. Active members carried most of the burden. In 1937, for example, Germany and the United Kingdom each paid nearly 25 percent of the budget.[18]

2.2 The Years of Growth: 1925-38

The IBU's creation in 1925 was an important event because it was the first time broadcasters of different countries had a permanent framework for attacking problems that could be dealt with effectively only by international collaboration. The new organization was a pioneer in a new field. Virtually every problem that arose required unique solutions. The IBU did find solutions. Indeed, by the time World War II broke out, the organization had pioneered many techniques used today by the EBU and OIRT for controlling the use of frequencies, for negotiating copyrights, and for exchanging programs. The IBU's record in dealing with technical, legal, and program exchange problems follows.

2.2.1 Technical Activities

The IBU was established principally to eliminate harmful interference between radio stations of different countries. This task was a major preoccupation of the agency until the start of World War II. Two primary activities were involved: drafting frequency allocation plans for broadcasting, and monitoring the uses of the spectrum.

Drafting frequency allocation plans for European broadcasting was the original and, at least until 1929, the primary task of the IBU. Today, it is a major function of the ITU. In the early 1920s, no international rules existed for radio broadcasting. Thus, the IBU proceeded to draw up frequency assignments to prevent harmful interference. Allocations were agreed upon in the IBU and submitted to national telecommunications administrations for approval. These regulations were frequently revised to accommodate the increasing number of stations in different bands.

In securing agreement on frequency plans, the IBU faced many of the problems which continue to be debated today. A major problem was reconciling the demands of existing stations with the rapid expansion of new ones. In preparing for Europe's first broadcasting plan — the so-called Geneva Plan — the BBC submitted a proposal based largely on the "first come, first served" principle.[19] But many IBU members disagreed with this proposal. Although many countries had not started broadcasting, they wanted frequencies reserved for them. In addition, multilingual nations such as Switzerland wanted more broadcast frequencies. Furthermore, early broadcasters knew little about the nature of the radio spectrum in order to make better allocations.[20] In the end, the Geneva Plan allocated a number of frequencies to each IBU member according to a formula which took into account the number of radio stations in the country, its population, topography, and "commercial importance" as measured by the volume of telecommunications traffic.[21]

The IBU made important strides in reducing harmful interference. The Geneva Plan, which came into force in 1926, allocated 83 exclusive and 16 shared frequencies (with a 10 kHz channel spacing) in the medium band to 168 stations in 28 countries.[22] It was effectuated by 80 percent of all European stations and resulted in an immediate reduction in interference.[23] In 1929, the IBU drafted the Brussels Plan which reshuffled new and existing stations on the medium and long wavebands as a result of the space reductions which governments imposed on broadcasters in the 1927 Washington Radiotelegraph Conference.[24] The IBU believed that producing allocation plans was its primary task. This was imperative in order to take full advantage of broadcasting technology.

But the non-governmental character of the IBU weakened its regulation activities. Each member had to submit all allocation plans negotiated within the IBU to its competent national telecommunications administration for approval. In addition, the IBU's plans were voluntary agreements. Because of the political importance of frequencies, the members of the IBU never granted the agency power to impose sanctions on stations which caused harmful interference.[25] Not all the IBU's members applied the Brussels Plan.[26] Most important of all, not all European countries such as the USSR took part in the IBU's work.

The IBU's inability to stop all interference forced governments to draft frequency allocations for Europe's broadcasters. At the 1929 Prague Radiocommunications Conference, European governments took it upon themselves to supplement the IBU's plans with formal agreements. The Prague Plan limited the IBU's role from drafting frequency plans to providing expert technical advice to governments in broadcasting matters.[27] IBU officials did not cherish the thought of politicians allocating frequencies for broadcasters for fear it would signal an end to the agency's integrity and independence.[28] But beyond the need for supplementing the IBU's plans with formal agreements, governments were prompted into frequency management because politicians increasingly realized the space in the spectrum was a valuable national asset.[29] In its new role as technical expert to governments, the IBU carried out frequency measurements and prepared for ITU radio conferences such as the 1933 Lucerne Plan and the 1939 Montreux Plan.[30]

Monitoring the uses of broadcasting frequencies was another key activity of the IBU. To check the effectiveness of frequency plans, the IBU in 1927 decided to create the Brussels Checking Center.[31] The Center monitored every European broadcasting station daily and intervened if a station went off its assigned frequencies.[32] It had no coercive power to impose sanctions, leaving conflicting parties to solve interference problems themselves. Still, the so-called "police of the air" eliminated many interference problems simply by notifying stations that they were not on their proper assignments. From 1927 to 1935, the Center made about 800,000 measurements and sent out roughly 10,000 interference notices.[33]

Broadcasters have found monitoring by an international organization to be a major tool in preventing harmful interference. The Brussels Center was the first frequency measuring station in the world to be run by an international organization. As we shall see, monitoring is also an activity of the EBU and OIRT. It should be noted that governments have never allowed the ITU to conduct monitoring for fear of losing control in this sensitive area.[34]

2.2.2 Legal Activities

Beyond frequency management, the IBU also offered the means by which broadcasters could protect themselves from exorbitant copyright fees and harmful radio propaganda. Broadcasters' concern for protecting themselves from high copyright fees was a primary reason for creating the International Broadcasting Union. At the 1925 London Conference, delegates agreed that the IBU should provide a forum for broadcasters to exchange information on ways to prevent higher fees.[35] In addition, the delegates agreed that the new organization should lobby not only for the inclusion of radio into existing national and international copyright acts, but also for uniform protection and royalty payments betweeen countries. In response to these concerns, the IBU created a Legal Committee in 1926 to study and issue recommendations on copyright and other legal questions.[36]

The IBU's solution was to lobby against exorbitant fees at international copyright revision conferences. The revision of the Berne Convention in 1928 is a case in point. The 1928 revision was critical to broadcasters. Although authors of literary, dramatic, and musical works were long protected by the Berne Convention, broadcasting was new, unknown during the 1908 Berlin revision. The IBU spent three years preparing for the revision conference which was held in Rome. Besides determining the existing copyright situation in each country, the Legal Committee, composed of jurists from all IBU members, prepared a memorandum advocating the position of broadcasting in regard to proposals formulated by governments, particularly Article 11bis which advocated giving authors exclusive rights on the communication of their work by broadcasting. The Committee's study argued that the economic interests of authors should be kept within reasonable limits. It also was against any scheme which required prior consent of the author each time a record is to be broadcast, arguing that this would render broadcasting impossible because of the difficulty of obtaining authorization in the necessary time.

The IBU's memorandum was submitted to interested governments and international organizations. In addition, the IBU asked members to send representatives to national preparatory discussions and try to secure positions in delegations to the conference so as to promote and protect the Union's views.[37] While the revision conference adopted Article 11bis, it also suggested that the member nations give special consideration to limiting the rights of authors so as not to prevent broadcasting from performing its public service duties.[38] The IBU was satisfied with the outcome of the conference, because it felt that governments now recognized the special character of broadcasting.[39]

Propaganda issues also arose frequently in the IBU. Because the IBU viewed propaganda to be harmful to international relations, it was active in resolving disputes between members and in adopting anti-propaganda resolutions. A conflict between German and Polish radio stations was brought to an end in 1931 through the good offices of the IBU. The IBU's secretary-general played a major role in bringing the broadcasters of the two countries to agreement.[40]

The IBU also adopted resolutions against harmful propaganda. In 1925, for example, at the request of Czech radio, a resolution was adopted urging members not to broadcast material on the internal affairs of other countries which might cause political problems.[41]

But the effectiveness of the IBU's anti-propaganda resolutions were limited largely by the fact that they were not binding on governments, who in many countries have the final say in broadcasting matters. To overcome this limitation, the IBU lobbied extensively for international governmental control before the League of Nations. A high point came in 1936 with the signing, under League auspices, of the International Convention Concerning the Uses of Broadcasting in the Cause of Peace. The IBU was a major initiator of the Convention. To get the issue on the League's agenda, the IBU prepared resolutions that were then submitted by members of national delegations.[42] Once the League decided to study the question, the IBU was active in meetings of the League's International Committee on Intellectual Cooperation which was responsible for drafting a convention. The Union's position was submitted to all the League's members.[43] After three years of work, the Convention was signed in 1936 and went into force in 1938. The Convention recommended the IBU sit on a special committee to resolve offenses among the signatories. But the IBU refused the invitation because its constitution prohibited involvement in political activities.[44]

The Convention did little to deter the increasing use of radio for propaganda and psychological warfare purposes, particularly after World War II. In the 1930s, many countries began foreign-language broadcasts particularly on shortwave for propaganda purposes. The growth continued during World War II and climaxed with the cold war. Today, the Convention is still in force, and the United Nations has continued the work begun by the League with respect to war propaganda. And interestingly enough, the international community is faced with many of the same questions on drawing up an international convention on regulating direct satellite broadcasting as were raised in 1930.[45]

2.2.3 Program Activities

The IBU's creation was also an expression of founding members' desire to organize program exchanges. As Captain Eckersley, one of the founders of the IBU, told the delegates at the 1925 London Conference, "to make broadcasting more interesting, the exchange of programs is going to be an important thing".[46] Members then agreed that program exchanges should be coordinated by an IBU program committee consisting of program executives.[47]

Organizing program exchanges was a primary task of the IBU as the "National Nights" program series shows. The idea behind the "Nights" series was that on a prearranged evening each month (except in summer) European IBU members would voluntarily broadcast musical and literary works of a particular country. The Geneva office translated and distributed all the necessary program material, including an introductory paper on the social life of the country, void of any "political problems", to participating members.[48] The preparation and broadcast of the "Nights" was the responsibility of the broadcasting organization of the country selected.

In addition to giving members access to one another's programs, the IBU viewed the value of the "Nights" as contributing to international understanding. The "Nights,"[49] the Council declared, gave "the listeners a simple and readily comprehensible example of efforts being made at present to create a better understanding between different peoples." From 1926 to 1931, 34 concerts were exchanged.[50] With the experience countries gained in simultaneously relaying programs over telephone lines, the IBU in September 1931, replaced the "Nights" with two different program exchange series: the "European Concerts" and the "International Concerts."[51]

Generally, the IBU's role as a "program clearing-house" was successful and went smoothly. One proposal which the IBU dropped was the creation of a center for exchanging recordings. In 1936, the Geneva office proposed that a recording studio be created and housed within the office to collect, record and distribute outstanding broadcasts. But in 1937, the council decided against the enterprise partly because of the high cost of buying additional equipment and hiring additional staff, and partly because the quality of recordings, which would be taken off of telephone cables, would be inferior to that of commercial studio recordings.[52]

Nevertheless, interest in the IBU's program activities was great as the growing number of offers received by the Geneva office illustrates. In 1932, 131 offerings (123 "International Concerts," 8 "European Concerts") were cleared by the Geneva office.[53] By 1938, the number of offerings had grown to 1,033 (957 "International Concerts," 4 "European Concerts," 2 "World Concerts," and 70 news events).[54]

But in 1939, with the start of World War II, many of the IBU's activities were abandoned. In fact, the IBU was nearly closed.

2.3 The Years of Conflict: 1939-45

The need for the IBU was tested by the start of World War II. In November 1939, two months after the start of hostilities, IBU President Antoine Dubois called for the closing of the Union largely because of a lack of funds. He feared that the Geneva secretariat could only operate for a short period if some of the conflicting nations did not resume their membership payments.[55] In addition, the closing of the Geneva office would permit the diversion of funds to keep the Brussels Checking Center running.[56]

But many member organizations and the IBU officials feared that the closing of the Geneva office would result in the union's death. Swiss broadcasters took a leading role in arguing that the closing of the Geneva secretariat would deprive the IBU of not only its effective management but also its legal existence as set forth in Swiss law.[57] IBU Secretary-General Arthur Burrows pointed out that although the Geneva office did not carry out any technical activities related to the application of international frequency plans, it nevertheless provided members with the machinery to exchange views, to defend themselves against opposing interests and to provide for the full development of broadcasting.[58]

In April 1940, the general assembly decided to continue the activities of both the Geneva and Brussels offices on a limited level. Beyond budget and staff cuts, the IBU was placed under the protection of Swiss neutrality in order to guarantee objectivity. The assembly also appointed Swiss broadcaster Alfred Glogg to assume the direction of the Geneva office and to act as interim Secretary-General until a successor to Burrows, who resigned to resume work with the BBC, was found. The assembly hoped these steps would ensure the IBU's existence for the duration of the war.[59]

Despite these measures, the Union found it increasingly difficult to work, particularly as the scope of the war grew. Indeed, some of its activities came to a complete halt. The "European" and "World" concerts, for example, died a quiet death in 1939,[60] and the last "International Concerts" offering which Geneva received was in 1940.[61] In addition, the IBU's Technical, Legal, and Program Committees failed to meet at all during the war.[62]

The experience of the Checking Center is a case in point. Six days after Hitler's armies invaded Belgium in May 1940, the Center's equipment and papers were evacuated first to France and then to Switzerland. But the Center's relocation to Geneva did not please the Germans who demanded that it be returned to Brussels partly for prestige reasons and partly for monitoring allied broadcasts. Although IBU officials insisted that the Center remain on neutral Swiss soil to serve all members equally, the Germans threatened to withdraw from the IBU and to use diplomatic pressure on Switzerland if the Center's equipment was not returned. In fact, the Center was so important to the Third Reich that the Germans started building another monitoring center in Brussels. In January 1941, the IBU allowed the Center to return to Brussels.[63]

Handing the Center over to the Germans, however, prompted charges of Nazi collaboration and a series of resignations from the IBU. Between 1940 and 1942, thirteen active and associate members from ten countries left the IBU.[64] In addition, several governments-in-exile in London informed the British government, and even announced over the BBC, that, although they would remain in the IBU, their national broadcasting organizations did not consider themselves bound by any of the Union's decisions made in the absence of all of its properly accredited representatives.[65] Aside from criticizing the IBU executives for allowing the Checking Center to be returned to Brussels, the governments of some of the occupied countries in exile suspected that the Germans were using the Center for military purposes.[66] The resignations left IBU membership largely confined to axis countries and axis-controlled organizations in other countries.

Despite becoming largely a Nazi-controlled organization, the IBU continued to meet and conduct limited activities during the war. The general assembly and the council met regularly except in 1945. The Checking Center continued its frequency activities.[67] Although its staff was reduced, the Geneva office continued to perform administrative tasks.

Significantly, by maintaining some of its activities throughout the war, the IBU did not die, thus providing a framework not only for its renewal after the end of the conflict, but also for the creation of the EBU and the OIRT.

2.4 The Years of Defeat and Rebirth: 1946-50

This section describes the fall of the IBU and the birth of the EBU and OIRT. It explains, for example, how cold-war politics made it necessary for broadcasters from Western and Socialist nations of Europe to have separate organizations — the EBU in the West and the OIRT in the East.

After the war, the IBU's leaders tried to secure a prominent place for the organization in influencing international broadcasting policy.[68] The IBU's primary problem at this time was not expansion, however, but survival. The major decisions about the postwar structure of European broadcasting collaboration were taken by Soviet, British and French broadcasters. France preferred an organization which would group broadcasters from around the world, particularly those of the USSR which never joined the IBU. It felt that this organization — whether a rebuilt IBU or a new body — should symbolize the prevailing postwar feeling of "international collaboration" that brought about the creation of the United Nations. The Soviets, however, were hostile to the IBU largely because of its questionable wartime collaboration with the Nazis. They preferred that broadcasting interests be expressed in a new world body. The BBC was skeptical about creating a new body because it felt that problems would be better solved by an experienced organization. It was also against granting membership to the Soviet republics.

At a meeting of broadcasters in Brussels in May 1946, the USSR came forward with proposals for a new international organization to be called the

International Broadcasting Organization (OIR).[69] These proposals included provisions to permit the OIR to become a world organization and envisaged that immediately following the OIR's birth, the IBU should be dissolved. The Soviet proposals were unanimously approved, with the abstention of the BBC.[70] The meeting sent out a draft constitution and invitations to the OIR's Constitutive Assembly.

At the OIR's Constitutive Assembly, which met in June 1946 in Brussels, considerable wrangling over questions of voting procedure and membership occurred. Disagreement first flared up during the Assembly's opening session when the Swiss delegation, supported by the BBC and Radio Nederland, proposed that only organizations from independent and internationally recognized nations should be allowed to vote.[71] But the Soviet delegate opposed the Swiss proposal, arguing that the radio services of the Soviet republics are independently controlled and operated and that the services from the Baltic States had been members of the IBU with full voting rights.[72] The problem was put to the Assembly's thirty-five delegations for a vote.[73] The Assembly voted twenty-seven to four (four delegates were absent) to give one vote in the Assembly to each of the invited delegates, until adoption of a definite voting article in the OIR's constitution.[74]

But agreement on a definite voting article in the OIR's constitution proved difficult. Most of the delegates, including the BBC, opposed the Soviet proposal that each OIR member have one vote for fear that serious disparities in influence would result. The BBC argued that a new voting formula was needed to prevent the USSR from having eight votes, France and its colonies in the European Broadcasting Area (Algeria, Morocco and Tunisia) from having four, while the United Kingdom would only have one vote.[75] The delegates of the USSR and Poland, however, argued that the voting issue had been settled earlier.[76]

The discussions grew so heated that the OIR's creation was placed in doubt. In fact, to prevent the Assembly from dissolving over the issue, the delegates agreed that a world conference of broadcasters would be called after the OIR's creation to define, among other things, the voting rights of OIR members.[77] It was hoped that this constitutional pledge to call a world conference would calm the complaints of the BBC and other Western broadcasters concerning voting rights and thus permit the creation of the OIR to go ahead. But the organizations from the following countries refused to sign the constitution: Denmark, Ireland, Norway, Portugal, Sweden, Switzerland, Turkey and the United Kingdom[78]

On June 29, one day after OIR became a reality, delegates from organizations of twenty-three countries attended the IBU General Assembly in Geneva to consider the question of dissolution. Most of the delegates favored dissolving the IBU because they saw no need for the existence of two international associations.[79] But some broadcasters, including those from Switzerland and Spain, wanted to keep the IBU alive until after the proposed world conference which the OIR was constitutionally required to call.[80]

The dissolution proposal, however, fell two votes short of being accepted. The voting, with fifteen for dissolution, two against, and six abstentions, did not produce the three-quarters majority stipulated in the IBU constitution.[81] After the vote, the organizations of Belgium, France, the Netherlands, and all the Soviet-bloc countries resigned. The BBC decided to remain outside both the IBU and OIR.[82]

The following day, the IBU declared that it dissolve itself after the proposed world conference.[83] But the conference was never held. In October 1946, the OIR decided that it was not necessary to call such a conference because the results of the Moscow and Paris Telecommunications Conferences, held in preparation for the 1947 Atlantic City Conference, suggested that future activities of broadcasting unions would be largely limited to regional matters, while international issues would be handled by the ITU.[84] Léo Wallenborn, in his study of postwar European broadcasting, notes that the decisions leading up to the Atlantic City radio conference reflected the desire of governments to regain sole control of broadcasting; thus any acts by broadcasters would have to be closely linked to those of the ITU.[85] In light of this situation, the OIR dropped the pledge to call a world conference from its constitution. This decision, however, freed the remaining IBU members from their decision to dissolve the Union. For the BBC, the OIR still remained unattractive largely because of membership and voting issues.[86]

Having decided against calling a world conference, the larger, stronger OIR set out to crush the IBU in hopes of becoming the sole organization representing European broadcasting interests. At the 1948 European Broadcasting Conference in Copenhagen, for example, the OIR argued that because the IBU was a dead organization, only the OIR should be appointed the international frequency expert to governments; a position of much institutional pride. As we have already seen, all previous frequency plans, since the 1929 Prague Plan, appointed the IBU as technical expert. But the withdrawal of most of its members crippled the IBU, leaving it with only eleven active members in 1948.[87] In contrast, the OIR, with its twenty-eight members, was active in attacking technical, legal, and program problems. In 1947, it rented the Brussels Checking Center from the IBU. In the legal field, the OIR began negotiating contracts with authors' and performers' organizations, providing a basis for contemporary model contracts.[88] In the program field, in 1947, the

OIR created an international program clearing center to facilitate the exchange of program offerings and requests.[89]

Although the Copenhagen Convention provided for an "international expert organization," no agreement could be reached on appointing either the IBU or the OIR. Both agencies failed to muster the necessary support of at least twenty-eight of the thirty-three countries of the European Broadcasting Area.[90] The Conference's failure to name an expert largely reflected the growing cold war clash between Socialist countries and the West.[91] The conference came at a time when the cold war was polluting the world political environment. The summer of 1948 saw the signing of the Brussels Pact and the start of the Berlin Blockade.

The failure to choose an expert at Copenhagen touched off collective actions — which grew more difficult as the cold war grew — to regroup European broadcasters under one roof before the Copenhagen Plan went into effect in March 1950. The first significant action came in the Spring of 1949 when the BBC, after talks with IBU and OIR officials at Copenhagen and at the 1948 Mexico City High Frequency Broadcasting Conference, declared that it would join the OIR, provided certain statutory provisions were changed. One major change which the BBC insisted upon was granting voting rights only to broadcasting organizations of countries which were members of the ITU,[92] thus excluding the five Soviet republics, Algeria, Morocco, and Tunisia from active OIR membership.

At the OIR's invitation, broadcasters from the IBU, the BBC, and the OIR met in Stresa, Italy, in August 1947 to discuss the British proposal as the basis for a single European broadcasting organization. Belgium, France, Italy, and the Netherlands felt that the BBC's proposal would prompt desertions from the IBU, thus assuring the OIR's appointment as technical expert.[93] But broadcasters from Czechoslovakia, Rumania, and the USSR were hostile to the proposal because the Soviet republics would lose their voting rights.[94]

In the face of seemingly irreconcilable differences, plans for a single organization for European broadcasting died. In the course of the talks, the representatives of Belgium, France, Italy, and the Netherlands agreed that they would leave the OIR.[95] Julien Kuypers, the chairman of the OIR, alluded to the impossibility of unifying European broadcasting at the close of the Conference, declaring that the talks were not "useless if only because it made our respective positions quite clear and dispelled certain illusions which we have cherished for many years in believing that it was possible in certain conditions to achieve a unity of European broadcasting."[96]

Moreover, East-West relations were strained at the time of the Stresa meeting. In 1949, the North Atlantic Treaty was signed and the United States began a military assistance program for its Allies. On the economic front, the Soviets countered the Marshall Plan with the creation of the Council of Mutual Economic Assistance. On the other side of the world, the civil war in China ended with the communists gaining control of the entire Chinese mainland in the fall of 1949. The following year the Korean War started.

It was against this backdrop of East-West antagonism that broadcasters from Belgium, France, Italy, and the Netherlands — all OIR members — as well as representatives from the BBC and an official from the IBU and the OIR met in Paris in October 1949 for two days of talks on creating a new agency of West European broadcasters. In the final report, the delegates unanimously agreed that the new agency should be a regional body with membership limited to broadcasting organizations from countries which were not only located in the European Broadcasting Area but also members of the ITU. They then invited the BBC to send invitations out to all broadcasting services of all countries in the European Broadcasting Area which were members of the ITU to attend a conference to be held in the United Kingdom in 1950 to create a new broadcasting union.[97]

The OIR General Assembly held in Brussels in November 1949 hotly debated the results of the Stresa and Paris meetings. One participant observed that the eleven-day meeting was the "most dramatic and disconcerting of all the sessions that the OIR had held..."[98] The Assembly atmosphere was further clouded by the resignations of eleven West European broadcasting organizations from the OIR. On November 17, 1949, the delegates of the organizations from Algeria, France, Italy, Luxembourg, Monaco, Morocco, the Netherlands, Tunisia, and the Vatican City announced or confirmed that they would withdraw from the OIR. The organizations from Belgium and Egypt soon did the same. They believed that no chance existed that the OIR would win recognition as the expert organization. In addition, they agreed that the OIR, in which West European countries were a minority, had not done all it could to unify European interests. Furthermore, in light of the consensus reached on forming a new international organization, they saw no need to stay in the OIR.

The Soviets were enraged by the resignations. They accused the BBC as largely responsible for the failure of the Stresa meeting, because the conditions set by the BBC on joining the OIR discriminated against some of the OIR's founding members.[99] The USSR's views were supported by other Socialist countries.[100] The resigning Western organizations, on the other hand, put the blame for Stresa on the USSR.[101]

The salient feature of the 1949 OIR general assembly was that despite three years of effort, European broadcasters could not merge the IBU and OIR. In the face of seemingly irreconcilable differences between East and West, plans for a unified European broadcasing agency gave way to plans for moving the OIR headquarters to Eastern Europe and creating the EBU to promote and protect the interests of West European broadcasters.

On January 5, 1950, an extraordinary OIR General Assembly was held in Prague to consider changes in the organization in order to reflect its new membership. The two-day meeting was attended by fifteen of the seventeen remaining OIR members, mostly from the socialist countries of Europe.[102] The organizations from Syria and Yugoslavia were absent. As the delegates got down to negotiations, the first task was to find a new headquarters for the OIR. The resignation of Belgium from the OIR legally prompted the agency to look for a new home.[103] The delegates unanimously accepted the invitation of the Czech government to move the OIR's administrative and technical headquarters to Prague.[104] They also agreed to other statutory changes. Besides electing new OIR officials, new representatives were elected to the administrative council to fill vacant seats. In addition, the organizations from Czechoslovakia and the USSR were given permanent council seats.[105]

The OIR's move to Prague was swift. At the end of January, the OIR began moving its own equipment and papers from Brussels to Prague. By the beginning of March 1950, the OIR's new monitoring station in Prague started conducting frequency measurements.[106] On February 23, 1950, by releasing the managers and staff in Brussels, the OIR gave the EBU an important "christening gift."

A new phase in the history of European broadcasting began on February 6, 1950, when West European broadcasters met formally in Torquay, England to create the EBU. Held at the invitation of the BBC, the broadcasting organizations from twenty-two West European, Mid-Eastern, and North African nations attended or were represented at the conference.[107] The broadcasting organizations from the Federal Republic of Germany and Spain were the only West European services not present. The reason for not inviting the Spanish and West German organizations was that both countries were not ITU members at the time.[108]

From the start, the atmosphere in Torquay was businesslike and friendly. On the first day of the conference, Sir Ian Jacob, director of the BBC Overseas Service, was elected president of the constitutive conference. The delegates also set up the following three conference committees: *1*) an Administrative Committee, *2*) a Technical Committee and *3*) a Drafting Committee. On February 9, the conference voted unanimously in favor of Jacob's proposal that the new body should be called the "European Broadcasting Union."[109]

Although the delegates adopted the articles of constitution almost unanimously, some disagreement arose concerning the seat of the EBU, the structure of the secretariat, and the linking of EBU membership with that of the ITU. Regarding the first issue, the INR/Belgium favored locating the seat of the Union in the same building as the Technical Center because it would provide members with a centralized, less costly agency.[110] But the Swiss delegation advocated a return to the pre-war arrangement whereby the IBU's technical center was in Brussels and the headquarters in Geneva. Aside from being located in neutral Switzerland, the Swiss argued that Geneva offered easy access to many international organizations which the EBU would have to deal with, such as the ITU. In addition, they claimed that the existing Geneva staff of the IBU would offer the EBU the advantage of not only starting operations sooner but also at less cost, thus permitting funds to be diverted to refurbishing the monitoring center.[111] On February 10, the conference put the choice between Brussels and Geneva to a vote. After a first vote, which revealed a tie, the delegates, by a vote of eleven to nine with one abstention, chose Geneva.[112]

The structure of the secretariat was another source of controversy. Several delegates, including France, favored a three-part secretariat consisting of a General Secretariat, an Administrative, Cultural, and Legal Directorate, and a Technical Directorate each headed by one elected official.[113] But most delegates opposed a third elected official. Sir Noel Ashbridge, director of the BBC's Technical Services, feared that three offices "would lead to doubt and argument at every meeting as to the precise division of functions." He also told the conference that perhaps a three-part secretariat could be created later, but that "no possibility of expansion in the near future (existed) because the budget would not allow it."[114] In the end, the three-part secretariat scheme was rejected. The conference voted thirteen to seven in favor of a two-part secretariat: an Administrative Office and a Technical Center.[115]

Another major problem resolved at the Torquay Conference was whether or not EBU membership should be limited to broadcasting organizations from countries that belong to the ITU. The dispute started when the Portuguese broadcasting service, ENR, proposed that the conference should restrict EBU membership to organizations from "sovereign nations" and not to ITU membership.[116] But many delegates felt that politics should not come into play when accepting members. "The purpose of the reference to the membership of the ITU was to exclude from the new Union all political discussions," said J.D.H. van der Toorn, director-general of the Dutch PTT. "If the Portuguese amendment were accepted, the door would be open again to the endless discussions of the last four years."[117] Broadcasters from Yugoslavia, the only Socialist country at the conference, also opposed the Portuguese proposal.[118] By the end of the conference, the delegates had adopted Article 3, para. 1, linking EBU membership to ITU membership.

Finally came the last and most memorable day of the conference. On February 12, representatives from the broadcasting organizations of twenty-two nations signed the Statutes of the European Broadcasting Union. Of the Torquay participants, the representatives of the broadcasting organizations from Finland and Israel did not immediately join the EBU.[119]

On February 13, the delegates remained in Torquay to attend the EBU's first extraordinary General Assembly. In two days, the delegates of the EBU's twenty-one active members set about giving life to their new agency. They elected important officials including members of the Administrative Council and the directors of the Technical Center in Brussels and of the Administrative Office in Geneva. Moreover, the Assembly decided to establish a Legal Committee and a Technical Committee to study questions and to make recommendations, in their respective fields, to the General Assembly and the Administrative Council.

On May 22, 1950, one month after its twenty-fifth anniversary, the IBU General Assembly met in Ouchy-Lausanne, Switzerland to discuss the issue of dissolution. The broadcasting organizations from Portugal opposed dissolving the IBU for fear that the EBU could break up like the OIR had.[120] But on the next day, the Assembly voted nine to one in favor of dissolving the IBU and transferring its assets to the EBU.[121]

2.5 Conclusion

The twenty-five-year-old IBU experiment taught European broadcasters important lessons about the degree to which an international organization could contribute to promoting and protecting their interests. The machinery and diplomacy of the IBU offered the means by which broadcasters could achieve many objectives. The IBU practiced one of the oldest ways of controlling frequencies. Broadcasters' desire for orderly European airwaves led the IBU to draft international frequency allocation plans. The IBU also created the world's first international monitoring station in order to police the "air" traffic. In the legal field, the IBU lobbied for international protection of copyrights in broadcasting, a difficult job since few existing laws specifically mentioned the new medium. In the program field, the IBU provided broadcasters of different countries access to one another's programs.

But the experience of the first international association of broadcasting organizations also showed that the extent of cooperation necessary to produce useful results depended upon the degree of common interest among the members. The IBU's informal frequency plans proved ineffective in stopping interference mainly because not all broadcasters adhered to them. The IBU's work in reducing interference had to be supplemented by formal agreements concluded by governments for the problem to be resolved. The IBU's aims of using radio to increase international understanding also proved to be a difficult undertaking. The Union's efforts in controlling international propaganda through resolutions, international lobbying, and offering its good offices did little to deter the increasing use of radio for propaganda and psychological warfare.

The most important lesson of the IBU experiment was the realization that cold war politics made it necessary for European broadcasters to have separate institutions — the European Broadcasting Union in the West and the International Radio and Television Organization in the East. Western broadcasters resigned from the OIR and created the EBU to avoid being dominated by the USSR, as measured, among other ways, by its voting majority. These events all but ended Socialist attempts to have the OIRT represent world broadcasting interests. To save face, the OIRT has been kept alive, despite its small membership, to group broadcasters from countries which embrace Socialism and which support the USSR's position in world affairs. As will be noted, however, the division of European broadcasting has not ended collaboration between the EBU and OIRT. Rather, EBU-OIRT collaboration has become imperative in order to take full advantage of the development of broadcasting.

Endnotes
Chapter 2

1. The IBU was known in French as the Union Internationale de Radiodiffusion (UIR). The literature on the IBU is fairly limited. The IBU itself published a general description of the organization's structure and activities entitled *Twenty Years of Activity of the International Broadcasting Union*, (Geneva: IBU, 1945). Charles E. Sherman has published articles on the IBU's history and activities; see "The International Broadcasting Union: A Study in Practical Internationalism," *EBU Review*, 25:3, (May 1974), pp. 32-36; and "Turmoil and Transition in International Broadcasting Organizations: 1938-50," *Journal of Broadcasting*, 15, (Summer 1971), pp. 265-273. See also D.H. Giesecke, "Der Weltrundfunkverein. Seine Entstehung und sein Wirken bis zur Luzerner Konferenz," *Studien Zum Weltrundfunk und Fernsehrundfunk*, 2, (1941), pp. 41-93. Important references to the IBU can be found in George A. Codding, Jr., *Broadcasting Without Barriers*, (Paris: UNESCO, 1959); and John D. Tomlinson, *The International*

Control of Radiocommunications, (Geneva: Imprimerie du "Journal de Genève," 1938). For a personal account of the IBU between 1939 to 1950, see Léo Wallenborn, "From IBU to EBU: The Great European Broadcasting Crisis," *EBU Review*, 29: 1, Part I, (January 1978), pp. 25-34; Part II, (March 1978), pp. 22-36. See also R. de Reding, *L'Activité de l'Union internationale de radiodiffusion de 1939 à 1946*, (Geneva: IBU, 1946).

2. Tomlinson, *The International Control of Radiocommunications*, op. cit., pp. 50-51.
3. Until 1927, the only international law dealing with radio was the International Radiotelegraph Convention of 1912 which was designed primarily for ship-to-ship and maritime communications. See George A. Codding, Jr., *The International Telecommunication Union: An Experiment in International Cooperation*, (Leiden, Netherlands: Brill, 1952), pp. 116-130.
4. IBU, Rapport sur la nouvelle répartition des longueurs d'onde, IBU Doc., Serial no. 247, August 18, 1926.
5. The idea of an international radio organization came from Maurice Rambert, a Swiss radio pioneer. In 1923, Rambert, who became increasingly irritated by the interference he received from foreign stations, asked Dr. Edmond Privat, president of the International Esperanto Office and radio enthusiast, for support in arranging a conference to discuss ways of solving the international problem. Privat agreed, and invitations were sent out to all the major European stations and interested groups to attend the 1924 Geneva meeting. See IBU, *Maurice Rambert 1866-1941*, (Geneva: IBU, 1941).
6. *Report of the Proceedings of the Preliminary Conference for an International Agreement on Wireless Telephony*, (London: Baynard Press, 1924).
7. Although the formation of a permanent international broadcasting body was recommended, the Geneva meeting was not as successful as its sponsors may have hoped, due mainly to the absence of the BBC — one of the most developed services in Europe at the time. Asa Briggs, in his study of British broadcasting, pointed out that one reason for the BBC's failure to attend was the belief that frequencies were matters for governments to decide, not broadcasters. Also the BBC and the British Post Office did not want to harm international acceptance of their frequency proposals to the 1927 Washington Radio Conference by premature talks with private bodies. Indeed, this difference of opinion about frequency allocations brought about a growing disaccord between John Reith, the BBC's first director-general, and Maurice Rambert which nearly prevented the creation of the IBU. See Asa Briggs,

The History of Broadcasting in the United Kingdom. 1st Vol.: *The Birth of Broadcasting*, (London: Oxford University Press, 1961), pp. 310-315. See also Andrew Boyle, *Only the Wind Will Listen, Reith of the BBC*, (London: Hutchinson & Co., 1972).

8. The following countries and their broadcasting services attended: Australia — Farmers Australian Radio; Belgium — Radio-Belgique S.A.; Czechoslovakia — Radiojournal; France — Le Petit Parisien; Germany — Ministerialrat im Reichs-Postministeruim; Netherlands — Nederlandsche Seintoestellen Fabriek; Norway — Kringkastingselskapet A.S.; Switzerland — Société des Emissions "Radio-Genève"; and the United Kingdom — British Broadcasting Company. Minutes of Proceedings of an Informal International Conference on Broadcasting, London, March 18-19, 1925. (unpublished).
9. *Ibid.*, p. 2.
10. *Ibid.*, p. 10.
11. *Ibid.*, p. 17.
12. *Ibid.*, p. 5.
13. See Appendix A for a list of IBU founding members.
14. IBU, *Problems of Broadcasting,* Geneva: IBU, 1930, p. 130.
15. Sherman, "The International Broadcasting Union: A Study in Practical Internationalism," *op. cit.*, p. 36.
16. Radio Luxembourg was never admitted to the IBU because of its illegal commercial broadcasts. In 1932, Luxembourg started broadcasting on a longwave frequency which had not been allocated to it by the 1927 Washington Conference. This led IBU Members, many of whom banned or severely limited advertising, to unanimously adopt a resolution condemning Radio Luxembourg's piracy and prohibiting it from joining the Union. IBU, *Resolution Digest of Guiding Decisions [1925-1937]*, (Geneva: IBU, 1938), pp. 109-110. The USSR never joined the IBU, although it did send observers to meetings.
17. IBU, Rapport de la Commission Technique au Conseil, IBU Doc., Serial no. 1268, February 20, 1929.
18. IBU, General Assembly, IBU Doc., Serial no. 680, June 25, 1937.
19. IBU, "Situation in Europe as Regards Wavelengths," Memorandum addressed by Captain Eckersley to the Bureau, IBU Doc., Serial no. 9, (no date).
20. P. P. Eckersley, *The Power Behind the Microphone*, (London: Jonathan Cape, 1941), p. 85.
21. IBU, Rapport sur la nouvelle répartition des longueurs d'onde, IBU Doc., Serial no. 247, August 18, 1926.
22. *Ibid.*

23. IBU, Rapport de la Commission Technique au Conseil, IBU Doc., Serial no. 1268, February 20, 1929.
24. IBU, *Twenty Years of Activity of the International Broadcasting Union, op. cit.*, p. 19.
25. Tomlinson, *The International Control of Radiocommunications, op. cit.*, pp. 51-52.
26. ITU, Documents de la Conférence radioélectrique européenne de Prague (April 1929), Bern, 1929, p. 31.
27. *Ibid.*, pp. 162-163.
28. Eckersley, *The Power Behind the Microphone, op. cit.*, p. 94-97.
29. Edward Pawley, *BBC Engineering 1922-1972*, (London:BBC, 1972), p. 211.
30. For an insight into the IBU's extensive preparations, see ITU, Documents de la Conference européenne des radiocommunications de Lucerne (May/June 1933), Bern, 1933, pp. 40-161.
31. The IBU's monitoring equipment was first located at the University of Brussels. It was built by Raymond Braillard, engineer of Radio-Belgique, and Professor Edmond Divoire, of the University of Brussels. In 1929, the equipment was moved to Braillard's home garage for better reception. That same year, the IBU named Braillard as the first director of the Technical Center, assisted by Divoire. In 1938, the Center was moved to a new building, which today is the home of the EBU Technical Center. After the EBU took over the IBU's operations in 1950, the monitoring station was moved to its present site at Jurbise in 1953.
32. IBU, *Twenty Years of Activity of the International Broadcasting Union, op. cit.*, pp. 20-21.
33. Lyman C. White, *International Non-governmental Organizations, Their Purposes, Methods and Accomplishments*, (New Brunswick:-Rutgers University Press, 1951), p. 56.
34. Harold K. Jacobson, "ITU: A Potpourri of Bureaucrats and Industrialists," *The Anatomy of Influence, Decision Making in International Organization*, ed. Robert W. Cox and Harold K. Jacobson (New Haven: Yale University Press, 1973), p. 75. See also David M. Leive, *International Telecommunications and International Law: The Regulation of the Radio Spectrum*, (Leiden, Netherlands: Sijthoff, 1970).
35. Minutes of Proceedings of an Informal International Conference on Broadcasting, London, March 18-19, 1925. (unpublished), p. 26.
36. IBU, Digest of Resolutions Adopted by the Council of the International Broadcasting Union from the Foundation of the Union (1925) to 8 December 1937, p. 28.
37. IBU, Memorandum au sujet du Congrès de Rome pour la révision de la

Convention Internationale de Berne ayant pour objet la protection de la propriété intellectuelle et artistique, IBU Doc., Serial no. 534, May 18, 1927.
38. Sherman, "The International Broadcasting Union: A Study in Practical Internationalism," *op. cit.*, p. 35.
39. IBU, Resolutions Digest of Guiding Decisions 1925-1937, Geneva, 1938, p. 44.
40. IBU, *Twenty Years of the International Broadcasting Union, op. cit.*, pp. 29-30. See John B. Whitton, "Radio After the War," *Foreign Affairs*, 22:1, (January 1944), and L. John Martin, *International Propaganda: Its Legal and Diplomatic Control*, (Minneapolis: University of Minnesota Press, 1958), and Institut International de Coopération Intellectuelle, *La radiodiffusion et la paix, études et projets d'accords internationaux*, (Paris: IICI, 1933), pp. 85-117.
41. IBU, Conseil de direction de l'Office internationale de radiophonie, 8 juillet 1925, IBU Doc., Serial no. 29, July 8, 1925.
42. IBU, Procès-verbaux du Conseil de l'Union internationale de radiophonie des 5 et 6 juillet 1926 a Paris, IBU Doc., Serial no. 231 (no date). See A.R. Burrows, "La Convention internationale sur l'emploi de la radiodiffusion dans l'intérêt de la paix," *Radiodiffusion*, 3:10, (October 1936), pp. 26-33.
43. See IBU, Memorandum on the Activities of the International Broadcasting Union for the Use of Broadcasting in the Cause of Peace, IBU Doc., Serial no. 5970, August 1936.
44. IBU, Rapport de la Commission Juridique au Conseil, juin 1939, IBU Doc., Serial no. 8235, June 20, 1939.
45. See EBU, "Memorandum on Direct Television Broadcasting by Satellite and the Legal Norms for its Use," *EBU Review*, 26:1, (January 1975), pp. 28-74; and Benno Signitzer, *Regulation of Direct Broadcasting from Satellites. The U.N. Involvement*, (New York: Praeger Publishers, 1976).
46. Minutes of Proceedings of an Informal International Conference on Broadcasting, London, March 18-19, 1925 (unpublished), p. 23.
47. The IBU had several program committees over the years. In 1926, the Committee of Intellectual, Artistic and Social Rapprochement was set up. Because international relays often involve artistic, legal and technical questions, the IBU decided in 1928 to create a second program group called the International Relay Committee. In 1936, the two committees merged into the Program Committee. IBU Doc., Serial no. 135; and IBU, Resolutions adoptées par l'assemblée générale et le conseil de l'Union internationale de radiophonie depuis sa fondation jusqu'au 5 septembre 1928, p. 32.

48. The series was also known as "National Concerts." See A.R. Burrows, "Efforts Made Collectively by Broadcasting Organizations (Members of the International Broadcasting Union) to Increase Understanding and Goodwill Between Nations," *Radiodiffusion*, 4:6, (July 1937), p. 88.
49. IBU, Procès-verbaux des réunions du Conseil, mai 1930, IBU Doc., Serial no. 1926, June 10, 1930.
50. Sherman, "The International Broadcasting Union: A Study in Practical Internationalism," *op. cit.*, p. 34.
51. See IBU, First Intercontinental Meeting of Broadcasting Organizations, Paris, February 27-March 6, 1936 — Preparatory Documents and Minutes of the Meeting, Geneva, May 1936.
52. IBU, Digest of Resolutions Adopted by the Council of the International Broadcasting Union from the Foundation of the Union (1925) to 8 December 1937, pp. 79-80.
53. Calculated by the author from the files on the "International" and "European" concerts at the EBU in Geneva.
54. IBU, Nombre de relais offerts aux membres de l'UIR par leurs collègues au cours de 1938, IBU Doc., Serial no. 8047, March 18, 1939.
55. de Reding, *L'Activité de l'Union internationale de radiodiffusion de 1939 à 1946*, *op. cit.*, Annex II-1.
56. *Ibid.*, Annex I-1 and 2.
57. *Ibid.*, Annex I-3. The IBU was governed by the Statutes and by provisions in the Swiss Civil Code concerning associations.
58. *Ibid.*, Annex II-5.
59. *Ibid.*
60. IBU, Concerts européens, IBU Doc., Serial no. 8139, May 22, 1939.
61. IBU, Nombre de relais offerts aux membres de l'UIR par leurs collègues au cours de 1938, *op. cit.*.
62. The Legal Committee resumed its meeting in 1943.
63. de Reding, *L'Activité de l'Union internationale de radiodiffusion de 1939 à 1946*, *op. cit.*, p. 24.
64. See Appendix A.
65. Wallenborn, "From IBU to EBU: The Great European Broadcasting Crisis," (Part I), *op. cit.*, p. 27.
66. *Ibid.*
67. When the Allies landed in Western Europe, the Checking Center once again became a pawn of the war. See Wallenborn, "From IBU to EBU: The Great European Broadcasting Crisis," (Part I), *op. cit.*, p. 29.
68. See IBU, *Activities of the International Broadcasting Union and Its Post-War Plan*, (Geneva: IBU, 1945).
69. Meeting of the Bureau and the Reduced Group (Technical) held in

Brussels, in the offices of INR on May 7,8,9,10, 1946, General Report, Doc. Br. 70, B./17, G.R./12. The OIR was known in French as the Organisation Internationale de Radiodiffusion. The abbreviation "IBO" was rarely used. Broadcasters from the following countries attended: Belgium, Czechoslovakia, France, Netherlands, United Kingdom and the USSR. For an account of the events leading up to the Brussels Information Meeting, see Wallenborn, "From IBU to EBU: The Great European Broadcasting Crisis," (Part I), *op. cit.*, p. 29.
70. *Ibid.*
71. Procès-verbal de l'assemblée constitutive de l'OIR, 1ère séance du 24 juin 1946, Doc. Br. 111, B./57, p. 15.
72. *Ibid.*, p. 17.
73. The organizations from the following countries attended: Albania, Algeria, Belgium, Bulgaria, Byelorussian SSR, Czechoslovakia, Denmark, Egypt, Estonian SSR, Finland, France, Hungary, Ireland, Italy, Karelian ASSR, Latvian SSR, Lithuanian SSR, Luxembourg, Moldavian SSR, Monaco, Morocco, Netherlands, Norway, Poland, Portugal, Sweden, Switzerland, Syria, Tunisia, Turkey, Ukrainian SSR, United Kingdom, USSR, the Vatican State and Yugoslavia. The following attended as observers: the Allied Control Council, Belgian PTT and the U.S. Department of State.
74. Procès-verbal de l'assemblée constitutive de l'OIR, 1ère séance du 24 juin 1946, Doc. Br. 111, B./57, p. 19.
75. Procès-verbal de la 13ème réunion du Bureau, 26 juin 1946 à Hotel Métropole, Doc. Br. 125, B./65, p. 1.
76. *Ibid.*, pp. 3-4.
77. Procès-verbal de la 16ème réunion du Bureau, 27 juin 1946, Doc. Br. 115, B./62.
78. The constitution was signed on June 27-28 by the broadcasting organizations from the following 26 countries: Albania, Algeria, Belgium, Bulgaria, Byelorussian SSR, Czechoslovakia, Egypt, Estonian SSR, Finland, France, Hungary, Italy, Karelian ASSR, Latvian SSR, Lithuanian SSR, Luxembourg, Morocco, Moldavian SSR, Monaco, Netherlands, Rumania, Syria, Tunisia, Ukrainian SSR, USSR and the Vatican State. Poland and Yugoslavia attended the Constitutive Assembly, but did not immediately sign the constitution. They joined the OIR before August 1, the statutory deadline, bringing the number of active members to 28; a figure that remained unchanged until December 31, 1949 when 11 organizations withdrew.
79. IBU, Minutes of the Meeting of the General Assembly, Geneva, IBU Doc., Serial no. 8904, June 29, 1946.
80. *Ibid.*

81. The vote went as follows: fifteen for dissolution — Algeria, Belgium, Bulgaria, Czechoslovakia, Egypt, Estonian SSR, Finland, France, Latvian SSR, Lithuanian SSR, Morocco, Netherlands, Poland, Tunisia, Yugoslavia. Two against — Spain, Switzerland. Six abstentions — Denmark, Ireland, Italy, Portugal, Sweden, Turkey. Palestine and the United Kingdom attended the meeting as observers.
82. Italy and Rumania did not resign until 1948, thus had dual membership.
83. IBU, Meeting du bureau de Conseil de l'UIR, IBU Doc., Serial no. 8941, December 3, 1946.
84. Julien Kuypers, "L'Organisation internationale de radiodiffusion (OIR)," *Journal des télécommunications*, 13:11, (November 1946), pp. 244-245. See George A. Codding, Jr. *The International Telecommunication Union, An Experiment in International Cooperation*, (Leiden, Netherlands: Brill, 1952), pp. 197-204. For more about the ITU, see George A. Codding, Jr. and Anthony M. Rutkowski, *The International Telecommunication Union in a Changing World*, (Dedham, Massachusetts: Artech House, 1982).
85. Wallenborn, "From IBU to EBU: The Great European Broadcasting Crisis," (Part I), *op. cit.*, p. 32.
86. Letter, Noel Ashbridge to George Conus, November 28, 1946.
87. They were the organizations from Austria, Denmark, Ireland, Italy, Norway, Portugal, Spain, Sweden, Switzerland, Turkey and the Vatican State. IBU Doc., Serial no. 9021.
88. Wallenborn, "From IBU to EBU: The Great European Broadcasting Crisis," (Part I), *op. cit.*, pp. 33-34.
89. OIR, "The OIR International Broadcast Clearing Center,"*OIR Documentation and Information Bulletin*, no. 22, (January 1, 1949), pp. 9-11.
90. Wallenborn, "From IBU to EBU: The Great European Broadcasting Crisis," (Part II), *op. cit.*, pp. 23-24.
91. See ITU, Documentation of the European Broadcasting Conference, Copenhagen 1948, Procès-verbal de l'assemblée plénière, réunion du mercredi 14 juillet 1948, Doc. no. 118, pp. 1-19.
92. IBU, Meetings of the Council and the General Assembly held on May 23 and 24 at Ouchy-Lausanne, IBU Doc., Serial no. 9073, June 23, 1949.
93. Minutes of the Third Meeting of the Plenary Assembly, Meeting of Information and Fellowship, Stresa, August 9, 1949, Doc. Str./6, p. 2.
94. *Ibid.*
95. IBU, "Creation of European Broadcasting Union," *Monthly Bulletin*, no. 290, (April 1950), p. 268.

96. Minutes of the Fourth Meeting of the Plenary Assembly, Meeting of Information and Fellowship, Stresa, August 10, 1949, Doc. Str./7, pp. 1-2.
97. Réunion de Paris des 31 octobre et 1er novembre 1949. "Broadcasting Union for the European Zone, Report by the Preparatory Committee."
98. Wallenborn, "From IBU to EBU: The Great European Broadcasting Crisis," (Part II), p. 27.
99. *Ibid.*
100. *Ibid.*
101. *Ibid.*
102. The resignations of eleven Western organizations meant that on January 1, 1950, OIR membership consisted of broadcasters from the following countries: Albania, Bulgaria, Byelorussian SSR, Czechoslovakia, Estonian SSR, Finland, Hungary, Karelian ASSR, Latvian SSR, Lithuanian SSR, Moldavian SSR, Poland, Rumania, Syria, Ukrainian SSR, USSR, and Yugoslavia.
103. Under Belgian law, the resignation of the Belgian organization from the OIR meant the union could no longer have civil personality in Belgium.
104. International Organization of Journalists, "30 Years of the OIRT," *Journalists' Affairs*, no. 22/23/24, (1976), p. 25.
105. See V. Strnad, "Vie de l'organisation," *OIR Bulletin de documentation et d'information*, no. 30/31, (May 15, 1950), pp. 7-17.
106. *Ibid.*, p. 14.
107. The organizations from the following countries attended: Belgium, Denmark, Finland, France, Ireland, Italy, Lebanon, Luxembourg, Morocco, Netherlands, Norway, Portugal, Sweden, Switzerland, Syria, Tunisia, Turkey, United Kingdom, the Vatican State and Yugoslavia. Monaco and Egypt were represented. Israel observed the conference.
108. The Federal Republic of Germany joined the ITU, and thus the EBU, in 1952. Spain adhered to the ITU's 1947 Atlantic City Convention in 1951.
109. European Broadcasting Conference, Torquay, February, 1950. Minutes of the Third Plenary Meeting of the European Broadcasting Conference. February 9, 1950, Torquay/22, p. 7.
110. *Ibid.*, Minutes of the Fourth Plenary Meeting of the European Broadcasting Conference. February 10, 1950, Torquay/26, p. 12.
111. *Ibid.*, Minutes of the Third Plenary Meeting of the European Broadcasting Conference. February 9, 1950, Torquay/22, p. 12.
112. *Ibid.*, Minutes of the Fourth Plenary Meeting of the European Broadcasting Conference. February 9, 1950, Torquay/26, pp. 11-12.

113. *Ibid.*, Minutes of the Sixth Plenary Meeting of the European Broadcasting Conference. February 12, 1950, Torquay/37, p. 3.
114. *Ibid.*, pp. 2-3.
115. *Ibid.*, p. 4.
116. *Ibid.*, Minutes of the Fourth Plenary Meeting of the European Broadcasting Conference. February 10, 1950, Torquay/26, pp. 6-7.
117. *Ibid.*, p. 7.
118. *Ibid.*
119. The original 22 EBU active members were: Belgium — Institut National Belge de Radiodiffusion; Denmark — Statsradiofonien; Egypt — Egyptian State Broadcasting; France — Radiodiffusion Française; Greece — National Broadcasting Institute; Ireland — Department of Posts and Telegraphs; Italy — Radio Italiana; Lebanon — Lebanese Broadcasting Service; Luxembourg — Compagnie Luxembourgeoise de Radiodiffusion; Monaco — Radio Monte-Carlo; Morocco — Radio-Maroc; Norway — Norsk Rikskringkasting; Netherlands — Stichting Nederlandse Radio-Unie; Portugal — Emissora Nacional de Radiodifusão; Sweden — Radiotjänst and Royal Telegraph Administration Bureau; Switzerland — Société Suisse de Radiodiffusion; Syria —Ministère des Travaux Publics et des Communications; Tunisia — Radio-Tunis; Turkey — Radio-Turquie; United Kingdom — British Broadcasting Corporation; the Vatican State — Radio Vatican; and Yugoslavia — Comité de Radiodiffusion près du Gouvernement de la RPFY. YLE/Finland became the 23rd active EBU member in June 1950. IBA/Israel was admitted to EBU active membership in October 1957.
120. IBU, Minutes of the General Assembly, Ouchy-Lausanne, May 22-23, 1950, IBU Doc., Serial no. 9112, June 14, 1950.
121. *Ibid.*

CHAPTER 3
INSIDE THE EBU AND OIRT

Before going into the specifics of Eurovision and Intervision, it is necessary to look at the agencies which have the job of planning, supervising, and coordinating European television program exchanges. Many organs of the EBU and OIRT deal with television program exchange activities including the standardization of equipment, negotiation for television rights, and collection and distribution of program offers and requests to members. Much of the structure and activities of the EBU and OIRT are similar, but also much is unique to each one. This chapter looks at the EBU's and OIRT's *1)* purposes, *2)* membership, *3)* general assembly, *4)* administrative council, *5)* secretariat, *6)* permanent committees, *7)* financing, and *8)* relations with other international organizations.

3.1 Purposes

Broadly speaking, the principal object of the EBU and OIRT, as expressed in their constitutions, is to promote and to protect the interests of broadcasters.[1] More specifically, the EBU's duties, as defined in Article 2 (2), are:

a) to support in every domain the interests of broadcasting organizations members of the Union and to establish relations with other broadcasting organizations or groups of such organizations;

b) to prepare and take all measures designed to assist the development of broadcasting in all its forms;

c) to promote radio and television program exchanges by all possible means, such as, for example, Eurovision, and any other form of cooperation among its members and with other broadcasting organizations;

d) to foster and coordinate the study of all questions relating to broadcasting, and to ensure the exchange of information on all matters of general interest to broadcasting organizations;

e) to use its best endeavors to ensure that all its members respect the provisions of international agreements on any matter relating to broadcasting;

f) to assist members in negotiations of any kind or itself negotiate at their request and on their behalf.

The OIRT's purposes are outlined in Article 2 of its constitution. The OIRT is obliged to:

a) establish links between the various organizations ensuring radio and television service, and being party to the present Statutes;

b) secure, as completely as possible, mutual exchange of information among members of the OIRT on the technical progress of sound and television broadcasting, on different schemes purporting to improve these techniques and, in general, on all measures taken in broadcasting activities;

c) ensure the all around protection of the interests of radio and television;

d) solve broadcasting problems by means of international cooperation;

e) study and work out all measures generally directed towards the development of radio and television, especially the development of broadcasting technology;

f) study and work out measures important for the rapid development of radio and television broadcasting technologies in insufficiently electrified regions and regions with specific climatic conditions.

These selections from the constitutions summarize the wide-ranging possibilities of the EBU and OIRT. Providing a forum for member organizations to carry on many different activities ranging from the exchange of views to the negotiation of program exchanges is one important emphasis. Another concerns providing services. Both have the statutory task to establish relations with other broadcasting organizations, to ensure the exchange of information and to promote measures furthering the development of broadcasting.

The scope of the EBU's functions has increased over the years while the OIRT's have remained the same. In 1966, largely in light of demands by developing countries, subparagraph (*b*) in Article 2 of the EBU Statutes was amended to allow the Union "to take all measures" to assist the development of broadcasting. Another change occurred in 1969 when the wording of subparagraph (*a*) was altered to permit the EBU to establish relations with other regional broadcasting unions. In 1981, the EBU's constitution was amended by the addition of subparagraph (*c*) which formally recognized the Union's long-established program exchange activities, particularly Eurovision. Previous amendments ignored the word "Eurovision," although the network was created in 1954. As we will see in Chapter Four, members have been reluctant to give the EBU control over their programs. Finally, subparagraph (*f*) was added in 1981 to formally give the EBU power to make decisions on behalf of members during its negotiations with television rights holders. In contrast to the EBU, the OIRT's formal tasks have remained largely unchanged since the agency's creation in 1946.[2]

3.2 Membership[3]

Not any radio, television or CATV station may join the EBU or OIRT. To be an EBU member, a broadcasting organization or a group of broadcasting organizations must (*1*) be from a country that is an ITU member, (*2*) be authorized by the competent authority as operating a broadcasting service, and (*3*) provide a service of national character and importance.[4]

The significance of these provisions is that the EBU is an association of broadcasting organizations, not states. The provision that EBU participants must hold dual membership in the ITU aims at ensuring that all EBU members operate a broadcasting service as defined in the International Telecommunication Convention. As already noted, the EBU's founders felt that the ITU criterion would exclude politics when admitting members. Furthermore, as Hans Brack notes in his study of the EBU, the IBU would not have fallen apart if its membership had been made conditional on ITU membership.[5]

Furthermore, EBU membership is restricted to national broadcasting institutions, not local or specialized stations. Cable operators, for example, are eligible, on condition that they either provide national coverage such as Ted Turner's Cable News Network or belong to a national association such as the Association of Independent Radio Contractors in the United Kingdom. In 1981, the EBU provided for "approved observer" status to allow "specialized" broadcasters such as INCA/France which provides considerable educational program material to take part in the Union's work, although it has no right to vote or hold office.[6] Stations which are not eligible include the numerous local Italian radio and television stations. Furthermore, the provision that members provide a service of national importance aims at excluding stations which broadcast largely to foreign audiences, such as Deutsche Welle and Radio Free Europe.

The OIRT limits membership primarily to government-run stations. Its membership, as set forth in Article 5 (1), is restricted to (*1*) state-operated organizations; (*2*) organizations of a civil character which, under government authority, ensure a broadcasting service; and (*3*) groups of national organizations of a civil character which fulfill the above conditions.

The EBU has two membership classes, active and associate. Active members are broadcasting organizations in a country located in the European Broadcasting Area.[7] Associate members are organizations from a country located outside of the European Broadcasting Area.[8] Associate members have the same basic rights as active members, but they can neither vote in the general assembly nor be elected to the administrative council.

It should be noted that organizations fulfilling active membership requirements but located outside "Europe" can apply for associate membership.[9]

This freedom of choice between active and associate membership allows the small, developing organizations from the Middle East and North Africa to participate in EBU activities without the financial burdens of active membership. It also offers political advantages. In 1958, for example, the Egyptian and Syrian organizations resigned from active EBU membership in response to the admission of Israel's organization. In 1975, however, the Egyptian service was readmitted as an associate member. In sum, because only active members have the right to vote in the general assembly and to be elected to the administrative council, EBU decisions are primarily made by West European broadcasting organizations, although recent years have seen greater representation of Middle East and North African countries on the administrative council.

OIRT Statutes also provide for active and associate members although not geographically defined as in the EBU. Only broadcasting organizations formed by competent authorities (i.e. governments) may be active members. Also only one active member per country may exist.[10] When a state organization co-exists with one or more private broadcasting organizations, the former will be admitted as an OIRT active member.[11] All other broadcasting organizations such as private commercial stations are admitted as associate members.[12]

The goal of EBU membership policy seems to be to attract as many members as possible into the organization. EBU has opened its doors to organizations from around the world. In fact, the number of its members has grown over the years. When the EBU constitution was signed in 1950, it had 21 members —all located within the European Broadcasting Area. In 1983, EBU had 42 active and 69 associate members — a total of 111 members from 78 countries.[13]

In addition, EBU members are varied. Government-subsidized broadcasting organizations sit alongside private commercial stations. This has led to problems as the admittance of the United Kingdom's Independent Broadcasting Authority (IBA) shows. Commercial stations like RTL had been active members of the EBU since Torquay, but IBA was a competitor of an EBU active member — the BBC. Initially, the BBC was reluctant to have IBA join the Union, partially because of the fear that it might endanger the EBU's non-commercial aims. IBA was admitted as an associate member in 1956 and later successfully pressed the EBU to modify its constitution to allow more than one active member per country. Had this decision not been taken, it would surely have left a tempting vacuum for commercial stations to create their own international organization.[14]

Members have withdrawn and have been expelled from the EBU, but no national broadcasting organization has ever been denied admission. Moreover, considerable sentiment seems to exist within the EBU favoring universality. It is important that, while Portugal was excluded from the ITU in 1973, its broadcasting organizations remained EBU members. This was a clear violation of the EBU constitution because membership is only open to broadcasting services from a country that is a member of the ITU.

Unlike the EBU, the OIRT has a political rather than a geographical or institutional base. OIRT membership is largely confined to those broadcasting organizations of countries that embrace Socialism and support the USSR's position in world affairs. Exceptions do exist. Yugoslavia's broadcasters are represented in the EBU rather than the OIRT.[15] Other exceptions are the dual membership of Finland in the EBU and OIRT[16] as well as TV Asahi/Japan, which is an associate member. Still, the nucleus of OIRT membership is the state-operated radio and television services from Eastern Europe and the USSR.

3.3 General Assemblies

The general assembly is the supreme organ of the EBU and OIRT. It has the ultimate responsibility for the overall direction the agency will take, as well as the supervision of the work of the various organs.

The functions of the EBU and OIRT general assemblies are similar. In both agencies, the general assembly considers the reports prepared by the administrative council on the activities of the organs of the union since the previous assembly. Also, the assembly must establish the basis for the budget. Furthermore, it elects the president, vice-presidents, and the members of the administrative council. These powers permit the assembly to closely look at the strengths and weaknesses of the agency's normal operations and to issue appropriate directives.

Structural differences, however, do exist. On the one hand, the OIRT's assembly meets irregularly, though the Statutes specify that it should be convened at least once every two years.[17] On the other hand, the EBU's general assembly is held annually.[18]

Moreover, unlike OIRT, EBU Statutes define the extent to which members are bound by decisions. The 1950 Torquay Statutes provided that assembly decisions were binding on all members. But, because of vast differences of interests and judgments among member organizations, this provision gradually gave way to allowing members to be excluded from EBU decisions for "imperative reasons."[19] The major impetus for change came from associate members who felt that they should not be bound by decisions on which they could not vote. After much discussion, the EBU in 1969 adopted a set of statutory provisions which not only defined the obligations of active and associate members but also recognized member sovereignty.[20] Today, the assembly may allow either derogations or temporary exemptions to its decisions in the event an active member deems it incompatible with domestic laws.[21] The only assembly decisions which associate members must observe concern administrative and financial operations of the EBU, but only to the extent the member deems it compatible with national legislation.[22] The OIRT charter does not formally define how members should observe the agency's decisions.

A final statutory difference concerns voting. In the OIRT, each member country has only one vote. But in the EBU, each country has twenty-four votes to divide among its member organizations as they see fit. Originally, only one active member per country existed with each member having one vote. But the Union broadened its admission rules to allow two active members per country, while any additional organization became supplementary active members. But this system made members with the greatest seniority more privileged. In 1981, the EBU abolished the supplementary active membership provision to allow a country as many active members as necessary. This change was prompted by the increasing decentralization and specialization of European broadcasting organizations such as in the United Kingdom and France. France, for example, has six government organizations covering various aspects of broadcasting. The twenty-four votes can be divided as each country sees fit.[23] West Germany's votes are shared with the ARD receiving fourteen and ZDF ten, while Switzerland's three organizations vote collectively.

3.4 Administrative Councils

The EBU and OIRT administrative councils are responsible for the administration of the organizations in the interval between the general assemblies. The EBU's council meets in spring and fall of each year and a third time during general assembly sessions. The OIRT's council meets once a year.

In both EBU and OIRT, the administrative council is subordinate to the general assembly, ensuring that assembly decisions are carried out. The council reports to the assembly on the agency's activities. Their usual duties include examining reports of committees and study groups[24], drafting the budget, and defining the duties of the secretary-general and the directors. Occasional jobs include proposing to the assembly the exclusion of members, the creation of new committees and the appointment of the secretary-general and directors. One important functional difference between the two councils is that decisions on the withdrawal of members and on membership fees in the EBU are made by the council, while, in OIRT, it is the general assembly's prerogative. Also, the EBU general assembly decides upon the admission of members, while it is the council's duty in the OIRT. Voting on the EBU and OIRT council is by simple majority.

The council of each agency consists of councillors who are elected by a majority of the general assembly. In the EBU, councillors serve staggered four-year terms.[25] In the OIRT, councillors serve two-year terms and may only be re-elected after a two-year waiting period.[26] In both agencies, only active members can sit on the council.

The number of seats on the EBU administrative council has grown over the years largely to meet the need for equitable representation of all parts of Western Europe. In 1950, EBU council seats numbered seven; in 1954, nine; in 1960, eleven; and in 1972, fifteen. A major factor in increasing the size of the council was to provide wider representation of West European broadcasting interests. Apart from Switzerland's permanent seat, the organizations of the Federal Republic of Germany, France, Italy, and the United Kingdom have sat on the council since 1955. The Big Four, however, have come to make up a declining proportion as the council's total membership has expanded. In 1954, the Big Four occupied four out of nine seats or 44 percent. In 1972, their proportion declined to 26 percent when the council was increased to fifteen members. The increases in the size and changes in composition have allowed the smaller services on the fringes of the European Broadcasting Area, such as Algeria, Cyprus and Tunisia, to occupy council seats.

Today, EBU's council consists of fifteen members. One seat is permanently given to Switzerland, where the seat of the EBU is located. Over the years, a certain practice has developed whereby the remaining fourteen elective council seats are allotted to major European geographical areas. Four seats are allotted to the Big Four; one to two seats are rotated among the Nordic services; one is given to a Benelux country; one is occupied alternatively by Portugal and Spain; one to Yugoslavia; and one to a North African member. The remaining seats are filled from among the other active members. Every two years, seven council seats are up for election.

EBU Statutes do not list qualifications of persons appointed to the council. But council meetings are usually attended by executive heads or directors of national broadcasting organizations. Also members often send the heads of their international affairs departments. Rarely are technicians or politicians sent.

The OIRT's constitution provides for a council of at least seven and no more than thirteen members. Since 1974, the council has consisted of eleven members. Almost without exception, OIRT councillors are presidents or ministers of state broadcasting committees. Besides the two permanent seats allotted to Czechoslovakia and the USSR, the services from Bulgaria, Cuba, the German Democratic Republic and Hungary have been regularly represented since 1971.[27]

Administrative council and general assembly meetings in both agencies are presided over by a president. EBU presidents are elected by the general assembly for two-year terms on the nomination of the council. OIRT presidents also serve two-year terms but are elected by the administrative council.

Although the duties of the presidents are similar, the statutory position of the EBU president seems stronger than that of his OIRT counterpart. The OIRT president can act on urgent matters only after conferring with council members by a mail or telegraphic vote. But the EBU president is in a position, in "case of urgent questions,"[28] to take decisions, normally the responsibility of the administrative council, thus becoming EBU's third decision-making organ.[29] The president often does make decisions between council meetings —subject to ratification by the council. Sir Charles Curran, president of the EBU, on several occasions had to make decisions on behalf of the organization during negotiations with the Canadian Olympic Games Organizing Committee for the European television rights and basic coverage for the 1976 Montreal Games.

3.5 EBU and OIRT Secretariats

3.5.1 EBU Secretariat

Administrative activities, including the coordination of live television transmissions, budgetary, secretarial, and housekeeping functions are performed by the EBU and OIRT secretariats. The EBU secretariat, called the "Permanent Services" in the Statutes, consists of five separate components: the Technical Center, the General Affairs Service, the Television Program Department, the Radio Program Department and the Department of Legal Affairs. The OIRT secretariat consists of a General Secretariat and a Technical Center. Each of these bureaucracies is headed by an elected official, and their senior staffs tend to be recruited from member organizations.

Of the EBU's five secretariat organs, the Technical Center, located in Brussels, is the largest. In 1983, the Center had a total staff of 118 persons. The Center, headed by a director, is the technical secretariat of the EBU. It provides the support services for the meetings of the Technical Committee. Another duty is publishing the technical edition of the *EBU Review*. In addition to secretariat tasks, the Center performs important operational duties. The Center runs the EBU's Receiving and Measuring Station (CEM) located in Jurbise, Belgium which monitors the occupation of the broadcasting bands.

Most important of all, the Center plans and coordinates Eurovision transmissions. Indeed, Eurovision is the Center's largest single activity. The supervision of transmissions and the switching of the vision and sound circuits is carried out in the Eurovision Control Center (EVC), while the Planning Unit and Finance Unit apply the agreed procedures for the coordination of transmissions. Of the Center's total staff in 1983, forty-six persons were fully assigned to Eurovision.

The Television Program Department is the second largest segment, with a total staff of fifty-one in 1983. Headed by a director, the Department provides the secretariat to the Television Program Committee. It also coordinates television program exchanges through the Television News Division, the Eurovision Program Division and the Specialized Television Program Division.

The third largest organ of the EBU administration is the General Affairs Service, which had a staff of thirty-two in 1983. In general, the General Affairs Service is an administrative and service organ, performing those budgetary, linguistic, secretarial, and housekeeping activities which are outside the competence of the Technical Center, Television Program Department, Legal Affairs Department, and Radio Program Committee. The General Affairs Service provides the secretariat to the general assembly and the administrative council, which typically involves establishing the contacts between members, collecting and distributing documents, organizing their meetings and preparing the reports. Furthermore, it keeps account of EBU and Eurovision costs. The General Affairs Service also maintains a library and archives, and is responsible for publishing the program, administrative, and legal edition of the *EBU Review*.

The General Affairs Service is headed by the secretary-general, who is also the coordinating figure of the EBU. The secretary-general is elected by the general assembly. The EBU does not define the length of office.[30] His functions include representing the EBU with third parties, coordinating the activities of the four directors, carrying out the decisions of the general assembly and the administrative council and, in association with the director of the Legal Affairs Department, concluding agreements for the EBU. One limit on the duties of the secretary-general is that he does not control the operations of the Brussels Technical Center.

The Department of Legal Affairs is the EBU's permanent legal organ. It provides the secretariat of the Legal Committee. The responsibilities of the director include advising the EBU on all legal matters and taking part in negotiations to televise international events such as Olympic Games. In 1983, the Legal Affairs Department was staffed with twelve persons.

Finally, there is the Radio Program Department, which had a total staff of twelve in 1983. The primary duty of the director and his staff is to coordinate the exchange of live and recorded radio programs among member organizations. The Radio Program Department also provides the secretariat for meetings of the Radio Program Committee.

The Permanent Services have evolved over the years. Originally, the EBU's secretariat, following the IBU's structure, consisted of an Administrative Office and a Technical Center. Although the delegates at Torquay in 1950 did not set up a Department of Legal Affairs, they did provide for a Legal Advisor within the Administrative Office, mainly to provide the secretariat for the newly created Legal Committee. Only in 1966 was the Department of Legal Affairs officially acknowledged as a permanent service in the EBU Statutes.[31] In 1976, the general assembly voted to reorganize the permanent services. The Administrative Office was replaced by the General Affairs Service, the Radio Program Department and the Television Program Department. The 1976 reshuffle also replaced the Director of the Administrative Office by a full time secretary-general supported by four directors. One reason for the reorganization was to prevent conflicts stemming from the lack of a clear-cut hierarchy and a consequent confusion over authority.[32]

The EBU staff has expanded over the years. From a total of 21 posts in 1950, the number increased to 70 after twelve years. Then from 1962 to 1983, staff numbers more than doubled, reaching 225.

3.5.2 OIRT Secretariat

The OIRT secretariat is divided into a General Secretariat and a Technical Center, both located in Prague. The General Secretariat, directed by the secretary-general, is responsible for the administrative and financial side of the agency's work as well as for publishing *OIRT Information* and *Radio and Television*. It is divided into a number of divisions including the Sound Broadcasting Program Section and the Intervision Program Coordination Center (IPCC). The secretary-general is elected by the general assembly for an unspecified term.[33] Like his EBU counterpart, the OIRT secretary-general does not manage the staff and the budget of the Technical Center.

The Technical Center, headed by a director, is the technical secretariat of the OIRT, operating the Monitoring Center and the Intervision Technical Coordination Center (ITCC). While no single post is formally the specific preserve of any one country, it is significant that all the directors of the Center since 1950 have been Soviet. Also from 1950 to the present, OIRT's secretaries-general have been Czechoslovak broadcasters. The OIRT has neither a legal director nor a legal department. In early 1983, the OIRT secretariat had a total of seventy persons of whom thirty-five served in the Technical Center.

3.6 The Specialized Committees

The activities of the permanent specialized committees, with their working parties, account for a high proportion of the EBU's and OIRT's work. These committees are established by the general assembly, upon recommendation of the administrative council, to examine particular questions. Each committee has its chairman and one or more vice chairmen. To assist committees in their work, working parties and sub-groups may be created. If a committee objects to a conclusion of its working party, the question goes back to the working party for further consideration. Once approved, committees make recommendations to the administrative council. Generally speaking, working parties are disbanded as soon as they have accomplished their mandates and made their reports.

The EBU committee structure (shown in Fig. 3-1) consists of the Technical Committee, the Legal Committee, the Radio Program Committee, and the Television Program Committee. The OIRT has the following committees: the Technical Commission, the Economic-Legal Commission, the Radio Program Commission, and the Television Program Commission (Fig. 3-2).

3.6.1 EBU Committees

Technical Committee

Created at Torquay in February 1950, the Technical Committee provides a forum for engineers to study technical broadcasting problems. It meets in the

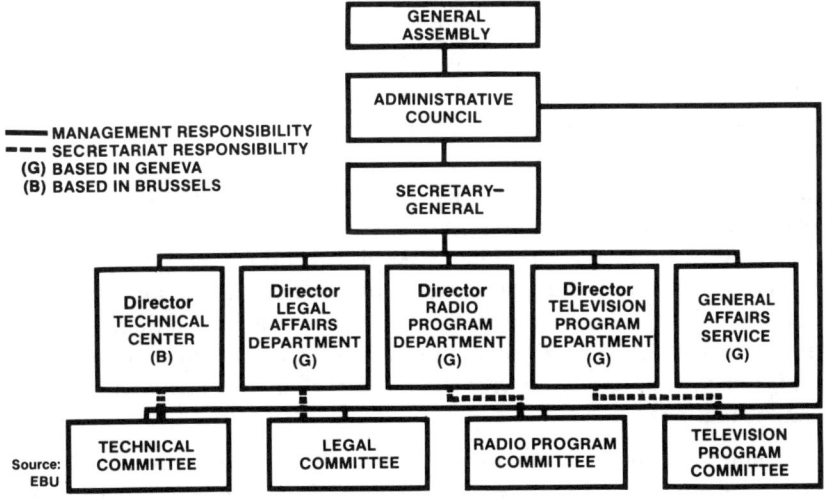

Figure 3-1: Organization of the EBU

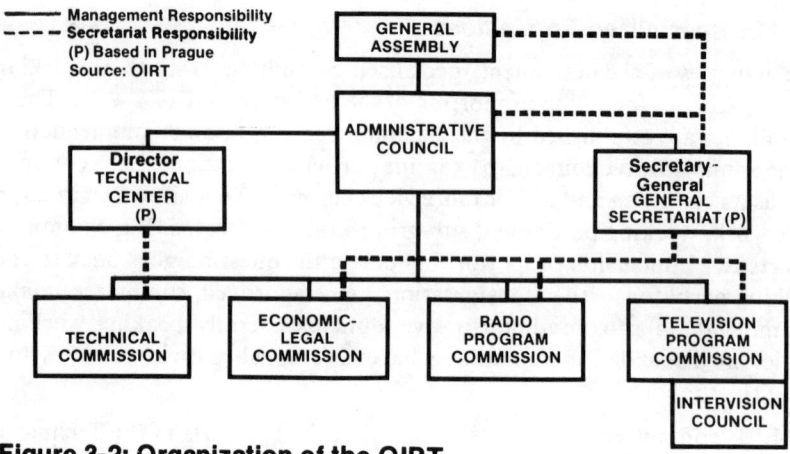

Figure 3-2: Organization of the OIRT

spring of each year. Plenary meetings are attended mainly by technical directors and chief engineers of member organizations. National telecommunications administrations, manufacturers, and other international organizations having allied interests look highly upon the Committee's work and often send representatives to observe meetings.

Studies made by the Committee and its working parties have largely dealt with *1*) broadcasting technology including spectrum utilization and *2*) Eurovision network transmission and operations.[34]

The study of broadcasting technology has been part of the Committee's functions since its origin. These studies deal with all aspects of new broadcasting developments from the compatibility of stereophonic reproduction to the danger of interference caused by microwave ovens to reception of satellite broadcasts in the 12-GHz band.

Other studies concern making efficient use of the spectrum to European broadcasting. EBU members have not given the agency power to cope with frequency difficulties as the IBU had.[35] As already noted, the 1948 Copenhagen Plan, and subsequent plans, went into effect without an appointed "technical expert." Today, the frequency spectrum is internationally managed by the International Telecommunication Union. In interference cases, the ITU may be asked by governments to carry out inquiries and to make recommendations.

The Committee works hard in preparing the EBU's position for ITU Administrative Radio Conferences. Although the EBU cannot vote to ratify treaties, the Committee's main aim in preparing for ITU conferences is twofold.

First, the EBU hopes that members will reach a consensus on problems. Second, the EBU hopes that members will put pressure on their own telecommunications administrations to adopt the proposals agreed to within the EBU.

The EBU spent six years preparing for the World Administrative Radio Conference on Broadcasting-Satellites (WARC-BS), held in Geneva in January 1977. EBU preparations began immediately after the 1971 World Administrative Radio Conference for Space Telecommunications. The Technical Committee undertook a variety of studies concerning broadcast-satellite service ranging from determining interference protection ratios to describing ground receiving equipment. It also did not ignore political and legal questions. The Committee, for example, agreed that the principle of "national coverage" was a way of avoiding serious copyright problems because copyright legislation is largely nationally controlled. In addition to conducting studies, EBU representatives also attended ITU seminars on WARC-BS. Ten months prior to WARC-BS, the EBU's final report *Satellite Broadcasting Design and Planning of 12-GHz Systems* was sent to all members, national telecommunications administrations, and the ITU as the formal conclusions of the EBU.[36] In addition, the EBU sent a three-member representing team, headed by the director of the Technical Center, to the WARC-BS.

In light of the extensive preparations, the EBU was not at all disappointed with the outcome of WARC-BS. The conference adopted an international plan which was based on the concept of national direct-broadcasting satellites transmitting within the 11.7-12.5 GHz band. Each government in ITU Regions 1 and 3 (Europe, Africa, Asia, and the Pacific) was given at least five satellite channels for television broadcasting at the national level.[37] But the EBU's work did not end with the WARC-BS conference. The results of the conference were published by the EBU in a five-volume, 1,913-page statistical document to help members implement the 1977 Geneva Plan for Satellite Broadcasting at 12-GHz.[38]

Studies on Eurovision network transmission and operations are clearly important to the Technical Committee. The use of the network depends directly upon how efficiently and effectively it can send members' programs across national boundaries.

The Committee has studied problems created by different transmission systems in an effort to facilitate Eurovision exchanges. A classic example of this involved color television standardization. European broadcasters have long been tackling problems created by different television standards. In 1950, when discussions about international television program exchanges started, the 405 line standard was used in the United Kingdom, the 819-line standard in France, and the 625-line standard in the few European countries which had television. No standards converters existed. For the broadcast of the first international transmission from France to the United Kingdom in August 1950, the BBC had to send one of its mobile broadcast units to France, so the program could be televised in 405 lines, enabling British viewers to see the program. In the late 1950s and the early 1960s, European broadcasters were again confronted with a host of problems including restricted live foreign telecasts, caused by the arrival of color television. They had three different systems to choose from: the American NTSC, the French SECAM, and the West German PAL.

To discourage EBU members from choosing different color systems, the Committee set up the Ad-hoc Group on Color Television in 1962 to evaluate the merits of NTSC, SECAM, and PAL.[39] Membership was open not only to EBU members but also to national telecommunications administrations and industrial organizations.[40]

The work lasted over four years. From 1962 to 1966, the Ad-hoc Group issued more than 220 documents comparing the characteristics of the three color systems and carried out numerous laboratory and field tests.[41] Because it was important that the same standard be adopted in Eastern and Western Europe, the OIRT and the EBU jointly organized transmission tests.[42] The results of the Ad-hoc Group's work were circulated to all members. These documents also served as a basis for the work of the 1964 and 1965 meetings of the CCIR Study Group 11 (Broadcasting Service-Television). The EBU hoped that its efforts would facilitate agreement, at least within the agency, on the choice of one of the three possible systems and that the favored system would be adopted as a common standard by the CCIR.

Despite the efforts made by the EBU, the 1966 Oslo CCIR conference could not prevent a division of Europe into three color television zones — two SECAM and one PAL. The conference degenerated into a shambles with technical criteria losing out to economic and political considerations.[43] The CCIR-approved system, for example, would have been guaranteed a near world monopoly in the manufacture and sale of color television sets. In addition, politicians became aware of the fact that a lack of standardization offered a way of protecting their own people from programs they did not want. In the end, the conference agreed simply to register NTSC, SECAM, and PAL as CCIR-approved systems and then left each country to make up its own mind.[44]

After the CCIR Oslo meeting, the EBU helped members to overcome the practical problems of starting color television service. The lack of color television standardization made program exchanges between countries using incompatible systems only possible with transcoders, which meant increased program costs. To promote exchanges, the EBU studied transcoding devices and concepts, including organizing demonstrations of converters for broadcasters.[45] The Ad-hoc Group on Color Television was disbanded in 1968. The Technical Committee decided not to replace the Ad-hoc Group with another body because it felt that operational questions of color television would be better handled in seminars with groups of specialists.[46]

Legal Committee

At Torquay in 1950, West European broadcasters were worried that they would have to pay higher royalties to directors, artists, authors and musicians. At the conference, the French delegation warned that if European broadcasters did not unite against demands of music publishers for compensation, RTF/France might be obliged to accept a new accord on music performances which, by creating a precedent, would harm the interests of broadcasting organizations, especially those in small countries. The Belgian delegation recommended that European b. oadcasters should take advantage of Austrian and Belgian court actions against special recording fees demanded by the Bureau International de l'Edition Mécanique (BIEM) by exchanging information to win not only other pending suits against BIEM but also copyright laws favorable to broadcasters. Moreover, the INR/Belgium stressed that urgent international action by broadcasters was needed to block demands of Belgian, French, and Italian authors' societies for higher copyright fees for the new medium of television.[47]

The seriousness of the matter made necessary a formal examination of ways by which broadcasters can protect themselves from higher program rights costs. As a result, the delegates at Torquay created the Legal Committee.[48] Composed of lawyers from all EBU member organizations, the Committee meets twice annually. In fact, it is the only professional forum in Europe for broadcast lawyers.[49]

Since its creation, a large part of the Committee's activities has concerned negotiations with international rights-holding bodies for rules regulating international program exchanges. The Committee's efforts in protecting broadcasters from high fees involve negotiating so-called "standard contracts" with international copyright holders. Since 1950, the EBU has negotiated four standard contracts. They are the EBU-IFPI contract governing the use of commercial records; the EBU-SACD contracts governing radio, television, and commercial films; the EBU-BIEM contract governing the exchange of recordings; and the EBU-UIE contract regulating the hire of musical material. Each of these agreements was negotiated by an EBU delegation consisting of selected members. Review or surveillance of standard contracts is done by periodic reporting by members to the Legal Committee. The contracts are revised periodically.

From the very beginning, the EBU found that copyright disputes involving television could lead to fewer program exchanges. This was made clear in 1954 when three international actors' unions — the International Federation of Musicians, the Federation of Actors, and the International Federation of Variety Artists — boycotted participation in Eurovision transmissions until an agreement for higher copyright fees could be reached with the EBU. As a result, all entertainment programs during Eurovision's first month of operation were canceled. The reason for the show of force by actors was to prompt higher compensation for the larger audiences which Eurovision would reach.[50] But broadcasters regarded the actors' demands as not only excessive but also damaging to Eurovision's growth. In 1957, however, an agreement between the EBU and the three actors' unions was reached.

Standard contracts agreed upon between the EBU and international rights-holding bodies set guidelines for sending programs across national boundaries. Standard contracts do not directly interfere in the matter of national fees. Each broadcasting organization negotiates its own rates with artists and authors on the national level. Rather, the contracts settle questions such as determining the percentages payable for international relays. The administrative council recommends EBU members to take standard contracts as the model for their own national agreements with artists' and authors' unions. Likewise, the international rights-holding bodies recommend their members to accept their terms when discussing conditions for international program exchanges with broadcasters. EBU officials hope that members will use standard contracts in their dealing with artists and authors, thus standardizing the rules governing the international exchange of programs.

Most broadcasting organizations seem willing to accept the contracts for their national agreements. Without a measure of international agreement on the standardization of payment procedures for relays, broadcasters would be faced with foreign program offers requiring different fees and different definitions of which programs require payments. These differences arise from varying national legal structures. Above all, the standardization of terms imposed on EBU members avoids excessive fees in any one country.[51]

In addition to standard contracts, the Legal Committee elaborates numerous model contracts which members apply among themselves and with third parties. In 1970, for example, the administrative council, upon the recommendation of the Legal Committee, approved a model contract for members to use in negotiating sports rights. One provision recommends that members require the organizer to list the advertising that will appear. The significance of this contract is that it ensures that sports programs sent over Eurovision may be negotiated on a uniform basis in all countries. It also serves to prevent offensive advertising.

Radio Program Committee

The Radio Program Committee traces its origins to the old EBU Program Committee created in 1953 to study both radio and television questions. Radio program makers, however, increasingly criticized the Committee's preoccupation with television, and particularly with Eurovision, demanding that a separate committee for radio program problems be created. Their demands were met in July 1964 when the general assembly split the Program Committee into the Television Program Committee and the Radio Program Committee.

The Radio Program Committee meets in the spring and the fall of each year.[52] Meetings of the Committee and its working parties are attended by radio program executives and program makers.

The Committee's competence "extends to all questions with sound broadcasting programs."[53] Two major activities are coordinating the free exchange of radio programs and organizing the annual "EBU Concert Seasons."

European broadcasters are no strangers to the free exchange of radio programs. Since the birth of broadcasting in the 1920s, broadcasters have been demanding and offering operas, concerts, and documentaries among themselves on a barter basis.[54] Although radio broadcasters realized that they do not need a centralized coordination center to exchange programs as was to be the case with live international television, the IBU still played an active role in promoting exchanges.

Radio program exchanges were institutionalized with the creation of the EBU. Supported by administrative council recommendations that members offer recordings without production reimbursement requests, the EBU Radio Program Department has become a "clearing house" for members' offers and requests.

The clearing procedure is as follows: a member which deems its production may be of interest to foreign broadcasters can send its offer to the Radio Program Department in Geneva. The Department processes the offer by first seeing if all the relevant information is included in the offer, such as the expiration date and whether individual works or parts of a program can be used separately. It then circulates the offer to all EBU members. A member wishing a particular offer usually contacts the member owning the program directly, although blanket requests are often channeled through the EBU. Typically, the Department processes about 1,000 program hours a year. All kinds of programs are exchanged, ranging from folk to classical music. Most offers come from the large organizations such as the BBC and are taken by the small ones such as the Swiss organizations.[55]

A second major activity of the Radio Program Committee is to coordinate a yearly concert broadcast series — the so-called "EBU Concert Seasons." Inaugurated in 1967, the "EBU Concert Seasons" involve the live relay of a member's orchestral concert to other EBU members who have helped finance it. The 1981-1982 Season, for example, consisted of six concerts which were transmitted to 14 organizations. The cost to each participant amounted to about 24,000 Swiss francs (about 12,000 dollars at the 1982 exchange rate).[56] Indeed, the cost savings to members is a major factor in explaining the "Seasons'" many years of operation. The economic appeal of the "EBU Concert Seasons" is also shown by the heavy participation of small organizations.

Planning begins in the Serious Music Working Party. Proposals for various concerts by members are submitted to the Working Party's meetings where they are discussed and approved. Once approved, the host organization undertakes to pay the production costs including conductors' and soloists' fees. The accommodation and travel costs of guest conductors and soloists are covered by the broadcasting organization they represent. The performance is broadcast by the host organization and relayed to foreign subscribers by the BRT/Belgium. Interestingly enough, the EBU Technical Center, which routes Eurovision transmissions, does not become involved in the routing of the "EBU Concert Seasons" except in a consultative capacity to the BRT. The Center is neither equipped nor staffed for routing of "EBU Concert Seasons" transmissions because it is not a full-time daily activity. Broadcasts of the concerts are usually taken live, although provisions have been made to permit organizations in countries either on the periphery of Europe or outside Europe to tape the "EBU Concert Seasons" for later broadcasts primarily because of the time-zone differences. The same exception also applies to organizations that operate only one service. At the end of a "Season," the production and transmission costs are sent to the Radio Program Department which calculates the total costs that participating members pay.

Significantly, the "EBU Concert Seasons" have brought live multilateral radio broadcasting back to Europe. As we have seen, the live relay of music programs among broadcasting organizations was a great feature of pre-war radio to which the IBU devoted considerable effort. Today, however, most of the concerts broadcast over radio are recorded. The "EBU Concert Seasons" have a "supra-national" value — simultaneously grouping audiences in many European countries to listen to a live performance.[57]

Generally speaking, it appears that the process of promoting radio program exchanges within the EBU has been successful and has gone smoothly. In recent years, only one program project has been rejected — the multilateral exchange of radio news over a permanent audio network. In 1971, several

European broadcasting organizations proposed that the EBU use its Eurovision network for a regular exchange of radio news. The Committee, however, decided that the project would be a costly operation requiring additional staff as well as a permanent sound network. In addition, it felt that the scheme was impractical because news items would be in different European languages, and because items, unlike television pictures, can readily be phoned in by national foreign correspondents.[58]

Television Program Committee

The Television Program Committee provides the overall direction to the EBU's work in promoting television program exchanges, particularly Eurovision. It works through annual meetings, a bureau, and working parties.[59] Meetings are open to all members as well as "approved observers" such as representatives from other broadcasting unions. The delegates are generally television program executives, directors, and producers.

As we shall see in the remaining chapters, much of the Committee's workload concerns Eurovision. But the Committee is also active in organizing *1)* non-Eurovision program exchanges, and *2)* screenings.

The Television Program Committee was principally established to promote the exchange of filmed or taped programs which did not require transmission on Eurovision.[60] Indeed, for many years, Eurovision took a back seat to EBU filmed program exchange series such as the eighteen-year-old "International Youth Magazine."[61] Early broadcasters were prevented from exchanging many programs on Eurovision because of the lack of national and international circuits and because of the high rental costs for vision circuits. In addition, language problems also made live transmissions unattractive. Foreign films could more easily be dubbed.

Admittedly, the Committee's major emphasis shifted from filmed exchanges toward Eurovision programming as the network grew more sophisticated and new uses were found such as regular news exchanges. Still, non-Eurovision exchanges make up a significant share of Committee's activities, as the "Documentary" series shows. In 1982, the Working Party for Programs for Children and Young People exchanged fourteen childrens' documentary programs among the services from thirteen countries.[62] Started in 1962, on a Swedish proposal to encourage home-produced material and so lessen dependence on American imports, the "Documentary" series calls on each participant to make a program on a predetermined subject which is then copied and sent to others.[63] This permits members to receive many programs at a lower cost than going it alone. If fifteen services are actively involved in the scheme, each service would get fourteen programs for one produced, paying only copying costs. Although in its fifteenth season in 1983, the series has met with some complaints by program makers. One frequent complaint is that some members take their contributions "out of the can," which means that rather than making a new program, a member may submit a program that has already been shown in order to save money and time.[64]

The Television Program Committee was also created, as set forth in Article 1 of its Rules and Procedures, to "encourage professional contacts and collaboration between television program experts." To this end, the Committee organizes the EBU Screening Sessions where members buy and sell programs. Indeed, the 21-year-old EBU Screenings, which are always held in October, have developed into one of the largest professional television markets in Europe.[65] The 1982 session, held in Milan, was attended by television programmers from all over the world. In just five days, they viewed 130 programs — totalling 115 hours — presented for sale by 41 active EBU members.[66] Although many programs are shown, EBU associate members such as the three major American networks (ABC, CBS, and NBC) have long argued that, since they contribute to the funding of the EBU, they should also be allowed to sell their programs at the sessions. The EBU recently responded by reorganizing the sessions to permit not only collective screenings but also small private screenings arranged by active members themselves.[67] To date, however, associate members are still not allowed to show their programs.

3.6.2 OIRT Commissions

Technical Commission

As early as 1946 when the Technical Commission was created, the OIRT recognized that collaboration among engineers of different countries is imperative if the potential of international broadcasts is to be fully realized. The Commission works through working parties, a bureau, and annual plenary meetings.[68]

In light of the basic link between scientific developments and international collaboration, it is not surprising to find that the bulk of the Commission's tasks are similar to those of its EBU counterpart. Like the EBU Technical Committee, the Commission has made studies dealing with all aspects of broadcasting, from descriptions of new digital techniques to the technical quality of international link-ups. In the field of spectrum utilization, the Commission concerns itself with equipping the OIRT Monitoring Station located near Prague (the EBU also has a monitoring center).

Indeed, the staffs of the OIRT and EBU technical centers can often be found preparing for the same ITU administrative broadcasting conferences. But joint preparations for such conferences is rare, if not non-existent. Calls to coordinate frequency proposals with the EBU, for example, were made to the

OIRT in advance of the 1975 ITU Regional Administrative LF/MF Broadcasting Conference and the 1977 WARC-BS. But both calls were rejected by the OIRT. The main reason for the lack of formal interunion collaboration is that OIRT members view the drawing up of frequency plans as a matter for governments, not broadcasters — the opposite viewpoint held by EBU members. Nevertheless, a considerable informal exchange of information often does take place through the Finnish broadcasting organization, YLE, which is a member of both the EBU and OIRT.[69]

While tasks may be similar, the two committees seem to focus their primary attention on different problem areas. A major problem area confronting the EBU Technical Committee tends to be standardization. The Committee's history can be seen as a consistent effort to keep EBU members from choosing different equipment. By contrast, the OIRT Technical Commission's main problem area seems to be development. Intervision's development, for example, was long hindered by the lack of two-way television links among members. Indeed, Intervision programs frequently had to be canceled because national circuits were occupied by other transmissions. Technical shortcomings also hindered the news exchange. It took six years of news exchanges before IVN became a daily operation in 1970.[70] The quality and reliability of Intervision transmissions, however, are improving particularly with the increasing use of INTERSPUTNIK satellites.

Economic-Legal Commission

The Economic-Legal Commission was established in 1968 to study financial and legal questions arising from OIRT activities and to issue recommendations concerning them. Unlike the three other OIRT commissions, the Economic-Legal Commission does not have any working parties.

Much of the Commission's work concerns drafting the OIRT's budget, which is voted on annually by the administrative council. The Commission also calculates membership fees, establishes development plans, and allocates construction funds. Another activity consists of providing members with a forum for discussing legal questions ranging from sports advertising to problems of satellite television transmissions.[71]

Compared with the EBU Legal Committee, however, the Commission's activities are few. The Commission has not become involved in either drafting or revising international treaties on copyright and neighboring rights, nor in negotiating standard contracts with international federations of artists and authors. Also, neither the Commission nor the OIRT has a permanent legal secretariat headed by an elected official, as the EBU does. Often the OIRT calls upon the services of the legal department of the Czechoslovak broadcasting service.

The Commission's limited activities reflect the importance which the Socialist governments of Europe place on controlling the performance of works. Copyrights do exist. But no performing rights collection agency rivals the state. This is reflected in the fact that while practically all the developed countries of the world adhere to the Berne Copyright Convention of 1886, and the subsequent International Conventions, the USSR does not. Also, Czechoslovakia is the only OIRT member party to the International Convention for the Protection of Performers, Producers of Phonographs and Broadcasting Organizations. Thus, legal aspects of Intervision are handled on a program-by-program basis, with the originating organization handling all the legal details so that the relaying organization will be protected.[72] The EBU, by contrast, standardizes many procedures through agreement with various federations which become involved when programs cross European boundaries.

Radio Program Commission

The Radio Program Commission is the principal body for promoting the exchange of radio programs. It was created in 1960 to overcome the neglect which radio was receiving in light of Intervision's creation. The Commission works through working parties, a bureau, and an annual plenary meeting.[73]

The Commission's main tool for promoting program exchanges is the publication, through the general secretariat, of catalogs listing programs available for exchange for the next six months. In 1982, a considerable number of offers concerned Socialist anniversaries and national days in OIRT countries including the 112th anniversary of Lenin's birth and the 65th anniversary of the Great October Revolution.

In addition, programs are exchanged at numerous concerts and festivals approved by the Commission. The annual OIRT Gala Concert, for example, was established in 1972 and permits members to offer operas for transmission. The "Galas" are organized through the Working Group for Musical Programs.

Representatives of the OIRT and EBU radio program committees meet every two years, alternating between Western and Eastern cities of Europe, to review cooperation between the two agencies in the radio field. The meetings are friendly, but the only areas where practical results have been obtained concern sports and music. OIRT and EBU representatives have arranged facilities for national commentators at international sports events and have exchanged music scripts. One reason for the limited cooperation is the difference in program values. Broadly speaking, EBU members do not take many OIRT offers because they find them either dull or full of political messages. On the other hand, OIRT members do not take many EBU offers partly because they are deemed to be too commercial.[74]

Significantly, program offers from OIRT members to EBU members are sent directly to the EBU by the individual OIRT member, not via OIRT headquarters. The reasons are partly due to the OIRT's small staff, and partly because some OIRT members such as the USSR seem to dislike the idea of working through an international secretariat.[75]

Television Program Commission

The Television Program Commission provides a forum where broad problems of television are discussed and where Intervision exchanges are planned. The Commission works through working parties, the Intervision Council and plenary meetings.

The Commission and all its working groups are mainly concerned with television program questions.[76] One recent achievement was the comparative study of the content and preparation of Intervision news programs. This work attempts to identify the kinds of news, particularly items making Socialist unity and integration attractive to news editors and viewers alike.[77]

The Commission established the Intervision Council in 1960 to deal exclusively with Intervision activities. The Council meets twice a year and is headed by the chairman of the Television Program Commission. Membership is open to those organizations which are linked to Intervision, although exactly how a member will be represented in Council meetings often depends upon the subject matter.[78] Representatives of international organizations and of non-member organizations may also participate in Council meetings.[79]

A major function of the Council, as set out in Article 4 of the Intervision Rules, is to draw up the television program exchange schedule. OIRT procedure for live exchanges over Intervision is based on a television program catalog which is regularly circulated to all members and other broadcasting unions. It contains lists of offers for the coming six months. It is important to note that the EBU generally does not circulate a program catalog except in cases of educational coproductions. Recent accomplishments include setting policy for Intervision coverage of the 1982 Madrid World Cup.

The Council also promotes the buying and selling of television programs, many of which are Socialist-oriented. Established in 1966, the Intervision Teleforum, which only screens productions from OIRT members, is held in the fall of each year in Moscow and attended by broadcasters from around the world. At the 1982 Teleforum, program-makers from 29 countries saw over 400 programs.[80] Many of the programs show Socialist achievements such as those in space and in tapping Siberia's rich resources.

3.7 EBU and OIRT Finances

Both the EBU and OIRT divide their overall operations into two budgets: the ordinary budget which covers the costs of the general assembly, the administrative council, the secretariat, and a "program exchange" budget which covers the costs of Eurovision and Intervision. The latter budget will be discussed in the next chapter.

The costs of the EBU are met from the subscriptions of the active members, each member paying a sum based on a unit class scale ranging from 1 unit to 107.[81] Active members are not free to choose unit classes. Rather, a unit class is assigned to each active member based upon the number of radio and television licenses in that country. Also, additional units are assigned to countries which have more than one active member.[82] Assessing countries with more than one active member not only defrays extra EBU costs but also signals that the country has the resources to finance a complex broadcasting system.[83] For members whose income does not come from license fees, subscription units are estimated by the administrative council.

Associate members do not pay subscriptions, but rather contribute to the ordinary budget according to the services rendered to them by the EBU and according to their financial resources. The amount due is fixed each year by the administrative council. Provisions exist in Article 16 of the EBU Statutes covering the financial contributions to be made by organizations and regional broadcasting unions whose participation is approved in EBU meetings.

In addition to membership dues, other sources of funds for the ordinary budget include interest from the EBU's own funds, rent from the Geneva building, and the sale of publications. In 1982, about 7 percent of the budget income came from the sale of publications.[84]

In 1981, the EBU's system of financing was changed to make membership fees more equitable and less arbitrary. The 1982 general assembly widened the range of classes from 55 units to 107. Several reasons were involved. First, the old system of 55 units did not account for the growth in the number of broadcasters in the same country.[85] Prior to 1981, organizations such as ZDF/West Germany and IBA/United Kingdom were arbitrarily placed on the scale, while ARD/West Germany and the BBC carried the most financial burden. The new system increased the fees of ZDF and IBA to a more realistic level. Second, the old system did not account for the growth of advertising activities.[86] The new system raised the subscriptions of commercial broadcasters, especially those of RMC/Monaco and RTL/Luxembourg who are located in small countries and broadcast largely to audiences in other countries. Third, the widening of the scale, based upon a mathematical formula, avoided the large and sudden jumps in fees which members faced with the growth in licenses.[87]

But the recent changes did not attack the problem of the critical financial situation which many members face. Many EBU members are struggling financially under the burden of adopting expensive new technology, compounded by the political unpopularity of increasing license fees. Furthermore, in countries like Italy, private broadcasters are cutting into members' budget. If the financial situation of members does not improve, the economic crisis could become a crisis for the EBU. Continuing economic weakness is likely to undermine members' ability to make and buy programs or to maintain Eurovision.

The non-Eurovision expenses of the EBU have steadily grown over the years. The EBU's ordinary expenditures have risen from 397,000 Swiss francs in 1950 to 4,630,000 in 1969 and to 12,592,000 in 1981 (approximately 7,407,000 dollars at the 1981 exchange rates).[88] The amount of a subscription unit for 1981 was determined by the general assembly to be 14,100 Swiss francs. Thus, the lowest class, 1 unit, to which only the Vatican subscribes, amounted to 14,100 Swiss francs, and the highest class, 128 units, to which only France subscribed, was 1,804,800 Swiss francs.[89] The Big Four (France, Italy, the United Kingdom and West Germany) paid about 45 percent of the ordinary budget.[90] The administrative council fixes the contributions of associate members. In 1981, the highest fees came from the four American networks (ABC, CBS, NBC and PBS) and from NHK/Japan, each paying 40,000 Swiss francs. The least amount, 1,800 Swiss francs, came from sixteen EBU associate members including the Congo and Qatar. Together, the contributions of associate members constituted only 5 percent of the EBU's ordinary budget income.[91]

The OIRT's budgetary arrangements are similar to those of the EBU. The OIRT ordinary budget covers all costs, except for Intervision activities which are covered in a special budget. Like the EBU, the OIRT's basic financial support is computed on the number of radio and television receiver licenses in OIRT member countries. Members are arranged in equitable financial groups by means of a table in which assessed units are pro-rated from one and one-half to fifty-five. The value of one unit in 1979 was 11,789 Czechoslovak korunas (about 2,400 US dollars at the 1979 exchange rate).[92] A member determines his obligation by multiplying the above figure by the number of units assigned to its group. In the case where revenue does not come from license fees, as is true of the USSR, assessments are determined by the administrative council.

The OIRT's expenses have grown. In 1969, the expenses were 4,356,300 Czechoslovak korunas.[93] By 1979, expenses had grown to 6,828,000 Czechoslovak korunas.[94] In 1979, the largest contributor was TSS/USSR, with 18 percent of the budget; Poland was second, with 11 percent. The Soviet Republics as a group paid 44 percent of the ordinary OIRT budget.[95]

OIRT's expenditures are almost entirely related to its forum role, while the EBU's expenditures are more service-oriented. A rough measure of these differing functions can be the distinction which both agencies make between the ordinary budget and the "program exchange" budget. In 1979, the EBU devoted 58 percent of its funds to service activities such as coordinating Eurovision operations, compared with only 10 percent by the OIRT. A further measure of the different degrees of EBU and OIRT activities is the size of their staffs. In 1983, the EBU staff numbered 225, while the OIRT had 70 employees.

3.8 Relations With Other International Organizations

The activities of the EBU and OIRT constantly bring them into contact with other international organizations concerned with broadcasting. They attend meetings of other international organizations as the occasion demands, particularly where questions of special interest to the agencies are discussed. Indeed, EBU and OIRT representatives often attend the same meetings.

EBU and OIRT maintain close relations with United Nations agencies which have special interests in broadcasting. They have been granted consultative status with ECOSOC, ITU, and UNESCO. EBU and OIRT also have working relations with ILO and WIPO.

Because frequency allocations directly affect broadcasters, the EBU and OIRT are most active with the ITU. They are represented in many ITU meetings in a non-voting advisory capacity when allocations are being considered. (In general, EBU and OIRT do not send observers to ITU Plenipotentiary Conferences.) At the Regional Administrative LF/MF Broadcasting Conference (1974 and 1975), for instance, the EBU and OIRT complained of harmful interference and requested changes of frequency assignments. Neither the EBU nor the OIRT attended the World Maritime Administrative Radio Conference (1974). Of the numerous CCIR and CCITT study groups, the EBU and OIRT tend to give high priority to the work of CCIR Study Group 10 (Broadcasting Service-Sound) and 11 (Broadcasting Service-Television). In fact, a director of the EBU Technical Center, Georges Hansen, was vice-chairman of Study Group 11 from 1953 to 1966. It is also worth noting that governments not belonging to the ITU have used the EBU and OIRT to gain access to ITU conferences and meetings.[96]

To a large extent, presentation of technical papers remain the EBU's and OIRT's most crucial asset in influencing ITU decision making. The EBU could presumably also use its Geneva headquarters for day-to-day contact with ITU officials, but this source of influence would likely be limited to nontechnical issues, since the EBU's technical experts are located in Brussels.

Outside the United Nations system, EBU and OIRT collaborate with other intergovernmental organizations, mainly with those whose memberships are compatible. EBU, for instance, has discussed satellite tariffs with COMSAT and CEPT, European broadcasting legislation with the Council of Europe, and European satellite communications projects with ESA. The OIRT has been represented in meetings of COMECON, INTERSPUTNIK, the World Federation of Democratic Youth and the World Federation of Trade Unions.[97]

In addition, both agencies have relations with a number of regional broadcasting unions. The most important of these are the Arab States Broadcasting Union (ASBU),[98] Asia-Pacific Broadcasting Union (ABU),[99] the North American National Broadcasters Association (NANBA), the Organización de la Televisión Iberoamericana (OTI)[100] and the Union of National Radio and Television Organizations of Africa (URTNA).[101] This cooperation ranges from inviting the other unions to general assemblies and exchanging daily television news stories, to negotiating the price for television coverage of Olympic Games and convening conferences of all broadcasting unions.

Significantly, the EBU has closer contacts with other international organizations concerning legal issues than does the OIRT. To standardize Eurovision legalities, the EBU has concluded standard contracts with the following international rights-holding bodies:

> International Bureau of the Societies Administering the Rights of Mechanical Recording and Reproduction (BIEM)
> International Federation of Phonographic Industry (IFPI)
> Society of Dramatic Authors and Composers (SACD)
> International Union of Editors (UIE)

The OIRT does not maintain relations with any of these bodies.

3.9 Conclusion

Our look inside the European Broadcasting Union and the International Radio and Television Organization has shown that much of their work involves planning, supervising, and coordinating Europe's television exchanges. Members have made studies and recommendations to permit new technologies to be integrated into the networks, to negotiate television rights and to exchange program offers and requests.

Indeed, the EBU's and OIRT's work is indispensible to most of its members. All broadcasting organizations must be concerned about what equipment other organizations adopt if they want to exchange programs with one another. By negotiating television rights on behalf of members, the EBU and OIRT hope to avoid excessive fees for any one country. Furthermore, most members seem to realize that, without a system for multilateral program exchanges, the national broadcasting fare would be duller and more expensive to make, especially for small organizations. The necessity of these functions to most members is also reflected in the cooperative arrangements between the EBU and OIRT.

Much of the structure and activities of the EBU and OIRT is similar. But significant differences also exist. One important difference is membership. The EBU considers it desirable to remain a regional body to achieve its goals, although it does not exclude broadcasters from outside "Europe" from participating in meetings. The OIRT, in contrast, as its name implies, has an "international" mission, although it groups politically like-minded countries. Also the majority of OIRT members are organizations of actual or near ministerial status, while EBU membership varies from private commercial organizations to state-run stations.

Other differences can be listed quickly. The EBU general assembly meets once a year, while the OIRT's assembly meets irregularly. EBU council members serve four-year terms, and members of the OIRT administrative council only serve two-year terms. The president of the EBU has a stronger position than his OIRT counterpart — often becoming a third EBU decision-making organ. Another difference is that outside the United Nations family, EBU and OIRT collaborate with other intergovernmental organizations whose memberships are similar. Moreover, the OIRT devotes the bulk of its efforts to forum activities such as promoting information exchanges, while the EBU allocates more than half of its expenses to service functions such as routing transmissions. The EBU's greater stress on service functions is also reflected in its larger staff and correspondingly larger budget.

Most important of all, serious differences exist in how salient the issues the EBU and OIRT deal with are for the central political authorities of members. Representatives of the EBU and OIRT technical committees have studied the details of color television together, but have not met in preparation for ITU conferences allocating broadcasting frequencies largely because OIRT members look at frequencies as a matter for governments, not broadcasters, to decide. In the legal field, EBU-OIRT collaboration is rare partly because of differing approaches in negotiating television rights. On the one hand, the EBU has concluded standard contracts with international federations of artists and authors to standardize payments. On the other hand, OIRT members have not concluded such agreements, requiring the originating station to handle all the legal details on a program-by-program basis. The limited commitment of OIRT members in the legal field is also reflected by the absence of a permanent legal organ. In the radio program field, OIRT offers to EBU members are sent directly to the EBU by individual OIRT members — not via OIRT headquarters. On the other hand, EBU offers to the OIRT are sent to Prague for further distribution. While the difference is partly due to the OIRT's small staff, it also reflects the limited commitment of OIRT members to work through their own secretariat.

As we shall see in the remaining chapters, EBU-OIRT collaboration is most extensive when it comes to Eurovision and Intervision activities. But the success of international television exchanges also depends upon the ability of members to retain their sovereignty over what their viewers will or will not see. We turn now to a closer look at how programs are transmitted over Eurovision and Intervision.

Endnotes

Chapter 3

1. An important source on the EBU has been written by a former chairman of the Legal Committee, Hans Brack, *The Evolution of the EBU Through Its Statutes from 1950 to 1976* (Geneva: EBU, 1976). See also Russell B. Barber, "The European Broadcasting Union," *Journal of Broadcasting*, 6:2, (Spring 1962), pp. 111-121; and Régis de Kalbermatten, "The European Broadcasting Union — Past, Present and Future," *Intermedia*, 5:6, (December 1977), pp. 25-30. EBU itself has published several official accounts of its structure and activities, including *Twenty-Five Years - European Broadcasting Union* (Geneva: EBU, 1974). Delbert D. Smith has several sections on the EBU in his *International Telecommunication Control* (Leiden, Netherlands: Sijthoff, 1969); as does Simone Courteix, *Télévisions sans frontières, un problème de coopération internationale* (Paris: Economica, 1975). A scholarly study on EBU was done by Charles E. Sherman, "The Structure and Functions of the European Broadcasting Union," (Wayne State University, 1967). A limited body of literature on the OIRT exists. Useful information on general structure and development can be found in Kenneth Harwood, "The International Radio and Television Organization," *Journal of Broadcasting*, 9:4, (Winter 1965), pp. 7-18, and Charles E. Sherman, "OIRT," *International Broadcasting*, (Washington, D.C.: Association for Professional Broadcasting Education, 1971), pp. 13-21. A recent work is Len Scott's, "OIRT: Far-flung Grouping of the Politically Like-minded," *BM/E's World Broadcast News*, (November 1982), pp. 21-28.
2. The exception was the addition of paragraph (*f*) in Article 2 in 1959.
3. The composition of EBU and OIRT membership is given in Appendices B and C respectively.
4. EBU, *Statutes*, (Geneva, 1981), Art. 3, (*1*). See EBU, *The EBU Statutes Revision*, (Geneva: EBU, 1982) for more about the changes in membership provisions.

5. Brack, *The Evolution of the EBU Through Its Statutes from 1950 to 1976, op. cit.*, p. 29.
6. EBU, *Statutes, op. cit.*, Art. 14, (*6*).
7. *Ibid.*, Art. 3, (*5*).
   The European Broadcasting Area, as defined in Article 8, section 1, para. 4 of the 1979 ITU Radio Regulations, is "bounded on the West by the Western boundary of Region 1 on the East by the meridian 40 degrees East of Greenwich and on the South by the parallel 30 North so as to include the Western part of the USSR and the Northern part of Saudi Arabia and that part of those countries bordering the Mediterranean within these limits. In addition, Iraq and Jordan are included in the European Broadcasting Area."
8. *Ibid.*, Art. 3, (*6*).
9. *Ibid.*, Art. 3, (*7*).
10. OIRT, *Statutes*, (Tampere, 1969), Art. 5, (*5a*).
11. *Ibid.*, Art. 5, (*5c*).
12. *Ibid.*, Art. 6.
13. The EBU regularly lists the composition of its membership in the *EBU Review*.
14. Brack, *The Evolution of the EBU Through Its Statutes from 1950 to 1976, op. cit.*, pp. 31-33.
15. The Yugoslavian broadcasting organization was a founding member of the OIRT. But, as a result of Tito's break with Stalin in 1948, and with the resignation of West European broadcasters from the OIRT in 1949, the Yugoslav organization withdrew from the OIRT on December 31, 1950. Ten months earlier, Yugoslavia had joined the broadcasters of 22 other nations in creating the EBU.
16. For an account of the benefits which Finnish broadcasters reap from being members of the EBU, the OIRT, and Nordvision, see Ville Zilliacus, "Where the 'Visions' Meet," *EBU Review*, 30:3, (May 1979), pp. 55-57.
17. OIRT, *Statutes, op. cit.*, (Tampere, 1969), Art. 10, (*3*). Since 1958, General Assembly sessions have been held in 1958, 1959, 1961, 1963, 1965, 1968, 1969, 1970, 1971, 1972, 1973, 1975, 1977, 1979 and 1981.
18. EBU, *Statutes, op. cit.*, Art. 6, (*3*).
19. *Ibid.*, Art. 12, (*1*).
20. See Brack, *The Evolution of the EBU Through Its Statutes from 1950 to 1976, op. cit.*, pp. 46-48.
21. EBU, *Statutes, op. cit.*, Art. 12, (*5*).
22. *Ibid.*, Art. 12, (*5a*).
23. *Ibid.*, Art. 6, (*2*).
24. Apart from the permanent committees, the EBU council has its own

study groups to study specific questions. In 1983, the following groups reported to the administrative council: the Consultative Group on Satellite Broadcasting, the Study Group on EBU Statutes, the Study Group on Financial Affairs, Interdisciplinary Group on Activities of International Organizations and Conferences Dealing with Questions Concerning Broadcasting, the Study Group on Technical Assignments, and the Telecommunications/Tariffs Exploratory Group. The OIRT's Council does not have any internal study groups.

25. EBU, *Statutes, op. cit.*, Art. 7, (*3*).
26. OIRT, *Statutes, op. cit.*, Art. 11, (*3*).
27. Author's analysis of *Radio-Television* and *OIRT Information* from 1958 to 1982. Article 24 of the Statutes still provides that one council seat be permanently assigned to the People's Republic of China, although that country has not attended council meetings since the early 1960s.
28. EBU, *Statutes, op. cit.*, Art. 11, (*3*).
29. Brack, *The Evolution of the EBU Through Its Statutes from 1950 to 1976, op. cit.*, p. 67.
30. The EBU has had four secretary-generals: Léo Wallenborn (INR/Belgium), 1950-57; Charles Guilliéron (SSR/Switzerland), 1957-65; Henrik Hahr (SR/Sweden), 1965-76; and Dr. Régis de Kalbermatten (SSR/Switzerland) from 1976 to the present (1983).
31. Brack, *The Evolution of the EBU Through Its Statutes from 1950 to 1976, op. cit.*, pp. 74-75.
32. *Ibid.*, pp. 74-80.
33. Six persons have been secretary-general of the OIRT: Leo Wallenborn (INR/Belgium), 1946-49; Theodore Zelezny (CST/Czechoslovakia), 1950-55; M. Broz (CST/Czechoslovakia), 1955-56; J. Weiser (CST/Czechoslovakia), 1956-57, Jaromir Hrebik (CST/Czechoslovakia); 1958-80; and Dr. Milena Balasova (CST/Czechoslovakia) from 1980 to the present.
34. In 1983, the following working parties reported to the Technical Committee:
    Working Party F   Technical Training
    Working Party G   Production-equipment Technology
    Working Party R   Sound and Television Broadcasting
    Working Party T   International Network Transmission and Operations
    Working Party V   New Systems and Services
    Works on the Technical Committee include Georges Hansen, "Evolution of the Activities of the Technical Center of the EBU Since Its Establishment," *ASBU Technical Review*, 1:1, (January 1974), pp. 9-15; and Edward Pawley, "The Work of the EBU in the Technical Field," *EBU Review*, 48A, (March 1958), pp. 43-46.

35. EBU, *Notification and Registration of Frequencies*, Doc. Tech. 3069, September 1956.
36. H. Mertens, *Satellite Broadcasting Design and Planning of 12-GHz Systems*, EBU Doc. Tech. 3220, March 1976.
37. ITU, *Final Acts of the World Administrative Radio Conference for Planning of the Broadcasting-Satellite Service in Frequency Bands 11.7-12.2 GHz [in Regions 2 and 3] and 11.7-12.5 GHz [in Region 1] Geneva 1977* (Geneva: ITU, 1977). See also A. Brown and H. Mertens, "The Work of the Conference on Satellite Broadcasting," *EBU Review*, 162, (April 1977), pp. 60-67. Region 2 (the Americas) adopted only preliminary provisions which were finalized in 1983 at the Regional Administrative Conference for the Planning of the Broadcasting-Satellite Service in Region 2.
38. EBU, *Analysis of the 1977 Geneva Plan for Satellite Broadcasting at 12-GHz*, Doc. Tech. 3222, April 1977. Volume I, *Summary Statistical Analysis [Regions 1 and 3] List of the Preponderant Interferers*. Volume IIa, *Detailed Analysis for Region 1 [Service areas A to L]*. Volume IIb, *Detailed Analysis for Region 1 [Service areas M to Z]*. Volume III, *Detailed Analysis for Region 3*. Volume IV, *Summary Statistical Analysis with Ideal Pointing of the Transmitting Antennae [Area covered by the Active Members of the EBU] Power Flux-densities Created in Region 2*. Volume V, *Graphical Results and Miscellaneous Statistics*.
39. As early as 1955, the EBU dealt with color television. The Technical Committee created Working Party H to examine the possibilities of agreeing to specifications for a single color system. After several meetings, however, it became clear that the situation was not far enough advanced to permit standardization. Most organizations were not ready to immediately start color television. Thus, the Working Party was disbanded a year later, and it was not until 1962 that the EBU resumed the study of color television.
40. EBU, *Report of the EBU Ad-hoc Group on Color Television, Second Edition*, February 1965.
41. Georges Hansen, "Color-Television Standards for Europe," *World Radio TV Handbook 1965* (Hvidovre, Denmark: WRTH Co., Ltd., 1965), p. 28.
42. CCIR, Study Group XI/45 (1965), EBU-OIRT.
43. See Rhonda J. Crane, *The Politics of International Standards: France and the Color TV War* (Norwood, N.J.: Ablex Publishing Co., 1979).
44. In 1982, countries in the European Broadcasting Area had adopted the following different color standards:

SECAM — Bulgaria, Czechoslovakia, Egypt, France, German Democratic Republic, Greece, Hungary, Libya, Luxembourg, Monaco, Morocco, Poland, Tunisia, and the USSR.
PAL — Algeria, Austria, Belgium, Cyprus, Denmark, Federal Republic of Germany, Finland, Iceland, Ireland, Israel, Italy, Malta, Netherlands, Norway, Portugal, Spain, Sweden, Switzerland, Turkey United Kingdom, and Yugoslavia.
Countries which have not yet decided are: Albania and Rumania.

45. EBU, "Meeting of the Conversion Sub-group of Working Party M (International Network Transmissions)," *EBU Review*, 113, (February 1969), pp. 51-52.
46. EBU, "Symposium on Preparations for Color Television," *EBU Review*, 107, (February 1968), pp. 46-48.
47. European Broadcasting Conference, Note on Various Aspects of Legal Work to be Carried Out by the Administrative Office and Why Such Work is Urgent, February 1950, Torquay/5, pp. 5-6.
48. Important articles on the Committee include Hans Brack, "The Place of the Legal Committee Within the EBU," *EBU Review*, 93B, (September 1965), pp. 60-61; Hans Brack, "Aspects of the Legal Committee's Work Within the Framework of the EBU 1965-1972," *EBU Review*, 24:1, (January 1973), pp. 37-43; Maurice Lenoble, "The Activities of the Legal Committee," *EBU Bulletin*, 6:5, (September-October 1955), pp. 503-505; Maurice Lenoble, "The Activities of the EBU Legal Committee," *EBU Review*, 85B, (May 1964), pp. 37-41.
49. In accordance with the spirit of the Statutes, the Legal Committee, unlike the other three committees, does not have standing working parties which meet regularly. Rather the chairman of the Committee will only create a working group to study a foreseen problem. Once the group has submitted its recommendations to the Committee, it is disbanded. Three working groups which have been active in recent years are the Working Party on Cable Distribution, Working Party on Secondary Uses of Broadcast Programs and Working Party on Satellite Questions.
50. See "8-Nation TV Faces Boycott by Actors," *New York Times*, April 26, 1954.
51. Madeleine Larrue, "Talk by Mrs. Larrue on the Legal Aspects of Eurovision," December 11, 1967, p. 2. (Unpublished paper).
52. In 1983, the following working parties reported to the Radio Program Committee:
Working Party on News and Current Affairs
Working Party on Serious Music

Working Party on Sports
Working Party on Broadcasts for Motorists
Working Party on Drama
Working Party on Light Music Ad-hoc Plenary Meetings of Experts in Various Program Fields
53. Sound Broadcasting Program Committee, Rules of Procedure, O.A./3042-Rad. Com./1-C.A./799.
54. Interview with G.C. Pellandini, Head of the Radio Program Coordination Department, SSR, Bern, May 1979.
55. Interview with Antony Dean, Director of the Radio Program Department, EBU, Geneva, July 1978.
56. *Ibid.*, January 1983.
57. Dean, *op. cit.*, July 1978.
58. *Ibid..*
59. In 1983, the following working parties reported to the Committee:
Working Party for Television News
Working Party for Television Sports Programs
Working Party for Educational Programs
Working Party for Programs for Children and Young People
Working Party for Television Music Programs
60. The Television Program Committee came into existence in July 1964 when the old Program Committee was split into the Radio Program Committee and the Television Program Committee.
61. See Heinz von Plato, "Eurovision and Youth Programs," *EBU Review*, 84B, (March 1964), pp. 6-7. The "Youth Magazine" ended in 1973 because of a lack of interest. See Paul Taff (ed.), *Report of the First EBU Workshop for Producers of Childrens' Television Programs, London, February 1968*, (Geneva: EBU, 1969), p. 81; and Doreen Stephens (ed.), *Report of the Second EBU Workshop for Producers and Directors of Television Programs for Young People, Stockholm, February 1970*, (Geneva: EBU, 1970).
62. Interview with Harry Dennis, Senior Assistant, Specialized TV Programs Division, EBU, Geneva, January 1983.
63. Stephens, *Report on the Second EBU Workshop for Producers and Directors of Television Programs for Young People, op. cit.*, p. 71.
64. Dennis, *op. cit..*
65. See Lars-Eric Kjellgren, "The EBU Screening Sessions — A Personal Report," *EBU Review*, 23:5, (September 1972), pp. 12-15; Paul Peyre, "The EBU Screening Sessions," *EBU Review*, 30:3, (May 1979), pp. 57-59; and "EBU: Sought-After Market," *TV World*, 5:1, (November 1981), p. 23. The EBU screenings are but one of several international television showings and festivals occupying the calendar of television

executives. See Jim Hodgetts, "Comparing MIFED and MIP," *TV World*, 1:12, (October 1978), pp. 25-26; and Jack Stockdale, "TV's World Market Place," *TV World*, 2:5, (March 1979), pp. 14-15.
66. Interview with Frank Naef, Head, Specialized TV Programs Division, EBU, Geneva, January 1983.
67. *Ibid.*.
68. In 1983, the following study groups reported to the Technical Commission:
    International Circuits for the Transmission of Sound
    Signals in Radio and TV Broadcasting
    Electro-Acoustics and Sound Recording
    Radio Wave Propagations
    Automation and Computer Techniques
69. Interview with Alan Brown, Technical Center, EBU, Brussels, April 1979.
70. See Waclaw Wygledowski, "IVN — Daily News Exchange on the International Network," *OIRT Radio-Television*, 1, (1972), pp. 3-4; Waclaw Wygledowski, "20,000 News Items Within 10 Years of IVN Exchange," *OIRT Radio-Television*, 4, (1974), pp. 3-6; and Waclaw Wygledowski, *Daily News Exchange on the Intervision Network 1964-1976*, (Prague: OIRT, 1977). This work is summarized in his article entitled, "Intervision: The Growth of an Exchange," *Intermedia*, 11:3, (June 1978), pp. 24-27.
71. Interview with Dr. Ales Poledne, Editor, OIRT, Prague, November 1975.
72. Sherman, "OIRT," *op.cit.*, p. 21.
73. The Radio Program Commission, as well as the Television Program Commission, trace their origins to the OIR Program Commission created in July 1947. In March 1957, the Program Commission was succeeded by the Commission for Programs and the Organization of Television. When Intervision was created in 1960, the Commission was reorganized into two separate bodies — the Radio Program Commission and the Television Program Commission. In 1983, the following working parties reported to the Commission:
    Working Party for Entertainment Programs
    Working Party for Musical Programs
    Working Party for Dramatic and Literary Broadcasts
    Working Party for Sports Programs
    Working Party for Science and Technology
    Working Party for Children's Programs
    Working Party for Youth Programs
    Working Party for Economic Programs
74. Dean, *op. cit.*.

75. *Ibid..*
76. In 1983, the following working parties reported to the Television Program Commission:
    Working Party for Children's and Youth Programs
    Working Party for Sports Programs
    Working Party for Literary-Dramatic Programs
    Working Party for Music Programs
    Working Party for Program Planning
    Working Party for News
    Working Party for the Protection of the Environment
    Working Party for Health Care
    Working Party for Educational Programs
    Working Party for Economy and Integration of National Economy
77. Waclaw Wygledowski, "20,000 News Items Within 10 Years of IVN Exchange," *op. cit.*, p. 6.
78. Correspondence with Raimo Arhela, International Relations Department, YLE, Helsinki, April 1979.
79. ORF/Austria, SR/Sweden and JRT/Yugoslavia — all EBU members — often send observers to Intervision Council meetings. Charles Sherman noted that ORF attends mainly because it is the junction point between Eurovision and Intervision, while SR and JRT seem to attend largely for information purposes. Sherman, "OIRT," *op. cit.*, p. 14. Representatives from INTERSPUTNIK have also participated in recent meetings.
80. OIRT, "Soviet Television and Radio," *OIRT Information*, no. 12, (1982), p. 12.
81. The subscription table can be found in Art. 16, (2b) of the EBU Statutes.
82. The EBU Statutes (Art. 16, (2cii) hold that a country with more than one active member faces a 35 percent increase for a second service, a further 12.5 percent for the third service and an additional 5 percent for each extra organization.
83. EBU, *The EBU Statutes Revision, op. cit.*, p. 30.
84. Interview with Bernard Briguet, Senior Assistant, Administration and Finance, EBU, Geneva, January 1983.
85. *Ibid..*
86. *Ibid..*
87. *Ibid..*
88. 1950 and 1969 figures from EBU Doc., 0.A./4147, A.G./330, July 3, 1970. 1981 figure from EBU Doc., A.G./522, S.P.G./1936/9, June 1982.
89. EBU Doc., A.G./522-S.P.G. 1936/9, June 1982.

90. Ibid..
91. Ibid..
92. OIRT, *Budget für 1979*, OIRT Doc., AS-53-5/78.
93. OIRT, *Budget für 1969*, OIRT Doc., AS-41-2/69.
94. OIRT, *Budget für 1979*, op. cit..
95. Ibid..
96. Perhaps the most successful delegate to the ITU in this regard was East Germany before it became an ITU member in 1973. In fact, this largely explains OIRT representation in numerous non-broadcasting meetings which the EBU did not attend. The OIRT, for example, sent representatives to the 1960, 1964, 1968 and 1972 CCITT plenary assemblies, while the EBU only attended the 1972 plenary. Though not necessarily related to the admission of East Germany into the ITU, the OIRT failed to attend the 1976 and 1980 plenaries. In addition, governments have been expelled from the ITU. This ITU connection through regional broadcasting unions could be useful in gaining access to ITU meetings.
97. Poledne, *op. cit.*.
98. See Douglas A. Boyd, "The Arab States Broadcasting Union," *Journal of Broadcasting*, 9:2, (Summer 1975), pp. 311-320; Abdallah Chakroun, "Maghrebvision: Aims and Realization of the Cooperation Between Tunisia, Algeria and Morocco in the Field of TV," *EBU Review*, 23:6, (November 1972), pp. 39-42; and Salah Abdel Kaker, "The Arab States Broadcasting Union and the Causes of Development, Popular Culture and Family Planning," *EBU Review*, 27:2, (March 1976), pp. 19-21.
99. See Yoshinori Maeda, "The Asian Broadcasting Union and What It Stands For," *EBU Review*, 23:1, (January 1972), pp. 14-17; and Charles E. Sherman, "The Asian Broadcasting Union," *Journal of Broadcasting*, 13:3, (Fall 1969), pp. 397-414.
100. See Felix Fernandez-Shaw, "Television Relations Between Europe and Latin America, (Part I)," *EBU Review*, 22:4, (July 1971), pp. 43-45; (Part II), *EBU Review*, 22:5, (September 1971), pp. 22-25; and his work *La Organización de la Televisión Iberoamericana [OTI]: Orígenes y Situación Actual*, (Buenos Aires: OTI), 1975. See also "OTI — Gets Things Done," *BM/E's World Broadcast News*, 2, (January-February 1979), p. 18.
101. See "URTNA Plays Vital Role in African Broadcasting Development," *BM/E's World Broadcast News*, 1, (September-October 1978), p. 22.

CHAPTER 4
EUROVISION AND INTERVISION OPERATIONS

Transmitting television programs across Europe's borders would be impossible without the procedures which the EBU and OIRT have created for linking stations and for routing transmissions as well as for exchanging offers and requests and for sharing costs. But the creation, structure, and procedures of Eurovision and Intervision also reflect the reluctance of countries to take any action affecting their programs which might derogate from their sovereignty. This chapter is divided into the following sections: *1)* the birth of Eurovision, *2)* the start of Intervision, *3)* the beginning of Eurovision-Intervision exchanges, *4)* a description of the administrative and technical routine for coordinating exchanges and *5)* financing.

4.1 Eurovision

Eurovision[1] was born on June 6, 1954, at 3:30 P.M., when television viewers in eight West European countries switched on their sets and saw live coverage of the Fêtes des Narcisses from Montreux, Switzerland. Technically speaking, that the Swiss picture traveled over 6,000 km (3,728 miles) of land lines and that eighty relays fed forty-four stations may not sound especially impressive by today's standards. But when it is realized that there were three different television line systems besides five different audio standards, that there were eight governments and twenty-five different administrations involved, plus a little matter of crossing the Swiss Alps, it begins to look like an engineer's nightmare. Moreover, the routing of the program was a curious one because of the lack of television links between adjacent countries. The picture going from Basel to Strasbourg involved transit via Cologne, Antwerp, Brussels, Lille, and Paris. Eurovision's first program would have been impossible without the EBU-operated program and technical coordination center in Lille, France, which routed the Swiss picture to Belgium, Denmark, France, Italy, the Netherlands, the United Kingdom, and West Germany, the only West European countries with television at the time.[2]

Despite the engineering obstacles, Eurovision's first program was a success.

The Fêtes des Narcisses program was followed by four weeks of Eurovision programs, during which over 65 million European viewers together saw ten World Cup Football (Soccer) Championship matches from Switzerland, eight programs produced by television organizations from Belgium, Denmark, France, Italy, the Netherlands, Switzerland, the United Kingdom, and West Germany, as well as a telecast from the Vatican featuring an address by Pope Pius XII.

Audience reaction was favorable to the exchanges. Dutch viewers numbered as many as thirty per set to see the World Cup finals.[3] The sale of television sets also jumped. In addition, the press hailed the exchanges as a way of uniting Europe.[4] By fall 1954, the word "Eurovision" was widely being used to identify the relay of live television among West European countries.[5]

If Eurovision can be said to have a father, he would be Marcel Bezençon, who from 1950 to 1972 served as director-general of the Swiss Broadcasting Corporation (SSR).[6] Bezençon believed that the existence of a coordinated program exchange network was necessary to take full advantage of television. But some broadcasters considered him an idealist and strongly opposed his attempts to use the EBU as a "bourse d'échanges de programmes" to plan and coordinate members' television program exchanges. The first day of Eurovision confirmed Bezençon's long-standing argument that broadcasters could not get one another's programs on a regular basis without an international organization capable of coordinating the exchanges.

The roots of Eurovision can be found in Bezençon's 1947 UNESCO proposal as well as in his proposals to the old IBU in 1948 and before the EBU in 1950.[7] But the most coherent presentation of his concept is found in a report entitled *Projet d'une bourse d'échanges de programmes de télévision* which Bezençon sent to the EBU Administrative Office in Geneva in October 1950.[8] Bezençon proposed that the EBU study the question of creating a so-called "program exchange market." His scheme incorporated the following three objectives: to promote the exchange of film offers and requests among EBU members, to circulate offers of live television transmissions, and to promote the rapid exchange of European and world news.

The major premise of Bezençon's plan was that program exchanges can be economically beneficial to large and small television services alike. Bezençon argued that large services would export their best productions — as much for reasons of prestige as for providing performers, producers, and writers with extra income. He also argued that small stations would profit from the exchange by getting programs which they could generally not afford to produce themselves.[9]

In addition, Bezençon's plan noted that because a television station cannot beam its programs across Europe, as radio can, broadcasters of different nations would have to link their stations together if they wanted to exchange programs on a live basis. Without an international network, national television stations would have to be content with mailing programs to one another.[10]

Moreover, Bezençon feared that a failure to create an EBU program exchange system would leave a tempting vacuum for the organization of a European commercial network. In the early 1950s, rumors were circulating in Europe that a network of private television stations might be set up being patterned largely on the United States example.[11] But Bezençon opposed such a development for fear that small television services would be exploited by large commercial stations. He argued that the creation of a noncommercial program exchange system among broadcasters would help keep the money flowing among themselves.[12]

Immediately Bezençon ran into opposition. France and the United Kingdom — the only West European countries operating television at the time — felt Bezençon's plan was premature. In response to a questionnaire sent out by the EBU Administrative Office in 1950, French broadcasters replied that numerous legal problems such as excessive fees for international television rights would have to be solved before a European network could be established. Also the French argued that such problems would be better solved by the existing EBU Legal and Technical Committees — rather than creating a new committee for programs. Finally, they felt that program exchanges should be initially limited to bilateral arrangements.[13] Indeed, the French and the British were planning to organize a week of live television exchanges in July 1952.

The BBC expressed the same worries as RTF/France about the practicality of international television exchanges. Although it favored program exchanges as a way of easing the shortage of television material and finances, the BBC stressed the necessity of negotiating rights and standardizing equipment before live international transmissions could go ahead. To attack common legal problems, the BBC suggested that the EBU enter into negotiations with international artists' and authors' organizations to make sure that agreements governing the exchange of television transcripts were concluded on reasonable terms.[14]

The EBU Legal Committee objected to the lack of international jurisprudence to permit the organization of television exchanges. It insisted that exchanges were restricted by a host of legal problems. The Legal Committee conducted a study which concluded that exchanges could not involve protected works or artists' performances because exporting such programs required special, often costly agreements. Without a legal regime for television, the Committee doubted that it would be possible to foresee live exchanges.[15]

Bezençon's plan was examined by the administrative council, meeting in Geneva in May 1951. Léo Wallenborn, director of the Administrative Office, noted that even though the replies of the BBC, RTF/France, and the Legal Committee identified many legal and technical problems to program exchanges, other problems including censorship, customs regulations, and language differences also merited attention.[16] By the end of the discussions, the delegates agreed that the study of Bezençon's plan constituted only part of the larger problem of international exchanges of television programs, and, if the EBU wished to deal with them, coordination of activities was essential. To this end, based upon the proposals of the director of the Administrative Office, the council instructed the committees to initiate the study of the legal and technical problems hindering television exchanges. Moreover, the council set up a study group to examine, among other issues, the creation of a permanent program committee. The council also instructed the Administrative Office to study the creation of a program department within the EBU for exchanging members' offers and requests.[17]

The council's decisions to put the EBU on the road to Eurovision were also prompted by the planned Franco-British week of television exchanges to take place in July 1952.[18] British and French broadcasters were no strangers to international television exchanges. On August 27, 1950, the BBC broadcast the centenary celebration of the laying of the first underwater telegraph cable between England and France live from Calais. Although this program was the world's first international telecast, French viewers did not see the show because of the different television standard used by the British and because the French television network had not yet reached Calais.[19] The success of the BBC's unilateral telecast prompted the planning of a Franco-British "Week of TV Telecasts." To this end, arrangements were made in November 1951 to establish a television link between Paris and London via Lille, Calais, and Dover, converting from 819 to 405 lines between Calais and Dover, to be in operation by July 1952. These arrangements would enable programs broadcast from Paris to be seen in London and vice versa.

The EBU came a step closer to creating Eurovision when the administrative council, meeting in Stockholm in May 1952, created the so-called "1952 Program Study Group." Unlike the program study group created in May 1951, this group had a larger scope of functions and structure. The council charged the group to "examine the various questions concerning television exchanges" and to "report... on the practical steps to be taken with a view to the organization and development within the shortest possible time of international exchanges of television programs." In addition, the new program group was split into a radio sub-group and a television sub-group, chaired by Théo Fleischman, INR/Belgium, and Marcel Bezençon, SSR/Switzerland, respectively.[20] But, to the objections of Bezençon, the group operated under the EBU Statutes as a study group, not as a permanent body of equal status with the Legal Committee and the Technical Committee.

Bezençon's group of television directors immediately proceeded to study ways of exchanging those programs which caused few legal difficulties. Its work largely centered on studying problems concerning the exchange of television newsreels and documentaries which were void of sound and performing artists. Accordingly, the television sub-group drew up a draft standard contract to govern the bilateral exchange of documentaries and outlined urgent legal and technical problems which inhibited greater film exchanges.[21] The administrative council, meeting in Lugano on September 22, 1952, adopted many of the group's recommendations.[22]

Despite the EBU's increased activities, European broadcasters preferred to organize international television exchanges outside the agency. From July 8 to 14, the BBC-RTF television week took place. Eighteen programs, totaling over thirteen hours, were telecast live between London and Paris.[23] The world's first two-way exchange spurred plans for the multilateral telecast of the coronation of Queen Elizabeth II. In preparation for the coronation, the television services from Belgium, Denmark, France, the Netherlands, the United Kingdom and West Germany set up a temporary network, complete with facilities for commentators and for standards conversion. It was not easy. Apart from different audio and video equipment, most national television networks did not extend over 200 km (124 miles) in 1952, often stopping short of national borders.[24] In fact, although Belgium had no regular television service, it routed the coronation transmission to neighboring Holland.[25]

The EBU encouraged broadcasters to work within the Union. The administrative council, meeting in Florence in May 1953, recommended that members should use the expertise of the EBU in establishing a permanent network. Also the council asked that members refuse to participate in meetings organized by other authorities, especially if they deal with issues normally discussed within the EBU. Despite these positive moves, the council postponed a decision to establish a permanent EBU program commmittee until after the broadcast of Queen Elizabeth's II's coronation.[26]

The telecast of the coronation of Queen Elizabeth II on June 2, 1953, was seen live by about 20 million viewers in France, the Netherlands, West Germany and the United Kingdom. It spurred the planning of other live international transmissions.[27] In July 1953, at a meeting in London, broadcast engineers from Belgium, France, the Netherlands, West Germany, and the United

Kingdom agreed to conduct a series of transmission tests in preparation for transmitting the World Football Championships in Switzerland in 1954. They also agreed to set up an international coordination center, in either Brussels or Lille, to link the participating services.[28] Two months later, a meeting in London of television program executives from Belgium, Denmark, France, Italy, the Netherlands, Switzerland and West Germany committed themselves to participate in the "International Television Week" in June 1954, starting off with the Montreux Narcissus Festival and closing with the World Football Cup.[29] The delegates wanted as many countries as possible to participate in the "Television Week." Indeed, they rejected a French proposal for organizing an earlier exchange, Christmas 1953, to allow Denmark, Italy and Switzerland to start television.[30] Furthermore, the delegates felt that the World Cup Championships in Switzerland would draw more viewers, thus providing a better opportunity for inaugurating a European television network.

The planning of further, more complex transmissions among European broadcasters gave added weight to Bezençon's argument that the EBU should urgently set up a program committee if it wished to occupy an important place in the broadcasting field. Bezençon told the representatives of the administrative council in Monte Carlo in November 1953 that a failure to create a permanent EBU program committee would further harm European broadcasting interests. He argued that the mandate and membership of his television sub-group prevented the study of increasingly complex problems raised by the start of international transmissions. Finally, he warned the council that if a program committee was not created, the EBU's activities would lag behind technical progress, a situation that would leave a tempting vacuum for the organization of a network outside the agency.[31]

The council adopted Bezençon's request and recommended that the general assembly create a program committee which would give priority to television questions. The council agreed that the new committee should concern itself exclusively with program questions, should not promote the division of television and radio broadcasting on the national level and should not conflict with the tasks of Legal and Technical Committees.[32] Finally, in November 1953, the general assembly decided to create a program committee. The scope of the committee's functions, the assembly declared, "would extend both to (radio) broadcasting programs and to television programs, and which, owing to circumstances, would give priority to television questions..."[33]

After the creation of the Program Committee, West European television representatives met, at the invitation of the RTF, in Paris on January 11, 1954 to finalize the Lille Experiment (the Summer Season of European Television Exchanges as it was officially named). The meeting, as a sequel to the two earlier London meetings, was attended by the program and technical representatives of the eight organizations operating television at the time — Belgium, Denmark, France, Italy, the Netherlands, Switzerland, the United Kingdom, and West Germany — as well as representatives of the national telecommunications administrations of some of those countries. At the end of the three-day meeting, the delegates had drawn up a calendar of nineteen program events, to be broadcast from June 6 to July 4, comprising the transmission of World Cup matches, as well as eight programs produced by each of the participating services, and one program telecast from the Vatican.

In addition, the meeting decided that these programs will be relayed over a European network of television links extending from Italy to the United Kingdom across Switzerland, West Germany (branching out from Hamburg toward Berlin and Copenhagen respectively), the Netherlands, Belgium, and France. To provide the necessary liaison between the eight television organizations, the delegates also decided to set up a program coordination center and a technical coordination center in Lille. Moreover, it was recommended that the Lille Experiment should be followed by a second experimental program exchange series.[34]

Bezençon and his new Program Committee set out to secure formal and practical recognition from West European television executives of the EBU's competence in managing their exchanges on a regular basis. At the Committee's first meeting in Geneva in February 1954, prominent television program executives — many of whom had been active in the planning of the Franco-British television week and the coronation telecast — were appointed to the Committee's eight-member bureau and as heads of the the two working parties — the so-called GTV/1 (film exchanges) and GTV/2 (direct exchanges). In addition, Bezençon was elected chairman, a post he held until 1969. The committee not only finalized the details for the first weeks of Eurovision but also initiated the study of film exchanges and began preparations for other special Eurovision transmissions.[35]

The Lille Experiment showed that programming across Europe's borders could only develop with the existence of an international administrative and technical coordination mechanism. That the EBU was able to provide the needed mechanism is reflected in the increasing number of members which linked themselves to Eurovision over the years. In 1954, eleven television services in eight countries participated in the Lille Experiment. In 1965, Eurovision linked twenty-two television services in seventeen countries, and, in 1983, it had thirty-five services in twenty-eight countries.[36]

Still, despite this growth, the cautious attitude of members, first evident in their reluctance to create an EBU program committee, has continued, and it is reflected in Eurovision's structure and authority. As noted in Chapter Three, Eurovision is not an institution, but an arrangement that has been internalized into much of the EBU's work. Another indication of the limited commitment of members is that Eurovision is not governed by any rules such as a constitution.

Furthermore, Eurovision members have not allowed the EBU to produce programs. All programs sent over the network are made by members, and each member is free to reject or receive the program. The EBU's role is that of a coordinator and not that of a program maker. "Jeux sans frontières," for example, is a game series which has been relayed over Eurovision since 1966. Planning and production of the "Jeux" is directly carried out among participating services, and the EBU only becomes involved for routing purposes. The EBU has even rejected a proposal that it judge disputes between "Jeux" members.[37] The EBU acts as an administrator, not as a direct employer of writers, producers, and actors.

All this shows that EBU members are reluctant to take any action affecting their programs which might derogate from their sovereignty, the same reluctance which Bezençon faced in proposing the creation of a program committee. The reasons for this reluctance are obvious. The control of broadcasting — its licensing and its content — is decided by each nation, through its own internal processes, and each regards it as imperative that the integrity of these decisions be protected. But, as Bezençon argued, the need to organize program exchanges among broadcasters of different countries is vital to ensure the full benefit of television.

Eurovision's founders realized that these conflicting pressures on members had somehow to be resolved, at least on an interim basis, to enable this new network to develop. Jean d'Arcy, one of the resourceful founders of Eurovision with Bezençon, wrote that because of the importance that every nation attaches to the right to determine for itself the nature of the television available to its people, "we could not, on the pretext of efficiency, create a joint central direction of the television services in Europe. In Eurovision, we have substituted coordination for direction, leaving each the complete freedom to offer, accept, or refuse a program."[38] The ingenuity behind Eurovision lies in the way the EBU handles members' offers and requests.

Despite the reluctance of members, Eurovision has made important strides since the Lille Experiment toward becoming a more efficient network while expanding its activities outside Europe. The construction of the Eurovision Control Center (EVC) in Brussels, to be manned by the staff of the EBU Technical Center, was a major turning point in this regard.[39] Initially, most member organizations felt that the Control Center itself would only be a temporary arrangement to be abolished when members learned how to organize and carry out their own bilateral and multilateral transmissions. In fact, the 1956 budget of the EVC was determined on the assumption that the Center would be closed in four years.[40] But the EVC, after opening on January 1, 1956, is still coordinating, planning, and supervising members' transmissions today. The significance of the creation of the EVC was that it was the first step in adding operational functions to the EBU's predominant forum activities.

A second turning point in Eurovision's development was the start of the permanent sound network in 1962 and the start of the permanent vision network in 1968. The results of these developments were that a collection of sound, vision, and control circuits were available at all times for the immediate use of Eurovision members rather than having to order them, well in advance, from the PTTs. In addition to gaining freedom from the PTTs, the renting of permanent networks made it much easier and more economic to rapidly organize transmissions. Moreover, the permanent networks offered the advantage of better and more consistent transmission quality.[41]

A third important turning point occurred in 1962 when the EBU began regularly to coordinate members' exchanges of newsfilm over Eurovision. Eurovision's early years were characterized by the occasional transmission of long programs concerning important events such as the 1956 Winter Olympic Games at Cortina d'Ampezzo and the Coronation of Pope John XXIII. But Eurovision, as a technique, changed in the wake of a new kind of broadcast journalism. Beginning in 1958, the entire orientation of broadcast news was altered by the invention of a series of technical and creative methods including the advent of the thirty-minute news bulletin.[42] News magazines accompanied by relevant pictures replaced the announcer reading from a script or telex. With the development of television news came the demand for more extensive and faster news coverage.

The Eurovision News Exchange (EVN) was an improved technique for collecting and distributing news. News stories could be transmitted electronically instead of sending prints by airfreight. Before EVN, airfreight was the primary means by which a national television organization could receive foreign newsfilm. But the problem with airfreight was that film often arrived a day or more after the event due to delays caused by factors such as bad weather and customs. Eurovision came to the rescue by cutting out most of the delays and thus permitting services to broadcast foreign news the day it happened. The first time European broadcasters appreciated the value of EVN for news transmitted the same day was the third day of EVN's existence when Pope Pius XII died on October 9, 1958.[43]

Following experiments in 1958, 1959, and 1961, a daily news exchange at 5:00 P.M. (EVN-1) started on January 1, 1962. The development of lunchtime and evening news shows in the late 1960s required more items and thus two more EVNs. A second Eurovision News Exchange (EVN-2) was created in January 1968 at 6:55 P.M., followed in March 1974 by a third regular exchange (EVN-0) at 12:00 A.M. [44]

Eurovision's evolution has also been marked by a greater role outside Europe. In 1970, the EBU established a permanent coordination office in New York to handle the news flow between Europe and North America. A year later, an agreement was reached between the EBU and the Organización de la Televisión Iberoamericana/Servicio Iberoamericano de Noticias (OTI/SIN) for the exchange of news between Latin America and Europe.[45] Finally in 1977, the so-called "satellite-EVN" was born, linking simultaneously the television networks of the Arab States Broadcasting Union and the Asia-Pacific Broadcasting Union to the daily EVNs by regular transmissions via the INTELSAT Atlantic and Indian Ocean satellites.[46]

Before Eurovision extended almost worldwide, the first inter-network exchanges were arranged with Intervision — the OIRT's television network.

4.2 Intervision

Intervision,[47] perhaps more than Eurovision, bears witness to an international effort to deal with the problems of organizing television relays. But Intervision is also the expression of its founding members' desire to promote program exchanges that support the policies of the party and the government.

The idea of Intervision can be traced to an informal meeting of television representatives from Czechoslovakia, East Germany, Rumania, and the USSR, which was held in Bratislava in November 1956 on the occasion of the start of Czechoslovak television. The delegates voted in favor of a Czechoslovak proposal that the OIR program commission study the establishment of a permanent body to ensure the maximum exchange of television programs among the Socialist countries of Europe and the rest of the world.[48]

Intervision's creation, however, had to await the establishment of international circuits. Although the USSR began experimental telecasts in 1931, all other East European countries entered the television age in the mid-1950s. Apart from geographical vastness and dispersed populations which made the construction of national television networks costly, television's slow development was due largely to the low priority which it received when measured against the budgetary needs of industry, the military, and agriculture. In addition, the already recognized social responsibilities of the established press and growing radio weighed against making heavy investments in television.[49] Nevertheless, the neglect of television's development did not last long. As soon as international television links were established, television exchanges began on an ad hoc basis. The first television transmission between two

Socialist countries took place in January 1956 when East German and Czechoslovak broadcasters linked their networks to relay about six hours of Eurovision coverage of the Cortina Winter Olympics.[50]

The success of the first TV transmission spurred links between other Socialist countries. In 1957, a permanent television link was established between East Germany and Czechoslovakia.[51] The same year saw the start of exchanges between Czechoslovakia and Hungary.[52] In 1958, program exchanges between Poland and Czechoslovakia occurred.[53] In fact, until the early 1960s, all live transmissions among East Germany, Hungary, and Poland had to pass through Prague. No television link existed between Poland and East Germany until 1960. But this also meant that because most of the television lines were single-channel circuits, it was impossible to exchange programs without disrupting Czechoslovak domestic programming. Still this ad hoc network permitted the exchange of many programs, including coverage of May 1 festivals and several Eurovision programs.[54]

While television links were being established, the OIR was active in establishing Intervision's machinery. In March 1957, the OIR took the first steps to create Intervision when the general assembly, meeting in Sofia, approved the creation of a television program exchange bureau within the OIR secretariat. Also, the assembly set up a Television Commission to study the development of television program exchanges. In addition, it instructed the secretary-general to publish a monthly list of programs available for exchange. Furthermore, the assembly charged the Technical Commission to elaborate norms for international television links and to urge national telecommunication administrations to speed up the construction of international television links.[55]

The announced construction of television links to the USSR provided the final impetus for Intervision's creation. In September 1958, the OIR was informed that television links, primarily to the USSR, would be established in either 1960 or 1961. Consequently, the administrative council directed the Television Commission and the OIR secretariat to prepare proposals for setting up a permanent technical and program coordination center.[56]

Action promptly followed. A statutory drafting group of the Television Commission was established in January 1959 to draw up rules governing the establishment and operation of a network.[57] This group later became known as the Intervision Council. To symbolize the agency's new television activities, the general assembly, meeting in Helsinki in July 1959, added "television" to become the "International Radio and Television Organization" (OIRT). Finally, on January 28, 1960, an extraordinary session of the administrative council in Budapest approved the constitution of Intervision.[58] The first Intervision transmission took place on February 2, 1960.[59] The Intervision administrative and technical centers in Prague began operations on September 1, 1960.[60]

Unlike Eurovision, Intervision members decided that a formal framework was needed to govern program exchanges. Intervision's founding document contains the normal attributes of a constitution such as provisions for an executive body (the Intervision Council) and a secretariat (the Intervision Coordination Center). Intervision even can have its own members (stations can join Intervision without joining the OIRT).[61]

Despite Intervision's institutional character, members have not given the organization a program-making role. Like Eurovision, Intervision members have been reluctant to give an international body control over its own programs. All programs sent over Intervision are made by members, and each is free to receive or reject what is sent over the network. Intervision's constitution is also void of rules on prohibited broadcasts. As we shall see in Chapter Six, the ultimate validity of Intervision programming is largely found in the requirements of Socialism — the idealogy common to all Intervision members.

Intervision has grown over the years in the number of members and in its geographical size. The original Intervision member states were Czechoslovakia, the German Democratic Republic, Hungary, and Poland. In 1961, the USSR joined, followed by Rumania and Bulgaria in 1962, Finland in 1965, Mongolia in 1972, and Cuba in 1979. In 1983, Intervision had thirteen members.[62]

Geographically speaking, Intervision is the largest land network in the world.[63] In 1960, Intervision extended about 3,000 kilometers (1,864 miles).[64] Today, Intervision reaches from East Berlin to Vladivostock, over 14,000 kilometers.[65] In addition, Intervision programs are increasingly being routed over INTERSPUTNIK satellites. In 1982, Afghanistan and Vietnam joined the Intervision news exchange with the aid of the "Statsionar 4" and "Statsionar 5" satellites covering Europe and Asia.[66]

4.3 Eurovision-Intervision Links

As we saw in Chapter Two, the hostility between Western and Socialist broadcasters of Europe resulted in the creation of separate broadcasting agencies. Today, however, Eurovision-Intervision exchanges are the most frequent and visible collaborative arrangements between the EBU and the OIRT. In fact, one of the first programs transmitted under the Intervision emblem was the Eurovision feed of the 1960 Rome Summer Olympics. The institutionalization of daily program exchanges between Eastern and Western Europe currently exists, but its evolution was not automatic.

EBU-OIRT relations were far from friendly in the early 1950s. Cold war politics greatly affected their relationship. At Torquay in February 1950, for example, the EBU issued a call for technical collaboration with the OIRT, particularly concerning the application of the Copenhagen Plan.[67] But the OIRT replied by accusing the EBU of being the violator of the Plan because it had allegedly not reported frequency violations of Allied forces in Austria and Germany. The OIRT also accused the EBU of collaborating with the Allies in transmitting anti-Socialist propaganda.[68]

Relations, however, began to thaw in the mid-1950s. The first sign of this thaw came when the OIRT, in 1956, asked Finnish broadcasters to call a meeting between EBU and OIRT representatives.[69] This meeting took place in February 1957 in Helsinki between representatives of the EBU and OIRT technical committees. By the end of the four-day so-called "informal talks," the delegates agreed to exchange lists of stations and to jointly study ionospheric propagation.[70]

The success of the Helsinki meeting and the start of regular television broadcasts in several East European countries spurred the OIRT to seek EBU cooperation in the program field. In March 1957, the OIRT decided to call a meeting between EBU and OIRT administrative, engineering, and legal experts. The reasons for seeking collaboration in the program field, the assembly declared, was to complement the already extensive bilateral exchange agreements between EBU and OIRT members. It also noted that increased program exchanges required the solution of common problems.[71]

The EBU, however, rejected the proposal. It felt that the results of the Helsinki meeting should first be evaluated before starting new arrangements.[72] In addition, an unstated reason was that the discussion topics proposed by the OIRT were too general. The EBU wanted to discuss specific program and operational questions rather than topics for a "catch-all" meeting.[73] Furthermore, these topics should fall within the comepetence of broadcasting organizations — not governments.[74] These same reasons led the EBU to reject other OIRT calls for collaboration.[75]

The creation of Intervision did, however, elicit a positive response on the part of the EBU and did lead to establishing program exchange procedures. In August 1959, several months before Intervision's creation, the OIRT persuaded the EBU to accept seven points as the basis of their future discussions.[76] In February 1960, in Geneva, upon the EBU's invitation, legal, program, and technical experts from the two agencies worked out procedures for institutionalizing East-West exchanges. To minimize legal obstacles to the exchange of variety shows, the experts agreed to exchange information on rights fees. In addition, it was announced that the agencies would jointly negotiate for the television rights to the 1960 Rome Olympic Games. In the program field, mechanisms were established for publishing and circulating lists of live and pre-recorded television programs suitable for exchange. In the technical field, the delegates agreed to establish numerous permanent Eurovision-Intervision junctions. They also reached a consensus for ordering and paying for circuits.[77] The significance of the Geneva meeting was that it defined the basic administrative and technical coordination procedures and principles for the first Eurovision-Intervision exchanges.

An obvious motive for linking Eurovision and Intervision was the practical need to get one another's programs. The first Eurovision programs taken by Intervision were transmissions of the Rome Olympics in August and September 1960. The first extensive Intervision operation in which Eurovision participated was coverage of the World Nordic Ski Championships in Zakopane, Poland, in February 1962. Some twenty-five radio and television services sent commentators to report on the events.[78]

The Eurovision-Intervision hook-up was also prompted by the shortage of international links among OIRT countries. Many early Intervision transmissions were often routed to a member via Eurovision. The first Intervision program taken by Eurovision was the coverage of Major Yuri Gagarin's Moscow welcome in April 1961. Interestingly, although this television program was seen by Eurovision viewers, its final destination was the television services of East Germany, Czechoslovakia and Poland, which were not directly linked with the USSR at the time. To get the picture from Moscow to Warsaw, signals first had to be relayed from Moscow to Helsinki, then to Stockholm, Copenhagen, West Berlin, East Berlin, Prague and finally to Warsaw. This transmission, as Jerzy Rutkowski, former chief engineer of Polish television, recalls, was organized by telephone only within a few hours' notice and made possible by a "chain of goodwill."[79] The Gagarin program also marked the start of USSR participation in Intervision.[80]

The 1960 Geneva meeting led to others. In 1964 in Helsinki, for example, EBU and OIRT representatives expanded the Eurovision-Intervision machinery in light of the growth in international satellite transmissions, the expansion of television channels and color television as well as the development of news exchanges.[81] This meeting also took place during a time of improving East-West political relations. In 1963, the Partial Nuclear Test Ban Treaty was signed in Moscow, signaling a détente between the Soviet Union and the United States. Also 1963 saw a relaxation of Soviet jamming of Western broadcasts.[82] Furthermore, 1963 saw the installation of the Washington-Moscow "Hot Line."[83]

Today, the two agencies are brought into frequent contact to negotiate television rights, to study and make recommendations on problems and to observe each other's meetings. Most important of all, daily contacts take place in coordinating program and news exchanges between Eastern and Western Europe.

4.4 Administrative and Technical Coordination

Coordinating, planning, and supervising international television transmissions is the largest single activity of the EBU and the OIRT. For the EBU alone, the number of coordinated news transmissions has increased from 213 in 1957 to 2,009 in 1967 and to 7,636 in 1982.[84] Broadly, the EBU and OIRT secretariats coordinate three types of television transmissions: multi-origin news transmissions, live program transmissions, and request transmissions.

Three times daily, seven days a week, the EBU coordination centers in Geneva and Brussels organize the Eurovision News Exchanges — EVN-0 at 12:00 P.M., EVN-1 at 5:00 P.M. and EVN-2 at 6:55 P.M.. Six actors may be identified as essential to making EVN work. They are the:

  News Coordinator
  Sports News Coordinator
  Eurovision Coordinator
  Duty Planner
  New York Coordinator
  Crisis Coordinator

The News Coordinator is a television news editor of a Eurovision member organization who makes EVN journalistic judgments for other members. His primary responsibility is preselecting, from all the news stories received by the EBU, those items which will be sent over EVN-0 and EVN-1 (items for EVN-2 are chosen by the member services themselves). The preselected items are received by all participating EVN services who then choose their own news items. In addition to preselecting offers, the News Coordinator has the power to order satellite circuits for EVN offers. If in doubt, however, he can consult with member services. In light of his supranational authority and duties, the News Coordinator is usually a senior journalist who has experience at the international news desk of his organization and with EBU news operations. This individual works from his home office, being connected to participating members and the EBU news staff in Brussels and Geneva via the Eurovision Program Coordination Circuits (PCC). The daily working hours of the News Coordinator average eleven hours. The position of News Coordinator is rotated every ten days.

Helping the News Coordinator preselect EVN news is the Sports News Coordinator. The Sports News Coordinator, like the News Coordinator, is a sports editor from a Eurovision member. But, while the News Coordinator largely specializes in hard news (politics, disasters), the Sports Coordinator preselects sports news items for the Eurovision News Exchange. The Sports Coordinator also holds a sports editorial conference over the Eurovision PCC every Tuesday afternoon during which sports experts of most participating EVN members make plans to exchange sports items for the following week. These items are then injected during the regular EVNs. The Sports

Coordinator remains in his home office, and the position is rotated every ten days. Typically, the Sports Coordinator is of a different nationality than the News Coordinator. Since both the News and Sports Coordinators make journalistic decisions, the rotation procedure avoids complaints that the exchange has a nationalistic slant.[85]

The actual EVN transmissions are coordinated and planned by the Eurovision Coordinator and the Duty Planner. The Eurovision Coordinator is an EBU employee located in the Eurovision newsroom in Geneva. He maintains contact with the individual television services, with the News and Sports Coordinators, with the Eurovision Control Center (EVC) in Brussels, and with the New York Coordinator. The Duty Planner is also an EBU employee who works at the EBU Technical Center. He plans the most efficient order for injecting EVN offers and arranges for vision circuits with the aid of a minicomputer.

Two final actors in coordinating EVN exchanges are the New York Coordinator and the Crisis Coordinator — both news editors from Eurovision member organizations. The New York Coordinator, as the name implies, is located in New York.[86] His primary duty is to edit the day's news stories from the American and Canadian networks. These stories are then transmitted by satellite to Europe. The Crisis Coordinator's position only exists during times of international crisis. Eurovision members may deem an event significantly important to warrant sending a news editor from a Eurovision member organization on location to coordinate multilateral coverage. The duties of the Crisis Coordinator include advising satellite bookings, making summaries of the best material and making on-the-spot decisions about clashes of similar offers. The first Crisis Coordinator was sent to Hong Kong in April 1975 to cover the U.S. pullout from South Vietnam.[87]

The timetable of a normal Eurovision News coordination day in the Eurovision newsroom in Geneva is as follows: the Eurovision news day begins at 8:30 A.M. when the Eurovision Coordinator in Geneva reads through the offer and request telexes received by the EBU from individual Eurovision services, from the New York Bureau, and from the international newsfilm agencies. The Eurovision Coordinator then discusses the technical feasibility of satellite offers from New York with the Duty Planner in Brussels, who then contacts national telecommunications administrations and Eurovision members with ground stations (as well as the INTELSAT Operations Center in Washington D.C. for short-notice transmissions). By 9:40 A.M., the Eurovision Coordinator for EVN-1 has received replies on possible satellite transmissions. The Eurovision Coordinator for EVN-0 informs the News Coordinator, by phone or over the PCC, of all offers and requests. The News Coordinator then proceeds to preselect items for the 12:00 P.M. exchange —EVN-0.

Informed of the News Coordinator's preselection, the Duty Planner starts planning for EVN-0 at 9:00 A.M.. He prepares the running order of the different origins chosen and then orders the necessary circuits, mainly taking into account economy, quality, and reliability.[88] The Duty Planner then sends a telex showing the items to be transmitted in EVN-0 to all participating members and the PTTs in the exchange. The EVN-0 telex normally totals about ten stories. The following details are given with each item: *1)* contents, *2)* place and date shot, *3)* whether color or black-and-white, and *4)* whether silent or with sound (natural or commentary). The deadline for organizations to opt out from EVN-0 that day is 10:30 A.M..

In Geneva, at 10:30 A.M., the Eurovision Coordinator sends a running order telex to all participants. Then, together with the News Coordinator, the Eurovision Coordinator prepares for the morning conference, which involves, among other things, checking offers available for EVN-1 from Intervision.

At 11:00 A.M., the morning editorial conference starts. The Eurovision Coordinator, over the PCC, begins by saying, "Good Morning, Bonjour, tout le monde," to the television editors listening all over Western Europe. As each story comes up, the News Coordinator asks, "is anyone interested?" An item normally requires the interest of at least three members before it will be included on EVN. After member interest has been established, the conference is then thrown open for anyone to request coverage from another organization of a story they had not proposed. The conference over, the Eurovision Coordinator draws up a list of the items to be transmitted in EVN-1 and sends it to all members. At 11:50 A.M., on cue by Geneva, services originating news times in EVN-0 read their dope sheets and shot lists over the PCC for recording by the receiving organizations.

At 12 noon, the EVN-0 exchange begins. The exchange lasts an average of fifteen minutes since EVN-0 has no editorial conference. Instead, television news editors are able to choose their own material after seeing it themselves. The switching for this "choice after viewing" exchange is handled by the EVC.[89] Besides Eurovision members, the EVN-0 feed reaches Intervision by land lines, as well as Arab (ASBU) and Asian (ABU) broadcasters by satellite. Broadcasters, particularly those with mid-day news bulletins, value EVN-O because it gives them early access to North American and agency material, as well as making for a shorter, less expensive EVN-1. On the average, EVN-0 consists of six stories. While EVN-0 is taking place, EVN-1 offers are confirmed. The deadline is 12:00.

At 2:00 P.M., the Duty Planner begins scheduling EVN-1. Simultaneously, the Latin American news exchange — the Servicio Iberoamericano de Noticias (SIN) — takes place.[90] RTVE/Spain, on behalf of Eurovision, offers items from EVN-0 and EVN-1 to the SIN members who in return offer items to Eurovision members. At 2:30, the Eurovision Coordinator informs the newsfilm agencies of their items taken by Latin American broadcasters. Accepted items are transmitted to SIN by satellite later in the day.

From 1:45 to 4:30 P.M., final preparations for EVN-1 and EVN-2 are made. After the deadline for withdrawing from EVN-1 has passed, the Eurovision Coordinator in Geneva informs the Duty Planner of participation. At 2:15, the Duty Planner tells all the participants of the EVN-1 transmission order and books the necessary circuits. From 3:45 to 4:00 P.M., the Duty Planner receives a list of origins and participation in EVN-2 and then proceeds to book the appropriate circuits. At 4:20, the Austrian broadcasting organization, ORF, in Vienna records items needed by Eurovision from Intervision for later injection into EVN-1. Finally, the Eurovision Coordinator sends a telex to all participants informing them of the EVN-1 running order. In this telex, EVN-1 offers are often split into two blocks, hard news first, followed by sports. This applies especially to weekends when many sports items are exchanged.

At 4:30 P.M., the afternoon editorial conference starts. On cue from the Eurovision Coordinator, services read out dope sheets and confirm items. The News Coordinator then discusses any late-breaking stories and offers an outlook for the following day's EVNs. The New York Coordinator also participates in the conference to see if coverage of North American news is desired.

At 5:00, EVN-1 picture transmissions begin. The Eurovision Control Center in Brussels supervises the injection and recording of the items. EVN-1 is the prime news exchange, which lasts about twenty-five minutes. On the average, eleven items are transmitted daily. In addition to Eurovision members and newsfilm agencies, EVN-1 items are taken by Intervision, ASBU, and ABU members. At 6:35 P.M., RTVE/Spain records items from the SIN exchange for injection into EVN-2.

At 6:55, the day's third EVN conference is held. For about ten minutes, dope sheets are read, and items are confirmed. Immediately afterwards, EVN-2 pictures are sent for about fifteen minutes. EVN-2 items are generally late-breaking offers, film that has been delayed and news items from Latin America. On the average, two stories are sent daily over EVN-2.[91] At 7:10 P.M., RTVE transmits Eurovision items to the SIN network.

At 9:00 P.M., the Eurovision news day ends. But the News Coordinator and the Eurovision Coordinator stay on duty if there are any further transmissions.

The coordination procedures for the Intervision News Exchange (IVN) are basically the same as EVN. The only difference between EVN and IVN operations is that IVN normally has just one daily exchange.[92] Also IVN maintains no links with other regional television exchange networks other than Eurovision. And because only seven Intervision members regularly participate in IVN, no rotating News and Sports Coordinators exist. Each member decides for itself what items shall be taken off the network.

Coordinating, planning, and routing of the daily IVN is the responsibility of the Intervision Program Coordination Center (IPCC) and the Intervision Technical Coordination Center (ITCC) in Prague. The IVN editorial conference is conducted by the IPCC Intervision Coordinator — an OIRT employee.

The IVN workday begins at 10:15 A.M. when the IPCC receives news offers from IVN members by telex, by the Intervision Program Conference Network (PKN), or by telephone. At 11:00, the IPCC sends a complete story list of all received offers, in Russian or German, to all members and to the ITCC. Prior to that, however, the IPCC sends the same list, normally in English, to the Eurovision Coordinator in Geneva for the EVN-1 morning editorial conference. From 11:00 A.M. on, IVN members inform the IPCC which items they will, or will not take.

At 12:00, the IPCC informs the ITCC of member interest. At 12:30 P.M., the IPCC receives a list of EVN news offers from Geneva which is then forwarded to IVN members. At 12:45, the ITCC determines which transmission circuits are available from national telecommunications administrations. The ITCC then sends a running order telex to all participants, starting with the Czechoslovak television organization.

Acceptances of EVN offers must be made by 1:30 P.M. Additional offers or changes in interest must be made by 2:00. By 1:45 P.M., the IPCC has informed the Eurovision Coordinator in Geneva of Intervision interest. At 3:00, the ITCC tells participants to clear the PKN circuit and, following a test, transfers the PKN to the IPCC Intervision Coordinator to start the IVN editorial conference.

From 3:30 to 4:20 P.M., the IVN editorial conference takes place, followed immediately by picture transmissions. The television news editors of Intervision countries are connected by the PKN, and the Intervision Coordinator conducts the conference. The total number of offers are confirmed, and new offers are given. The individual services then describe the content, shot sequences, and running time of each item. Future events are also discussed. When the conference ends, the IPCC gives the PKN circuit back to the ITCC.

At 4:20, the ITCC signals each participant when to inject and record. In 1982, an average of fourteen items a day were sent over IVN. Of course, the above timetable, as that of the EVN exchange, can vary from day to day, depending on the amount of news. On Sunday, for example, a day when the amount of news is generally less, the IVN transmission takes place from 1:00 to 1:30 P.M. During the IVN, ORF/Austria records the entire transmission. It then sorts out the items requested by Eurovision members for injection into EVN-1. Intervision members receive a direct feed of EVN-1.[93]

In addition to IVN exchanges, the IPCC and ITCC coordinate the transmission, usually during IVN, of unilaterals and news bulletins. Also the electronic IVN exchange is supplemented by airmail exchanges of newsfilm and videotape of non-timely events. In 1982, 464 items were exchanged by air.[94]

The coordination, planning, and supervision of live television transmissions — a ski race, an opera, a variety show — is another prime activity of the EBU and OIRT secretariats. Although the details can vary according to the kind of program, the overall routine followed by the EBU and the OIRT is similar. Let us look at how a European Cup soccer game between France's Sochaux and Switzerland's Grasshoppers was telecast from Zurich over Eurovision.

Coordination of the European Cup soccer match from Zurich began when the Swiss broadcasting organization, SSR, feeling that other Eurovision members would be interested in the game, sent an offer telex to the Eurovision Program Exchange Service in Geneva. In the telex, the Swiss informed the EBU of the date and time of the game, its duration, the nature and content of the program, the number of available commentary positions, a description of the nature and locations of advertising and, as in most cases, how much the Eurovision rights would be. The Swiss also indicated that the program would be available to Intervision. In principle, all Eurovision programs are offered to Intervision, except in cases where Intervision already has a television rights contract.

The Eurovision Program Exchange Service then passed the Swiss offer around to other Eurovision members. This was done through various circular letters sent to all Eurovision members.[95] Eurovision circular letters are also sent to the Intervision Program Coordination Center in Prague, which includes the EBU offers in its own circular letter. Program offers from Intervision are handled in the same manner as offers from Eurovision members. If the Swiss offer had arrived at the EBU less than four working days before the telecast, it would have been telexed to members because the EBU normally needs a gestation period of about three weeks from when the offer is received. In addition to informing members of the time, place, content of offers and acceptance deadlines, the EBU also tells interested members how much their shares for Eurovision rights will be.

Members must inform the Eurovision Program Exchange Service in Geneva whether they are interested in the offer or not. Interested stations must tell the

EBU of their commentary requirements (whether it will send a reporter or relay another station's commentary) and whether it will take the event live or tape it for later use. The EBU then forwards this information to the offering organization. Generally, at least two organizations must accept an offer if the Eurovision Exchange Service is to coordinate. If only one station is interested, the transmission can be bilaterally arranged. But the Eurovision Control Center (EVC) still can become involved in the actual routing of the program.

Once participation is definite, the Eurovision Program Exchange Service notifies the EVC in Brussels, which plans the actual routing of transmissions. This work is done by the Planning Unit, which selects the routes to be used and determines which members must order occasional circuits. The EBU administrative council has authorized the EVC to plan Eurovision transmissions, taking into account both security and economy.[96] The detailed transmission plans are published in the Synopsis of Technical Arrangements which is sent to the relevant PTTs, members' engineering departments, and network operators. The Synopsis is also used to determine how costs, if any, of transit, conversion and the like should be shared. Often, the Synopsis has to be prepared on short notice and sent by telex.

Meanwhile, the Swiss start preparing for the telecast, which includes playing host to the foreign announcers. More specifically, the SSR/Switzerland must supply foreign broadcasters with the following three forms of technical assistance: announcer booths, a mobile switching center, and handle relations with the Swiss PTT.

When the foreign radio and television reporters arrive at the stadium in Zurich, an audio booth is made available to each. The audio booth is the reporter's workshop. A typical booth will have one television monitor and a two-way telephone link directly to his home studio. In addition to providing announcer booths, the SSR provides liaison officers (usually one to every third reporter) who serve as a link between the production staff and the foreign reporters. It is his duty, for example, to hold a pre-production meeting with foreign broadcasters to discuss subjects as opening and closing shots, program running order and any last-minute changes. Normally, this meeting is held a day before the game.

The second technical aid to foreign broadcasters is the mobile control van which collects the pictures and commentaries from the stadium and switches them to different countries. The inside of the control is small and cramped. The seven-meter motor home is bisected by a bank of television monitors from which the director calls the camera shots. The director sits with two engineers who man the video control panel. The back half of the control van contains the video crew and more monitors. The engineers in the back ride the levels on all the cameras, ensuring that the colors and contrast are right.

The originating organization is also responsible for relations with the national telecommunications administration. Foreign broadcasters book the sound circuits from their home PTT, but the host broadcaster may have to request his PTT to ensure local connections between the stadium and the switching center.

Transmission day arrives. It is two hours before the 8:00 P.M. game when the Swiss production crew and foreign announcers arrive at the stadium. Earlier that day, the Swiss director held a camera-talk meeting in which he stated his battle plan, giving the cameramen and videotape-playback recorder men their assignments and going over which elements of the action he wants stressed during the telecast. Some of what he tells them will be based on the information and suggestions put forth by the Swiss and foreign announcers during yesterday's production meeting.

The preparation pays off almost immediately. It is only thirty seconds before air time when the Brussels EVC tells the Swiss and the relaying television services that the international vision circuit is open. Each relaying service must then have a blank screen and have no sound. The Swiss television service then cuts to its own Eurovision caption for thirty seconds. It also starts the Eurovision tune (an extract from Marc-Antoine Charpentier's Te Deum) for thirty seconds on the sound circuits. Meanwhile, each relaying station cuts to its own Eurovision tune or takes the sound from the SSR. Then, fifteen seconds before air time, each relaying service cuts from its own Eurovision caption to the one coming from Zurich. The first Eurovision picture shows the players of the two teams coming out onto the field. On the sound network, the foreign announcers are cued to start.

During the entire program, the Swiss production crew and the foreign announcers are covering all angles of the game. In the control unit, the director is watching his monitors. Wearing a head set, he also listens to engineers and talks to his cameramen and video operators. Meanwhile, the announcers are on top of the action, passing information and anecdotes that pertain to the game on to the viewers.

At the end of the game, the SSR cuts to its Eurovision caption for thirty seconds. Then, each relaying station either starts its Eurovision tune or takes the Swiss sound fifteen seconds later. During the next fifteen seconds, after each relaying station has cut from the incoming caption to its own and has ensured that no cross-fading of sound occurs, all services leave the international vision and sound network. The Eurovision transmission has ended. After each transmission, when the exact details of the usage of circuits and other facilities are known, the Finance Unit of the EBU Technical Center divides the estimated costs among the participating services.

Although Eurovision members pay their share of EBU coordination costs, of Eurovision rights and of circuits costs, all coverage between members is free of charge. Each member offers the picture and technical service (audio booths, mobile switching van, and liaison) free to participating foreign stations. Because of the tradition of reciprocity, a service may agree to incur the additional expense of providing a program for the network because it knows that, in the future, it will be offered similar events from other members which would involve similar costs.

The third type of transmission coordinated by the EBU and OIRT secretariats are request transmissions between members. A television organization in one country may ask another organization to cover an event for it, although it is of no interest to anyone else. This type of transmission requires a special link-up involving the setting up of a video channel, two sound circuits, and a program coordination circuit between the origin and destination. Individual members may also request a series of transmissions from a single origin. During the European Summit Meeting in Paris on March 12-13, 1979, for example, the Eurovision Control Center coordinated about fifteen programs each day between 6:00 and 9:00 P.M.[97]

4.5 Eurovision and Intervision Finances

Whether a television station accepts or rejects a program offer often depends upon cost. Because very few events exist in which all Eurovision or all Intervision members are interested, the EBU and OIRT have established complicated accounting systems which guarantee that the large services help pay the way for the small ones.

Eurovision and Intervision costs have grown over the years. The cost of Eurovision has increased from 7,733,000 Swiss francs in 1961 to 51,773,000 Swiss francs in 1969 to 56,600,000 Swiss francs in 1981 (approximately 33,294,000 dollars at 1981 exchange rates).[98] Intervision costs have risen from 767,450 Czechoslovak korunas in 1969 to 2,284,000 Czechoslovak korunas in 1979 (approximately 466,122 dollars at 1979 exchange rates).[99]

Eurovision has three major costs. The first is the cost of the permanent Eurovision coordination staff in Brussels and Geneva, of meetings, of equipment, and of renting space for the EVC from the Belgian broadcasting organization. These costs comprise the Eurovision budget (for the Brussels operations) and the Television budget (for the Geneva operations).[100] Both budgets are financed by Eurovision members. The Eurovision/Television budget has risen from 596,000 Swiss francs in 1961 to 5,218,000 Swiss francs in 1969 and to 23,100,000 Swiss francs or 13,588,000 dollars in 1981.[101]

The second is the cost of buying rights for various events and of producing them. Either a member organization or the EBU (particularly for Olympic Games and the World Cup) can negotiate Eurovision rights on behalf of all members. The rights for televising important events such as Olympic Games are becoming increasingly expensive. The EBU, for example, paid 20 million dollars for the rights to the 1984 Los Angeles Games, while the 1980 Moscow Games cost six million dollars. Except for such special events, the EBU has been able to stabilize Eurovision program costs by concluding long-term contracts, by paying in installments and by maintaining an operating fund based on member contributions. The amount advanced by members varies from year to year depending upon the occurrence of important events. In some years, for instance, as much as 20 million Swiss francs (about 10 million dollars at 1983 exchange rates) has been set aside for buying and producing Eurovision programs.[102]

The third — and most expensive — Eurovision cost is for the permanently leased and occasionally rented sound and vision circuits. From Eurovision's start in 1954, sound and vision circuits had to be rented individually for each transmission from national telecommunications administrations. But the high cost of this method led many members to use other less costly means such as air freight for exchanging programs.[103] To reduce circuit costs, in 1962 the EBU succeeded in negotiating the creation of a permanently leased sound network from national telecommunications administrations belonging to CEPT. A permanent vision network was established in 1968. Eurovision's permanent sound and vision network not only made rapid transmissions and better circuit testing possible but also lowered annual vision costs by 30 percent.[104] Not all of Eurovision's circuits are permanently leased. Circuits which are used less than twenty hours a month are rented as the need arises. But this practice is becoming rare as the continuing expansion of the Permanent Vision Network (PVN) shows. In 1968, the PVN reached over 1,600 km (994 miles) connecting Milan, London, and Malmo, Sweden.[105] In 1982, the network went from Finland in the north to Morocco in the south and from Portugal in the west to Turkey in the east: a total of 17,600 km.[106] The actual costs of Eurovision sound and vision circuits totaled 33,500,000 Swiss francs or 19,705,800 dollars in 1981.[107]

The bulk of Eurovision's costs are borne by the large television organizations. Because members pay according to the number of television sets or licenses in their countries, the "Big Four" (France, Italy, the United Kingdom, and West Germany) paid about half of the total Eurovision/Television budget in 1981.[108] As already noted, the Big Four also pay about half of the EBU ordinary budget.

Having the large organizations paying the way of the smaller ones has long been one of Eurovision's pillars. Eurovision's founders realized that although the small television stations had the most to gain from the network, the budgets of the small organizations could not afford the costs of transmitting programs across Europe's borders. Thus, it was agreed that for Eurovision to work, the larger, more affluent organizations would have to ease the burden of the small and peripheral stations.

This idea was first incorporated in the so-called Rossi Scale which was established in 1961. With the Rossi Scale, devised by Swiss banker and former EBU councillor Riccardo Rossi, members paid according to the number of television sets or licenses in their countries.[109] In other words, the more television sets or licenses in a member country, the larger the share in the costs. In 1971, for example, the Big Four were liable for 51 percent of the Rossi units, while the television stations from eighteen countries were responsible for the remaining 48 percent.[110] The significance of the Rossi Scale was that it ensured that countries like Belgium and Denmark would get exactly the same caliber of coverage as the wealthier West Germans and British, who could, if needed, afford to go it alone. But it also meant that at least one of the Big Four would have to participate to get an event off the ground.

The Rossi Scale worked well when most of Eurovision's members were located in the "core" of Western Europe where small countries either bordered or intersected the Big Four. But the Scale became increasingly shaky as Eurovision expanded to countries located on the periphery of the European Broadcasting Area. In the 1960s, Spain, Yugoslavia, Portugal, Finland, Ireland, Tunisia, Algeria, Morocco and Greece joined Eurovision. Not only did most of the new small television services contribute little to Eurovision financing, particularly the expensive vision circuits, but they also took more Eurovision transmissions than they were giving.[111]

But the rising costs of linking the small, remote stations to Eurovision led the Big Four to cancel scheduled transmissions. The Big Four argued that they could not bear the high costs of Eurovision's expansion to the small stations. In fact, they found that it was cheaper to pay for unilateral foreign receptions outside Eurovision rather than help assume the costs involved in a multilateral transmission shared with some relatively poor system on the network periphery.[112]

To keep Europe's television giants from returning to less costly autonomous program-making and transmission, the Rossi Scale was replaced with the Eurovision Basic Sharing Scale in 1974. Like the Rossi Scale, the Basic Sharing Scale uses the number of licenses or sets registered in each country. But the Rossi Scale was more the result of bargaining than reality because the number of licenses in several countries were only estimates.[113] With the Basic Sharing Scale, cost-sharing is linked to an open-ended scale of television licenses which can be expanded, upon decision by the administrative council, to accommodate license increases. Each Eurovision participant is assigned a number of so-called Basic Units (BUs) to pay for the costs incurred by the EBU secretariat for coordinating, planning, and supervising transmissions, for the costs of buying program rights and for the costs of sound circuits.[114] As a result, the least affluent Eurovision members pay a large share of the costs, although still maintaining a relative advantage.

Vision circuits, however, are financed differently. The expensive vision circuits are handled in a special manner involving a measure called Vision Units (VUs). VUs are computed by adding so-called Excess Cost Units (the per-minute cost of the vision circuit linking a member to the network) to the BUs. This tends to place a greater burden on the more remote television services. For example, in the case of Portugal with six BUs, Excess Cost Units amounted to 4.5; for Ireland with six BUs, they amounted to eight; and for Morocco with four BUs, six Excess Cost Units were alloted. The end result of this complex fiscal scheme is that the eight smallest Eurovision member countries pay over 50 percent of their vision circuit costs compared with 13 percent in 1973.[115]

Other schemes exist for sharing vision circuit costs for Eurovision news transmissions. The EBU fixes the monthly sharing of EVN-0 and EVN-1 terrestrial and satellite vision circuit costs by multiplying VUs by the number of items available for exchange.[116] Another formula exists allowing members to know the approximate cost for each EVN item.[117] Applying these formulas to several countries with different sharing units, the approximate cost per EVN-0 and EVN-1 item available in 1983 was: Italy, 274 Swiss francs (approximately 137 dollars at 1983 exchange rates); the Netherlands, 155 Swiss francs; Switzerland, 111 Swiss francs; and Ireland, 66 Swiss francs.[118]

Because EVN-2 does not permit "choice after viewing" as do EVN-0 and EVN-1, the cost-sharing scheme differs. Vision costs for EVN-2 are determined by adding the number of news transmissions in which a member participates during one month to the number of items taken in the transmissions.[119] As with EVN-0 and EVN-1, members can also estimate how much each item sent over EVN-2 will cost. But unlike EVN-0 and EVN-1, a sliding scale encourages the acceptance of more than one item. Applying another formula, the approximate costs for the first EVN-2 item for Italy in 1983 was 429 Swiss francs, the Netherlands 243 Swiss francs; Switzerland 174 Swiss francs, and Ireland 104 Swiss francs. The second item costs half as much.[120]

Intervision's accounting methods are easier to explain. The Intervision budget covers the administrative and technical costs for Intervision. This budget is financed only by Intervision members based on the number of television sets. The largest share of the Intervision budget is borne by the USSR. For 1979, its assesed contribution was 752,149 Czechoslovak korunas

Eurovision and Intervision Operations 121

(approximately 153,500 dollars at 1979 exchange rates) or 29 percent of a total assessment of 2,598,300 Czechoslovak korunas. The Ukraine was second with 15 percent, followed by Poland with 10 percent. The Soviet Republics, as a group, paid over 56 percent of the Intervision budget.[121]

Charges for circuits and program rights are not included in either the OIRT's regular budget or the Intervision budget, but are covered in government budgets. Intervision circuits are generally booked on a program-by-program basis, although key vision links have been permanently rented for prolonged coverage of events such as Olympic Games.

The EBU and OIRT have established a cost-sharing agreement for program costs. When the EBU and OIRT jointly buy television rights, as for the Lake Placid Olympics, 67 percent of the cost is borne by the EBU and 33 percent by the OIRT, based on the number of television sets in each region. In addition, a table of individual shares has been established for Intervision members. This table is used when the EBU, the EBU and the OIRT jointly, or an individual EBU member negotiates the rights for a Eurovision-Intervision transmission against payment of a lump sum for both agencies. It is also used when organizers do not specify a sum for transmission to Intervision countries.[122]

Of course, Intervision operates in an environment of a planned economy, but its operations have frequently been limited by members' inability to freely spend hard currency. Indeed, a major limit to expanded Intervision activities outside Socialist Europe is that broadcasters are restricted in spending hard currency, so badly needed by governments.[123] Intervision, for example, finds it difficult to get advances to buy television rights to Olympic Games because agreement has to be first reached among the finance ministers of the six East European countries and the Soviet Union.

4.6 Conclusion

Western and Socialist broadcasters have seen that sending television programs across Europe's borders is impossible without the operations of the EBU and OIRT. To this end, technical coordination centers were set up to transmit programs over international television networks. European broadcasters also have agreed to administrative procedures for coordinating offers and requests and for sharing costs. Moreover, the necessity of these operations to most broadcasters leads to arrangements connecting Eurovision and Intervision. Members of both networks benefit from the lower cost and the greater efficiency of EBU and OIRT television services.

But the founders of the networks saw one major roadblock to the growth of international television exchanges: resistance to the new technique by political entities that feared it. Eurovision and Intervision members, respectively, refused to give the EBU and OIRT power to produce programs. They also refused to draw up rules on prohibitive broadcasts. Their reluctance stemmed from the high priority they give to controlling the reception of foreign programs. The problem of safeguarding national sovereignty was solved by having the various editorial powers vested in member organizations. While Eurovision and Intervision operate to give all members access to programs from other countries, the networks also respond to the needs of most countries to protect their sovereignty in the vital and sensitive field of television.

Endnotes

Chapter 4

1. Major sources on Eurovision's history include: Paul Bellac, "L'Origine de l'Eurovision," unpublished mimeograph (Bern, June 1962); this work is summarized in his "Origin and First Steps of the EBU Program Committee, Start of Eurovision," *EBU Review*, 85B, (May 1964), pp. 21-24. See also Marcel Bezençon, "Eurovision Under Examination, *EBU Bulletin*, 3, (May-June 1956), pp. 349-352; and Marcel Bezençon, "The Birth of Eurovision," *EBU Review*, (May 1979), pp. 20-24.
    Other important articles include: Jean d'Arcy, "Eurovision," *EBU Review*, 56B, (July 1959), pp. 6-12; Georges Hansen, "Some Technical Aspects of Eurovision," *Telecommunication Journal*, 28:7, (July 1961), pp. 441-448; E.L.E. Pawley, "Eurovision: An Idea Becomes a Reality," *EBU Review*, 55A, (June 1959), pp. 3-5; M.J.L. Pulling, "Eurovision Technical Operations: A Survey," *EBU Review*, 55A, (June 1959), pp. 6-15; and Donald K. Pollack and David Lyndon Woods, "A Study in International Communication: Eurovision," *Journal of Broadcasting*, 3:1, (Spring 1959), pp. 101-117.
2. Because of the critical role of the Lille center, broadcast engineers called Eurovision's first month the "Lille Experiment." For more about the Lille Experiment, see EBU, "Summer Season of European Television Exchanges June 6-July 4, 1954," *EBU Bulletin*, 5 (May-June 1954), pp. 345-358; EBU, "First Summer Season of European Television Relays," *EBU Bulletin*, 5, (July-August 1954), pp. 497-498; EBU, "The European Television Relays," *EBU Bulletin*, 5, (September-October 1954), pp. 645-647; Alvise Zorzi, "Twenty Years After — The Story of Italy's Contribution to the First Day of Eurovision Programs," *EBU Review*, 25: 3, (May 1974), pp. 20-22 and "8-Nation TV Network in Europe Opened by Pope," *New York Times*, June 7, 1954.
3. EBU, "The European Television Relays: Audience Reaction in the Netherlands," *EBU Bulletin*, 5, (November-December 1954), p. 713.
4. See L. Marsland Gander, "Eurovision Achieves a Successful Start," *New York Times*, July 13, 1954.

5. The word "Eurovision" was coined by British journalist George Campey in an article in London's *Evening Standard* describing a Dutch telecast of a prerecorded BBC program three years before the official start of Eurovision. Not until May 1954, at a meeting of journalists from the eight nations involved in the Lille Experiment in Santvoort, Netherlands, did Campey use "Eurovision" to describe live European television transmissions.
Interestingly, some EBU staff members initially disliked the word. Gilbert Trolliet, Swiss journalist and EBU employee wrote in the May-June 1954 issue of the *EBU Bulletin* that "it is probably under this (somewhat barbaric) heading that the programs of the (Lille Experiment) will be presented." In the September-October issue, he again held that "we, personally, do not much like its somewhat 'telegraphic style'." But the term became increasingly popular with the press and the public, and the EBU inevitably followed suit. Correspondence with Charles Gilliéron and Léo Wallenborn, former directors of the EBU Administrative Office, May 1977.
6. The EBU recognizes Bezençon as the Father of Eurovision. But the creation and operation of this new way of exchanging programs would not have come about without the help of many other broadcasters. They include: Jean d'Arcy, of RTF, and Imlay Newbiggen-Watts, of the BBC, who demonstrated the feasibility of Eurovision by organizing the first international television link-up in August 1950 between France and the United Kingdom as well as the British-French television week in July 1952. Eduard Haas, of the SSR/Switzerland, Louis-Philippe Kammans and Bert Leysen, of INR/Belgium, Henk Maas and J.W. Rengelink of NTS/Netherlands, and Heinz von Plato, of ARD/West Germany, all played important roles not only in televising Queen Elizabeth's coronation but also in convincing their respective organizations that it was in their interest to exchange programs and that the EBU should patronize Eurovision. Other broadcasters which helped set up the technical machinery of Eurovision are Jack Treeby Dickinson, E.L.E. Pawley and Martin J.L. Pulling, of the BBC, and Stéphane Mallein, of RTF.
7. On July 1, 1947, Bezençon, as director of Radio Lausanne, sent a letter to UNESCO in which he proposed the creation of a central documentary and news service to encourage international radio program exchanges. But the proposal, one among many calling for UNESCO action in the communications field, failed to come about. Bezençon remembers that he got some of his ideas from an American plan for a UNESCO radio network submitted to the First General Conference in 1946, which also received little response. In 1948, he called upon the

IBU to adopt the project. But the IBU, with its handful of members, was having its own problems in unifying European broadcasters under one roof. Bezençon's project died along with the IBU.

On September 28, 1950, Bezençon, who had meanwhile become director-general of the Swiss Broadcasting Corporation (SSR), put his proposal before the EBU general assembly. He stressed the need to immediately study the problems relating to the exchange of television programs. Unlike his earlier proposals, Bezençon explained the idea of a clearing house solely in terms of television, not radio. Interview with Marcel Bezençon, Lausanne, November 1976.

8. EBU Doc. no. O.A./157, December 9, 1950.
9. *Ibid.*
10. *Ibid.*
11. *Ibid.*
12. Bezençon also hoped that the creation of an international network would spur Swiss politicians to rapidly introduce television. Miroslav Vilcek, "Twenty-five Years of TV Exchanges Via Eurovision," *Television*, 27:4, (July-August 1979), p. 7.
(July-August 1979), p. 7.
13. Fourth Session of the Administrative Council, May 23, 1951, EBU Doc. no. O.A./193-C.A./76, Annex 2.
14. *Ibid.*, Annex 3. See R.C. Robbins, "Some Legal Problems of Television in England," *EBU Documentation and Information Bulletin*, 1, (September 15, 1950), pp. 226-229.
15. EBU Doc. no. O.A./174-Com. J./44, p. 10.
16. EBU Doc. no. O.A./193-C.A./76, p. 3.
17. Fourth Session of the Administrative Council, May 25, 1951, EBU Doc. no. O.A./218-C.A./99, pp. 9-11.
18. EBU Doc. no. O.A.193-C.A./76, p. 2.
19. See "Proposed Cross-Channel Television Link," *EBU Documentation and Information Bulletin*, 1, (July 15, 1950), p. 119; and "Outside Broadcasting Developments," *EBU Documentation and Information Bulletin*, 1, (November 15, 1950), p. 398.
20. Sixth Session of the Administrative Council, May 26, 1952, EBU Doc. no. O.A./356-C.A./173, p. 2.
21. Report from the "1952 Program Study Group" — "Television Sub-Group," EBU Doc. no. O.A./380, G.E. Pro. TV/4-C.A./183.
22. Seventh Session of the Administrative Council, September 29, 1952, EBU Doc. no. O.A./411-C.A./220, pp. 3-4.
23. See R. Felletier, "Paris Comes to Britain," *London Calling*, September 18, 1952, pp. 14-16; "The Week of Franco-British Television," *EBU Documentation and Information Bulletin*, 3, (September 15, 1952), p.

550; and BBC, *Annual Report and Accounts of the British Broadcasting Corporation for the Year, 1952-53*, (London: BBC, 1953), p. 20.
24. Bezençon, "The Birth of Eurovision," *op. cit.*, p. 22.
25. F. Williams and M.J.L. Pulling, "Engineering Arrangements for Broadcasting on Sound and Television the Coronation of Her Majesty Queen Elizabeth II," *EBU Documentation and Information Bulletin*, 4, (July 15, 1953), pp. 391-397.
26. Eighth Session of the Administrative Council, May 12, 1953, EBU Doc. no. O.A./465-C.A./240, pp. 4-6.
27. Pollock and Woods, "A Study in International Communication: Eurovision," *op. cit.*, pp. 103-104. See "The Relay of the Coronation Television Programs to Western Europe," *EBU Documentation and Information Bulletin*, 4, (July 15, 1953), pp. 461-467; and Y. Angel, "Some Practical Lessons of the London-Paris Television Relay of the Coronation," *EBU Documentation and Information Bulletin*, 4, (July 15, 1953), pp. 545-548.
28. "Conference of International Television Relays," *EBU Documentation and Information Bulletin*, 4, (September 15, 1953), pp. 599-600.
29. "International Television Exchanges in Europe," *EBU Documentation and Information Bulletin*, 4, (November 15, 1953), p. 741.
30. d'Arcy, "Eurovision," *op. cit.*, p. 7.
31. Ninth Session of the Administrative Council, November 10, 1953, EBU Doc. no. O.A./528-C.A./269, p. 2-3.
32. *Ibid.*, pp. 3-5.
33. Fourth Ordinary Session of the General Assembly, November 13, 1953, EBU Doc. no. O.A./532-A.G./95, pp. 12-13.
34. First Plenary Session of the Program Committee, February 4-5, 1954, EBU Doc. no. O.A./543-Com. Pro./11, pp. 2-3. See "International Television Exchanges in Europe," *EBU Bulletin*, 5, (January-February 1954), p. 117.
35. EBU Doc. no. O.A./543-Com. Pro./11.
36. The composition of Eurovision membership is given in Appendix D.
37. Interview with Miro Vilcek, Director, Television Program Department, EBU, Geneva, November 1978.
38. d'Arcy, "Eurovision," *op. cit.*, pp. 10-11.
39. Originally, the coordination of Eurovision was done from the Lille Technical Center set up in 1954. Responsibility for the Center was entrusted to RTF/France. In January 1955, the EBU agreed to move the center to Brussels — more specifically to the Palais de Justice. Apart from being the seat of the EBU Technical Center, Brussels offered a strategic site for monitoring and switching transmissions because Belgian television lines to and from France, the Netherlands,

the United Kingdom, and West Germany ended in the dome of the Palais de Justice. In addition, the Palais was the tallest building in Brussels, thus permitting easy signal reception. EVC began operating on January 1, 1956. The EVC's cramped quarters and the desire to install new equipment led to the construction of a new center in the basement of the headquarters of the Belgian broadcasting organization. The new EVC began operations on April 12, 1979.

For more about the EVC's history, see "New International Coordination Center," *EBU Bulletin*, 7:1, (January-February 1956), p. 109; "New Brussels 'Eurovision' Coordination Center," *EBU Bulletin*, 7:2, (March-April 1956), pp. 266-267; Georges Hansen, "The Technical Adventure of Eurovision," *EBU Review*, 143, (February 1974), pp. 2-3; Edward Pawley, "Eurovision: Faith and Works," *EBU Review*, 30:3, (May 1979), pp. 30-35; and W. Potter, "The New Eurovision Control Center," *EBU Review*, 175, (June 1979), pp. 128-131.

40. J. Treeby Dickinson, "Birth and Growth of Eurovision," *EBU Review*, 175, (June 1979), p. 109.
41. See J.N. Douglas, "Quality Control of the Eurovision Permanent Vision Network," *EBU Review*, 175, (June 1979), pp. 120-127.
42. See Anthony Smith, *The Shadow in the Cave, A Study of the Relationship Between the Broadcaster, His Audience and the State*, (London: Quartet Books, 1976), pp. 144-164.
43. See Carel Enkelaar, "We Want the Dead Pope Live," *Behind the Screen, the Greatest TV Stories Never Told*, ed. Carel Enkelaar, (Hilversum: NOS, 1979), pp. 11-16.
44. For a history of EVN, see J.W. Rengelink, "Operation Eurojournal," *EBU Review*, 10B, (July 1959), pp. 15-17; J.W. Rengelink, "The Eurovision News Transmission," *EBU Review*, 85B, (May 1964), pp. 12-13; and J.W. Rengelink, "Origin and Development of the News Exchange," *EBU Review*, 30:3, (May 1979), pp. 25-28.
45. See "OTI-Gets Things Done," *BM/E's World Broadcast News*, 1:3, (January-February 1979), p. 18.
46. See "Arabvision News Exchange to Start in 1979," *BM/E's World Broadcast News*, 1:4, (November-December 1978), p. 19.
47. The word "Intervision" is attributed to Czechoslovak broadcaster Jaromir Hrebik who was the secretary-general of the OIRT from 1958 to 1980. It was adopted to denote Inter(national) (tele)vision as opposed to a Euro(pean) (tele)vision program exchange system. Correspondence with Ferenc Benkö, Deputy Director of the Technical Center, OIRT, Prague, February 1977.

The literature on Intervision is sparse. Still, useful information on the structure and development of Intervision can be found in Kenneth Harwood, "International Radio and Television Organization," *Journal of Broadcasting*, (Winter 1960), pp. 61-71; Burton Paulu, *Radio and Television Broadcasting in Eastern Europe* (Minneapolis: University of Minnesota Press, 1974); Charles E. Sherman, "OIRT," *International Broadcasting* (Washington, D.C.: Association for Professional Broadcasting Education, 1971), pp. 13-21, and Ales Suchy, "Intervision," *World Radio TV Handbook-1964* (Hvidovie: Billboard A.G., 1964), p. 26 and 54. A recent work is "L'Intervision a vingt ans," *OIRT Information*, 1, (1980), pp. 1-3.

48. J. Hrebik, "Sur les travaux de la commission des programmes," *OIR Bulletin de documentation et d'information*, 2-3, (July 1957), p. 78. See also Kaarle Kohout, "Emploi du film à la télévision," *OIR Bulletin de documentation et d'information*, 2-3, [July 1957], p. 80.
49. Mark W. Hopkins, *Mass Media in the Soviet Union*, (New York: Western Publishing Company, 1970), p. 251.
50. "Expérience de l'exploitation technique du réseau de l'Intervision," *OIRT Radiodiffusion Télévision*, 2, (1963), p. 28.
51. *Ibid.*
52. *Ibid.*
53. *Ibid.*
54. *Ibid.*
55. "Conference de l'OIR-Sofia," *OIR Bulletin de documentation et d'information*, 2-3, (July 1957), pp. 61-74.
56. "30éme session du conseil d'administration de l'Organisation internationale de radiodiffusion," *OIR Bulletin de documentation et d'information*, 6, (December 1958), pp. 485-486.
57. "Compte-rendu final de la IIe réunion des directeurs de programmes des télécentres des pays-membres de l'OIR," *OIR Bulletin de documentation et d'information*, 2, (April 1959), pp. 53-55.
58. "A propos de la création de l'Intervision," *OIRT Radiodiffusion Télévision*, 1, (1960), p. 71.
59. "L'Intervision a vingt ans," *op. cit.*, p. 1.
60. "Expérience de l'exploitation technique de réseau de l'Intervision," *op. cit.*, p. 29.
61. OIRT, *Intervision Rules Governing the International Television Program Exchange Among OIRT Member Countries*, (Prague: OIRT, 1960).
62. The composition of Intervision membership is given in Appendix E.
63. France has established an extensive television network connecting

Paris to its overseas territories. See Jim Hodgetts, "France's 'Dom Tom' Network — Biggest in the World," *TV World*, 2:2, (February 1979), pp. 18-19.

64. "A propos de la création de l'Intervision," *op. cit.*, p. 71.
65. Wilson P. Dizard, "Europe's TV Networks," *Television Quarterly*, 4:4, (Winter 1965), p. 14.
66. For more about INTERSPUTNIK, see V.S. Vereschetine, "Interspoutnik: organisation et système internationaux de télécommunications spatiales," *La Recherche spatiale*, 2:1, (March-April 1973), pp. 16-19; S.V. Borodich, L.Y. Kantor, and S.P. Kurilov, "The Intersputnik International Communications Satellite System," *Telecommunication Journal*, 45:3, (March 1978), pp. 116-123; and V.P. Romantsov, "Intersputnik — Taking Part in the Olympiad — 80 Coverage," *OIRT Radio-Television*, 1, (1979), pp. 15-20.
67. First Extraordinary Session of the General Assembly, February 13, 1950, EBU Doc. no. O.A./15-A.G./2.
68. "Résolutions de l'assemblée générale-VIIIe session," *OIR Bulletin de documentation et d'information*, 33, (December 20, 1950), pp. 310-313.
69. "Rapport d'activité du conseil d'administration de l'OIR depuis la XVe session ordinaire de l'assemblée générale et projet de programme d'activité pour les années a venir," *OIR Bulletin de documentation et d'information*, 4, (August 1958), p. 299.
70. "Helsinki: Unofficial Meeting Between Technical Delegates of the EBU and OIR," *EBU Bulletin*, 8:2, (March-April 1957), p. 249.
71. "Rapport d'activité du conseil d'administration de l'OIR depuis la XVe session ordinaire de l'assemblée générale et projet de programme d'activité pour les années à venir," *op. cit.*, pp. 294-296.
72. 16ème réunion du conseil d'administration, June 1, 3 and 4, 1957, EBU Doc. no. O.A./1102-C.A./482.
73. Interview with Henrik Hahr, Director of the Administrative Office, EBU, Geneva, July 1975.
74. Twentieth Meeting of the Administrative Council, May 29-June 1, 1959, EBU Doc. no. O.A./1364-C.A./572.
75. *Ibid.*, EBU Doc. no. O.A./1344-C.A./558.
76. The OIRT proposed that an agenda be based on seven points as follows: *1)* the organization of television program exchanges, *2)* the study of problems in transmitting sports programs, *3)* the coproduction of radio programs, *4)* the establishment of procedures for film exchanges, *5)* the problems of international circuits, *6)* the methods for testing international sound and vision circuits and *7)* the creation of procedures for exchanging music tapes. Twenty-first Meeting of the

Administrative Council, October 24-26, 1959, EBU Doc. no. O.A./1401-C.A./578.
77. EBU-OIRT Meeting, February 3-6, 1960, EBU Doc. no. O.A./1446-Com.T./25-Com.Pro./377-Com.J./295, Annex I.
78. Interview with Jerzy Rutkowski, former chief engineer of Polish Television, Geneva, November 1976.
79. *Ibid.*
80. *Ibid.*
81. Thirty-first Meeting of the Administrative Council, November 13, 14 and 16, 1964, EBU Doc. no. O.A./30 36-C.A./771. A published account of this meeting can be found in "EBU/OIRT Meeting-Helsinki, June 29-July 1, 1964," *EBU Review,* 85A, (August 1964), pp. 194-195.
82. "Rumania Halts Radio Jamming," *New York Times,* August 3, 1963. See Gerhard Wetting, *Broadcasting and Détente, Eastern Policies and Their Implications for East-West Relations* , (New York: St. Martin's Press, 1977).
83. See "US-USSR 'Hot Line' Now Via Satellite," *Communications News,* 15:3, (March 1978), pp. 32-33.
84. The figures for 1957 and 1967 from Georges Hansen, "Evolution of the Activities of the Technical Center of the EBU Since Its Establishment," *ASBU Technical Review,* 1:1, (January 1974), p. 14. 1982 figures are from EBU Doc. no. SPG 2279, June 1983.
85. The importance of the News and Sports Coordinators has increased with the growth of sports news. The Sports Coordinator's position was created in January 1975 in response to members' increased interest in getting sports newsfilm. But in light of the large exchange of sports — as many as eleven items daily over the weekends — the journalistic decisions of the Sports Coordinator can have significant financial consequences. Too much sports can lengthen EVN running time and thus increase vision circuit costs for members. In addition, too much sports can disrupt inter-network exchanges (with ASBU, OTI/SIN) by increasing satellite costs to other regional broadcasting unions. To avoid overruns, time restrictions have been placed on the News and Sports Coordinators.
86. For more about the New York Coordinator, see "EBU to Open New York Bureau," *Telecommunication Journal,* 37:9, (September 1970), p. 652; and Jean-Pierre Weinmann, "New York: The EBU's Television News Exchange Satellite Office," *EBU Review,* 26:3, (May 1975), pp. 23-25.
87. EBU, *Weekly Liaison Bulletin,* no. 27, (June 28, 1975).
88. EBU, *Eurovision, EBU Administrative Council Rulings on Cost-Sharing,* September 1975.

89. For a description of EVN's technical arrangements, see Gaston van Larebeke, "Technical Side of Television News Exchanges," *EBU Review*, 26:3, (May 1975), pp. 15-20; and F. Pisseloup, "Technical Progress and the Growth of Eurovision," *EBU Review*, 175, (June 1979), pp. 114-119.
90. To participate in SIN, a station must be a member of the Organizacion de la Televisión Iberoamericana (OTI). For more about the Eurovision and Latin American exchange, see Xavier Alonso Lennard, "The Conquest of Distance," *EBU Review*, 26:3, (May 1975), pp. 28-30; and "OTI-Gets Things Done," *BM/E's World Broadcast News*, 1:3, (January-February 1979), p. 18.
91. One reason for the small number of items in EVN-2 is that services seem to prefer EVN-2 items in the next day's EVN-0. This is only natural because few services start their evening news shows at 7:00 P.M. Also those who prepare 7:30 bulletins do not want to take the risk of not being able to edit EVN-2 material in time. EBU, *Weekly Liaison Bulletin*, no. 37, (September 18, 1979).
92. When special events take place, a second exchange (IVN-2) is implemented.
93. For more about the role of ORF, see Horst G. Jancik, "The Exchange of News Between Eurovision and Intervision," *EBU Review*, 26:3, (May 1975), pp. 26-27.
94. OIRT, *Statistik des Aktualitätenaustausches zwischen den Intervisionsländern and zwischen der Intervision und Eurovision und anderen FSO 1981 und 1982* (unpublished OIRT document).
95. The Eurovision Program Exchange Service issues five kinds of circular letters, each identified by a different color of paper. First comes the "Green Letter" which contains a calendar of projected offers for a specific month, and a tentative list of interested members for each offer. The "Green Letter' is followed by the "Pink Letter" which contains projected offers and provisional interest of a more definite nature than the former. The "Pink Letter" appears one month before the event. The third circular is the "Blue Letter" which lists only definite offers and participation. It is published three weeks before the telecast. The "Blue Letter" often contains "Yellow Sheets" which denote changes that have occurred not less than one and not more than three weeks before transmission. The final circular is the "White Letter" which published a week before the event, lists last-minute changes, information on programs already offered, new offers, enquiries, and future events.
96. EBU, *Eurovision, EBU Administrative Council Rulings on Cost-Sharing, op. cit.*

97. Pisseloup, "Technical Progress and the Growth of Eurovision," *op. cit.*, p. 117.
98. 1961 and 1969 figures from J.B. Broeksz in an address to the 21st Ordinary Session of the General Assembly, Paris, July 3, 1970, EBU Doc. no. O.A./4147-A.G./330. The 1981 figure from interview Bernard Briguet, Senior Assistant, Administration and Finance, EBU, Geneva, January 1983.
99. 1969 figure from OIRT, Budget für 1969, OIRT Doc. AS-41-2/69; 1979 figure from OIRT, Budget für 1979, OIRT Doc. AS-53-5/78.
100. The name difference is due to the fact that the television budget also covers non-Eurovision expenses of the Television Program Department.
101. 1961 and 1969 figures from Broeksz, *op. cit.*, and 1981 figure from Briguet, *op. cit.*
102. Briguet, *op. cit.*
103. J. Treeby Dickinson, "News Exchanges in Eurovision," (Paper presented to the 2nd International Television Symposium April 30-May 4, 1962, Montreux, Switzerland), p. 75. See also "Eurovision Permanent Network Scheme. Implementation of Stage 1," *EBU Review*, 71, (February 1962), pp. 46-47; and "Extension of the Eurovision Permanent Network," *EBU Review*, 111, (October 1968), p. 226-227.
104. Interview with Alan Brown, Engineer, EBU, Geneva, February 1977.
105. "Extension of the Eurovision Permanent Network," *op. cit.*
106. Interview with Michael Type, Head of the Permanent Secretariat, EBU, Geneva, February 1983.
107. Briguet, *op. cit.*
108. *Ibid.*
109. Before 1961, the EBU unsuccessfully tried numerous cost-sharing schemes ranging from dividing costs equally to requiring payment only for circuits used in a member's country. For more about early Eurovision account methods, see Russell B. Barber, "Eurovision as an Expression of International Cooperation in Western Europe," (Ph.D. diss., Northwestern University, 1963).
110. For a good description of the Rossi Scale, see Brack, *The Evolution of the EBU Through Its Statutes from 1950 to 1976*, *op. cit.*, pp. 98-100; and Konrad M. Kressley, "Eurovision: Distributing Costs and Benefits in an International Broadcasting Union," *Journal of Broadcasting*, 22:1, (Spring 1978), p. 185.
111. Sherman and Ruby, "The Eurovision News Exchange," *op. cit.*, p. 483.
112. Kressley, "Eurovision: Distributing Costs and Benefits in an International Broadcasting Union," *op. cit.*, pp. 185-187.
113. *Ibid.*

114. The Basic Sharing Scale is derived from the following formula:
$$BU \sqrt{\frac{\text{licenses}}{10,000}}$$
115. Briguet, *op. cit.*.
116. EBU, "Eurovision Clearing — EVN-0/EVN-1, Application of Formula (VU x A) as from 1.7.78," EBU Circular SG/AF/2332, March 14, 1979.
117. Cost estimates for participation in EVN-0 and EVN-1 transmissions are obtained by this formula: Gold franc (2VU EVN x 6A) where VU is Vision Units, EVN is EVN rating units (doubled vision units), and A is items available.
118. Briguet, *op. cit.*
119. Vision circuit costs for EVN-2 transmissions are estimated by the following formula: Gold franc (4T + 4N) U where T is the number of news transmissions in which a member participates during one month, N is the total number of items taken in the transmissions, and U is the Vision Units multiplied by two. EBU, "Eurovision Clearing-ENA (EVN-2) Cost-Sharing Formula," EBU Circular SG/AF/2282, February 16, 1979.
120. Briguet, *op. cit.*
121. OIRT, Budget für 1979, OIRT Doc. AS-53-5/78.
122. USSR-13.5 percent; German Democratic Republic-6.2 percent; Poland-6.2 percent; Czechoslovakia-4.7 percent; Hungary-3.2 percent; Rumania-2.6 percent; and Bulgaria-1.6 percent.
123. Generally, when coverage occurs outside Europe, Eurovision and Intervision members pay in the currency where the program originates. Inside Europe, the Swiss franc is normally used as the reference currency.

CHAPTER 5
EUROVISION PROGRAMMING

Eurovision programming is, in the ultimate sense, European. Viewers throughout Western Europe often see the same international sports events at the same time. They also see many of the same political and disaster news stories. But Eurovision's founders expected the exchange of a wider range of content. Members do not accept all that the network sends out. Sports are preferred over arts and culture, while political items are reported more often than economic news. Eurovision has united European viewers, but the prerogatives of national sovereignty, as well as economic and social barriers, have slowed Eurovision's evolution toward a higher level of programming.

The purpose of this chapter is to see how members use Eurovision and to see why members choose the programs they choose. It is divided into the following sections: *1*) the rate of participation and exchange, *2*) the content of the Eurovision program exchange, and *3*) the content of the Eurovision news exchange.

5.1 Eurovision Traffic

The number of programs exchanged over the Eurovision network have ballooned over the years. Figure 5-1 shows this quite well. From 1972 to 1982, the Eurovision program exchange has grown at an average annual rate of over 3 percent. Growth is strongest in Olympic years and in those years designated for World Cup (soccer) championships, as in 1978 and 1982. The big jump in 1961 is attributed mainly to the fact that figures of the European news exchange were included with those of the Eurovision program exchange.

Eurovision news traffic has shown greater growth (Figure 5-2). The volume of news items sent over the network increased at a 6 percent annual rate from 1972 to 1982.

The volume of program and news traffic is influenced by many factors. While the installation of new Eurovision equipment has increased the quality, reliability, and economy of routing transmissions, it does not seem to have

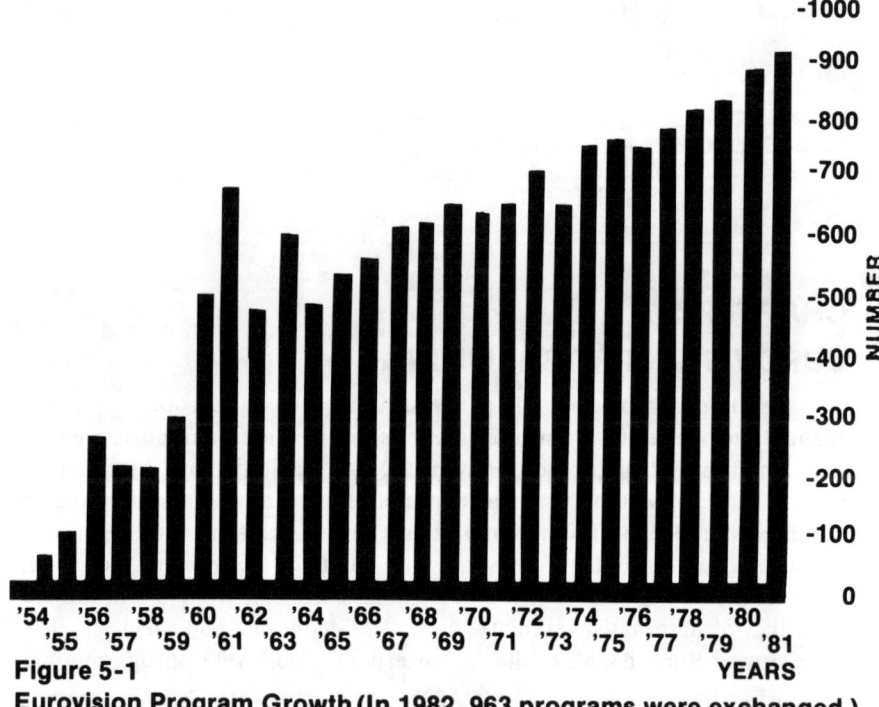

Figure 5-1
Eurovision Program Growth (In 1982, 963 programs were exchanged.)
Source: EBU

directly caused the increase in traffic.[1] Still, technology has facilitated the growth in traffic. The advent of videotape recorders in 1958 helped prompt the start of the Eurovision news exchange because it eliminated editing problems and stimulated demands for request transmissions.[2]

In addition, the recent arrival of electronic news gathering equipment (ENG) in Europe has permitted broadcasters to offer more stories more quickly to Eurovision than ever before.[3] What's more, ENG combined with quick satellite booking allows new stories to break almost simultaneously with the event's occurrence. In June 1979, Eurovision had pictures of Israeli ships sailing through the Suez Canal two hours after the event, and Pope John Paul II's motorcade through Warsaw was televised a few minutes after it occurred.[4] Aside from new television technology, the start of the permanent vision network in 1968, which permits the organization of short-notice transmissions, helped to meet broadcasters' demands for news of the big events of 1968: the
"Prague Spring," the Paris student demonstrations in May, and the Vietnam War protests at the Democratic National Party Convention in Chicago in August.[5]

Eurovision Programming

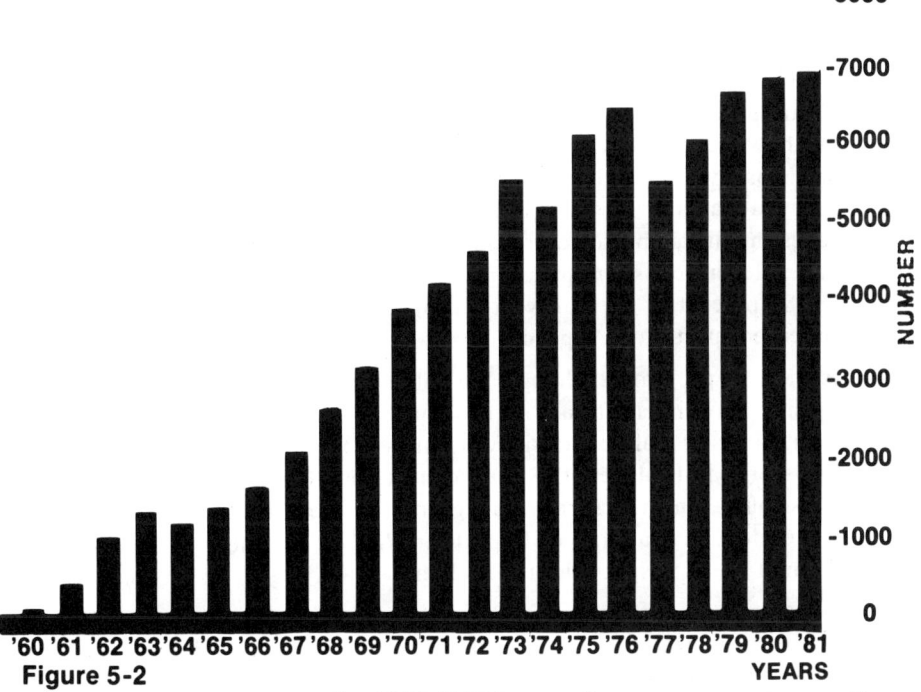

Figure 5-2
Eurovision News Growth (In 1982, 7,636 news items were exchanged.)
Source: EBU

The participation of worldwide newsfilm services has also increased traffic. The agencies offer Eurovision members access to stories from around the world. Agency library film is also frequently used by Eurovision members to provide background items. Typically, the agencies contribute about half of the items transmitted during the EVNs. Of the 7,636 items transmitted during the 1982 EVN's, 3,828 (50 percent) were originated by television news agencies.[6]

Moreover, the volume of Eurovision program and news traffic depends upon major international events and upon the sports calendar. One type of event which most Eurovision members regard as important are international championships, cups, and tournaments of popular sports. All thirty-two Eurovision members (plus six Intervision members), for example, relayed the opening ceremony and the first match of the 1982 World Football Cup in Spain.[7] Most European sports championships also draw heavy participation. The 1982 European Champion Clubs Football Cup Final between Aston Villa and Bayern Munich was relayed by thirty Eurovision members (plus four Intervision members).[8] Other 1982 championships which attracted more than fifteen Eurovision members included the European Winners' Football

Cup Final, European Indoor Athletics Championships, Grand Prix of Monaco, and the British Tennis Championships at Wimbledon.[9]

Not all sporting events are taken. In 1982, for example, no Eurovision interest was shown for the World Doubles Tennis Championships from Birmingham, the "Moscow News (Gymnastics) Prize," and the Toboggan World Cup in Czechoslovakia.[10] The popularity of a sport and whether a national team makes the finals appear to be important criteria in determining Eurovision usage. Nevertheless, broadcasters' hunger for sports is reflected by the fact that 82 percent of all Eurovision program exchanges from 1972 to 1982 concerned sports (see Appendix H).

As with the program exchange, the volume of Eurovision news traffic also depends upon international events. Eurovision news traffic is its heaviest during times of political crisis, war, strikes, and elections. Among the top EVN stories in 1981 were U.S. President Ronald Reagan's inauguration, the release of U.S. hostages from Iran; events surrounding attempts on the lives of President Reagan and of Pope John Paul II, the successful launch and return of the U.S. space shuttle "Columbia," and the events in Poland.[11]

A clearer picture of Eurovision's growth can be seen by comparing which member organizations give and take the most programs and news items. To simplify this comparison, Eurovision membership may be divided, based upon the number of television sets in each country,[12] into the following categories:

Big Four (with over 10 million sets): Federal Republic of Germany, France, Italy, United Kingdom.

Medium states (under 10 million sets): Austria, Belgium, Denmark, Finland, Greece, Netherlands, Norway, Portugal, Spain, Sweden, Switzerland, Turkey, Yugoslavia.

Small states (under 1 million sets): Algeria, Cyprus, Iceland, Ireland, Israel, Jordan, Luxembourg, Libya, Monaco, Morocco, Tunisia.

The chief originators in the Eurovision program exchange are the Big Four (Figure 5-3). In 1982, the Big Four as a group contributed 454 programs, or 47 percent of the 963 programs originated for Eurovision.[13] The largest program originator of the Big Four in 1982 was West German television with 138 programs (264 h 12). The British networks were second with 115 programs (311 h 40), followed by the Italian service with 103 programs (169 h 29), and by the French networks with 98 programs (170 h 06).[14] In terms of air time, British television ranked first.

The dominant position of the Big Four largely reflects the fact that the British, French, Italian, and West German networks are the largest and among the richest in Europe. Because the Big Four (except for ITV/United Kingdom)

Eurovision Programming 137

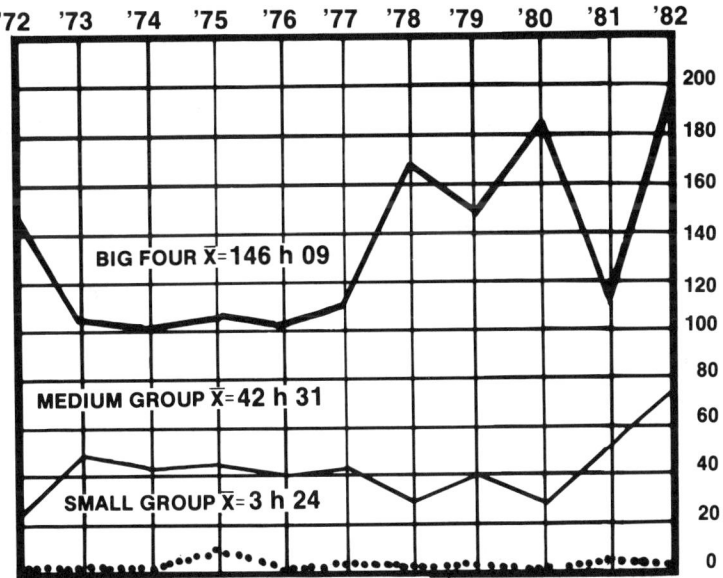

**Figure 5-3
Average Hours Originated with the Eurovision Program Exchanges 1972-1982**

Source: EBU

are financed mainly by license fees, the funds for technique and content are generally greater. In 1981, the Big Four had over 61 percent of the Eurovision total of about 113 million sets.[15] Another reason for the Big Four's strong position is that most European sporting events are staged in these countries. Large countries have the resources to hold such events. In addition, profit-minded sports federations and other organizers seek to have events staged where large audiences can be attracted.[16]

Figure 5-4 shows a distinct upward trend in program reception for all Eurovision members. The first observation to be made is that all program reception curves are similar, with peaks occurring in Olympic years and in those years designated for World Cup (soccer) championships. Moreover, the Big Four slightly surpassed the mid-sized nations in program reception. At first glance, this may seem to contradict one of the basic aims of Eurovision's creation, i.e. to give the smaller organizations access to programs which might normally be beyond their financial, staff, and technical resources. But the medium and small nations individually are the biggest receivers. In the ten years preceding 1982, Swiss television has taken the most Eurovision programs (except in 1980 and 1982 when it was ranked second). The EBU's

1982 annual program statistics show that, of the 963 programs sent over Eurovision, France took the most, with 389 (844 h 37) or 40.3 percent. Switzerland was second with an average of 386 programs (684 h 31) or 40 percent, followed by the Netherlands with 382 programs (774 h 17) or 39 percent.[17] One reason for the high reception by the Big Four, as a group, is that the financing of rights and often of vision circuit costs of many European programs, chiefly sports, requires the participation of at least one of the organizations of the Big Four.[18]

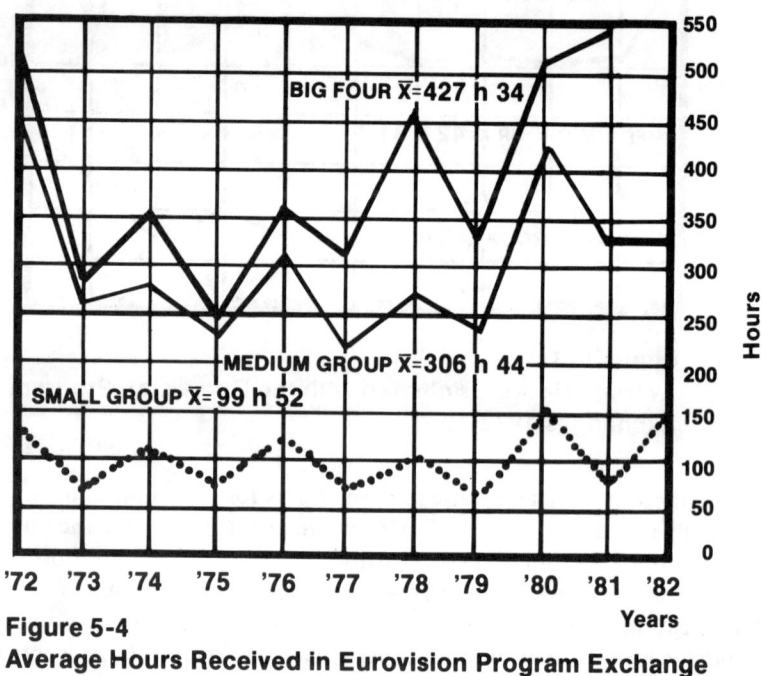

Figure 5-4
Average Hours Received in Eurovision Program Exchange
Source: EBU

In addition, the smallest Eurovision members often take more programs than they give (Table 5-1). Significantly, the television services from Cyprus, Jordan, and Morocco failed to give any programs to Eurovision from 1976 to 1982. As has already been noted, the heavy reliance of the small, poorer organizations on the reaches of the Eurovision network caused a crisis when the Big Four began canceling scheduled transmissions rather than helping subsidize the expensive circuit costs to link the remote services.

Moreover, Eurovision makes up for a larger share of the total annual program output of the small and mid-sized stations than of the Big Four (Table

Table 5-1

Participation of Eurovision's Smallest Members: 1976-1982 (Excludes the Eurovision news exchange)

Country	Total Number of Programs and Hours of Programs Originated		Total Number of Programs and Hours of Programs Received	
	No.	Hours	No.	Hours
Algeria	28	38 h 59	678	1,316 h 35
Ireland	66	109 h 46	879	1,738 h 45
Israel	10	13 h 13	239	424 h 07
Jordan	-	-	196	355 h 25
Libya	2	6 h 40	285	514 h 33
Luxembourg	6	9 h 36	516	567 h 15
Monaco	12	26 h 18	278	725 h 13
Morocco	-	-	425	749 h 08
Tunisia	6	13 h 45	635	1,037h 53

Source: EBU

5-2). In 1981, Dutch television output comprised the highest share of Eurovision programs, with over 11 percent; Norway came in second, with over 9 percent, followed by Denmark with over 7 percent. For all Eurovision members, the network accounted for over 4 percent of total air time.

As in the Eurovision program exchange, the Big Four traditionally supply the most items to the Eurovision news exchange. Admittedly, the exact contribution can vary from year to year. Still, as Figure 5-5 shows, the Big Four contribute roughly half of all the items exchanged in the EVNs. Of the 7,636 news items originated for EVN in 1982, the television networks of the Federal Republic of Germany, France, Italy, and the United Kingdom supplied 2,431 items or 32 percent. The largest EVN originator was the United Kingdom (BBC, ITN, and the newsfilm services) with 13 percent. Italy's RAI was second, with 7 percent, followed by France's networks with 6 percent, and by West German services with 5 percent.[19]

The domination of the Eurovision news scene by the Big Four cannot entirely be explained by the phenomenon that more newsworthy events happen in the large West European countries. A great deal of news comes from the three international newsfilm agencies regularly participating in EVNs — the American CBS News, the British-American United Press International Television News (UPITN), and the British Visnews Ltd. In 1981, 42 percent of the 6,820 EVN items came from the newsfilm agencies.[20] Of the total contribution, Visnews supplied over 49 percent, UPITN slightly more than 32 percent, and

CBS News just over 18 percent.[21] Partly because of British financial holdings in two of the agencies, and partly because London is the main EVN injection point for agency as well as North American items into EVN, the United Kingdom has a dominating position in the Eurovision news exchange.

Table 5-2 Contribution of Eurovision to National Program Output in 1981

Country	Annual Program Output (Hours)	Eurovision Reception (Hours)		Eurovision Reception as a Percent of Program Output
Algeria	3,510	154 h	52	4.4
Austria	7,608	567	53	7.4
Belgium	7,639	434	29	5.6
Denmark	2,559	196	51	7.6
Federal Republic of Germany	12,198	664	45	5.4
Finland	4,860	264	15	5.4
France	11,334	604	54	5.3
Greece	3,331	186	21	5.5
Ireland	5,616	203	02	3.6
Italy	11,124	386	54	3.4
Libya	3,456	28	47	0.8
Luxembourg	6,555	80	16	1.2
Monaco	4,050	152	28	3.7
Morocco	2,268	59	21	2.6
Netherlands	4,860	582	45	11.9
Norway	2,500	248	59	9.9
Portugal	5,184	226	04	4.3
Spain	5,961	215	39	3.6
Sweden	4,860	223	43	4.5
Switzerland	9,936	646	37	6.5
Tunisia	2,970	131	18	4.4
Turkey	1,944	67	03	3.4
United Kingdom	17,091	503	11	2.9
Yugoslavia	7,830	373	43	4.7
TOTAL	149,244	7,199	30	4.8

Sources: Annual program output calculated by author from "Expansion of Television During 1981," *EBU Review*, 193, (June 1981), p. 145. Eurovision reception figures are from "Statistics of Eurovision Programs and News Exchanges, 1.1.1981-31.12.1981," *EBU Review*, 33:3, (May 1982), p. 39.

Eurovision Programming 141

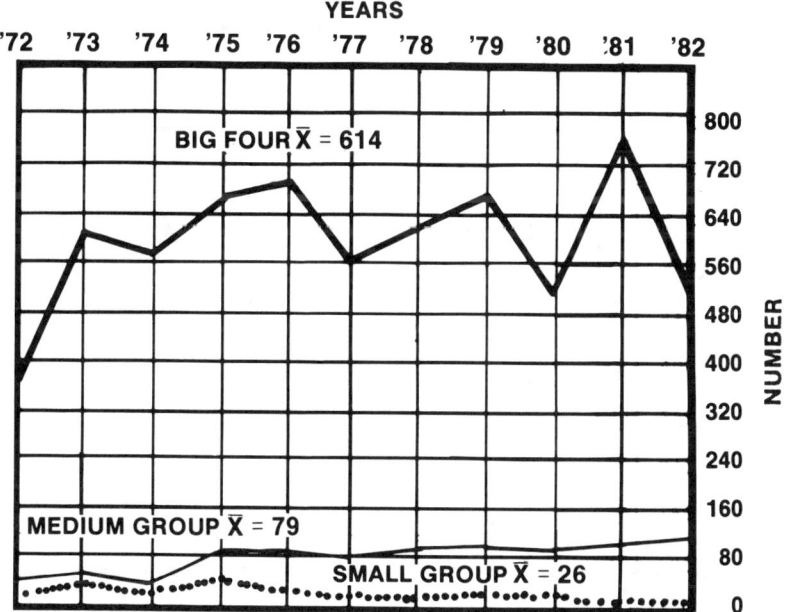

**Figure 5-5
Average Number of News Items Originated in Eurovision
1972-1982**

Source: EBU

The steep growth curves for all participants in Figure 5-6 shows that West European television stations depend greatly on Eurovision for getting the news. The medium-sized group of nations lead the Big Four in news reception. In 1982, Swiss television took the most, with 7,338 items or 96 percent of all the material offered. Austria's ORF was second, with 95 percent, followed by JRT/Yugoslavia with 93 percent. As already pointed out, Swiss television also tends to take the most Eurovision programs. Of the Big Four, France took the most news items, 6,907 or 90 percent, followed by Italy with 6,767 items or 88 percent.[22]

None of this is to say that the Big Four are less news conscious. When compared with small television organizations with a tiny population and an accordingly small budget, the Big Four have a larger capability — in terms of reporters and camera crews — to get the news themselves. In 1982, for example, the BBC had twenty-two full-time foreign correspondents and a worldwide network of fifty freelancers, while Swiss television kept no reporters abroad.[23]

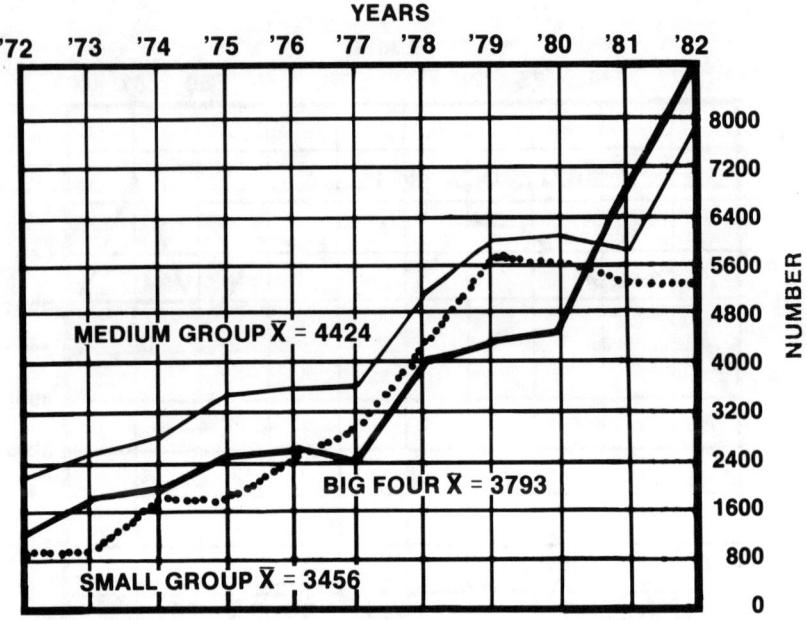

Figure 5-6
Average Number of Eurovision News Items Received 1972-1982
Source: EBU

5.2 Eurovision Program Exchange

As broadcasters began using television, Eurovision seemed to have the magic formula for making good use of the new medium. We have already seen that the rise of Eurovision owes a lot to the fact that taking full advantage of television technology requires international collaboration. Because of television's limited propagation range, signals could not cross political boundaries without linking stations by either terrestrial or space facilities. In addition, satisfying broadcasters' hunger for regular and rapid access to programs and news from abroad meant that there would have to be at least a measure of agreement on acquiring international circuits, standardizing equipment, and coordinating exchange procedures.

The sharing of costs also plays a big role in explaining the appeal of Eurovision. In fact, for television executives in many countries, the use of Eurovision is a simple budgetary necessity. To buy the television rights to a European football championship (nations) can cost the EBU as much as 1.5 million dollars, yet after the costs have been shared among participating members, a television network in, say Finland, may pay as little as 5,000 dollars to televise the event.

Eurovision Programming 143

Beyond technical and economic factors lies a much more altruistic cause for creating Eurovision. Eurovision's founders had hoped that the network would exchange a wide variety of programs in Europe, thus helping to reduce international misunderstanding and to create new bridges between the peoples of different nations.

But the number and variety of Eurovision programs could certainly be greater. Members do not accept all program offers. Indeed, the largest single receiver of Eurovision programs — France — took only 40 percent of all 1982 offers. Moreover, in the same year, members canceled 197 Eurovision programs partly because organizations withdrew their offers and partly because of a lack of interest.[24] Today, the network accounts for only about 4 percent of all television air time in Western Europe (see Table 5-2).

Members exchange little beyond sports in the Eurovision program exchange. Sports have long dominated any other kind of Eurovision programs (see Appendix H). Over a ten-year period ending in 1982, sports averaged 82 percent of all transmissions. And second only to sports in international penetration are current affairs — averaging 9 percent of transmissions from 1972 to 1982. Light entertainment programs were the third most frequently exchanged program type, with 4 percent, followed by religion with 2 percent, drama/music with 2 percent, and folklore with 1 percent.[25]

Exchanges of culture and arts are few and far between. But when drama, folklore and light entertainment programs have been transmitted, many have become Eurovision traditions, appearing yearly on West European screens. Programs such as ORF's "New Year's Concert from Vienna," RAI's Christmas and Easter masses from the Vatican, BBC's "Billy Smart's Easter Circus," "Jeux sans frontieres," "Interneige," and the "Eurovision Song Contest" are seen regularly by viewers in many Eurovision countries. Often, they are also seen in other parts of the world. On April 24, 1982, the 16th annual "Eurovision Song Contest" was relayed live from Harrogate, U.K., to twenty-three members and recorded by several non-Eurovision services in countries such as Poland and the USSR.[26]

One of the reasons for a certain sluggishness in the number and kinds of Eurovision programs is the increasingly high costs of buying television rights. In 1981, for example, several of the BBC's "Promenade" concert offers drew no Eurovision interest mainly because members considered the cost of the rights to be too high.[27] As we have seen, the EBU has concluded numerous agreements to protect broadcasters from excessive fees. The Model Contract for the International Televising of a Sporting Event, for instance, recommends that no EBU member can negotiate independently to buy exclusive rights to a sports event without offering it to others. In addition, any negotiations must be held directly with the sports federation responsible for the event. Normally, the EBU negotiates on behalf of Eurovision members.[28]

Sports federations have been largely content to negotiate with the EBU because Eurovision has given sports a wide audience. But in light of the rising costs of television rights in recent years, a dispute has developed between international sports federations and the EBU over the role of third persons in the negotiation process. Some sports federations have contracted so-called "third-party" middlemen — such as independent public relations firms — to negotiate the rights for them to ensure both a good fee from broadcasters and a wider marketing of their sports. But the EBU sees no need for "third-party" companies, insisting on dealing directly with the federations. Part of the EBU's mistrust appears to stem from the close ties the companies have with advertisers — whose products will be aired during sports programs. This dispute has already cut down the amount of international sports on Eurovision. European viewers did not see the first World Swimming Cup in Tokyo in September 1979 because the EBU refused to deal with a London-based public relations company which was under contract by the International Swimming Federation.[29]

The EBU often coordinates its actions with other broadcasting unions in an effort to lower prices. During negotiations for television rights to the 1976 Montreal Olympics, the EBU joined five other broadcasting unions in threatening to black out coverage of the Games outside North America if the 18 million dollar price demanded by the Canadian Olympic Organizing Committee was not lowered. In the end, the television rights were sold to the EBU for about 10 million dollars.[30]

The costly Eurovision machinery also can inhibit the live transmission of timeless programs such as arts and culture. In June 1982, for example, Eurovision members did not exchange any cultural programs despite numerous offers.[31] One reason for the reluctance of members to exchange operas and plays is that most Eurovision members are held accountable for program-making. Thus, they are understandably cost-conscious when offering and accepting Eurovision transmissions. Generally, members give priority to immediately transmitting sports and current affairs programs, because drama, concerts, opera, and ballet are not timely items: they can be easily sent by the cheaper mail service.[32]

In addition, Eurovision programs have cultural and social limitations. The opportunities for the live exchange of programs are often restricted by language barriers. Quite obviously, language barriers can be technically overcome by having a commentary on what the viewer sees in the language of the country taking the event. Although this is widely done for international sports, it is rarely done for operas, ballet, and drama.

Some "non-sports" Eurovision programs are only taken by television services sharing the same language. One such program is "Aktenzeichen XY...üngelost," a re-enacted true-life crime investigation telecast live monthly in Austria, German-speaking Switzerland, and West Germany. Surely neither the EBU nor Eurovision was created to promote the exchange of programs only among broadcasting organizations with linguistic, and cultural similarities.[33]

Beyond language barriers, the more serious problem of differing viewer tastes and interests exists. Of course, the importance of the role played by a national team in any international sporting contest — champion or likely winner — is a major deciding factor in accepting or rejecting a Eurovision offer.[34] Nonetheless, different countries tend to have different sports interests and tastes. For example, in descending order of viewer ratings, football, boxing, and horse racing dominate the Italian sports television scene, while in France, horse racing, football, and rugby get high ratings.[35]

Partly because of this diverse interest, it is not surprising to find that the greatest interest of most Eurovision members is confined to a few kinds of sports. Of the 476 sports programs transmitted over Eurovision during the first six months of 1982, 82 (101 h 25) were football, 63 (76 h 55) were skiing, 48 (113 h 20) were hockey, 38 (46 h) were handball, 35 (38 h) were cycling, and 31 (154 h 08) were tennis. The remaining 179 programs (37 percent) were divided among twenty-four different sports.[36] Obviously, unlike drama and other programs, the importance attached to sports television is relative to the practice of sports in a particular country. Moreover, a popular sport in one country may be construed as objectionable to another, as the telecast of a Spanish bullfight to India surely shows.

Even with sports that elicit European-wide interest, such as Olympic Games, one program for the whole of Europe cannot be made without compromise, particularly between the big services and the small. At the Montreal Olympics, for example, the entire 10,000-meter run could not be covered because the cameras could only get three sections of the track. While small and big services alike wanted to see the winner, the big services also wanted to see the performance of their own competitor, even if he did poorly.[37] To meet special desires and interests, broadcasters can unilaterally transmit an event. In fact, unilaterals are increasingly being used to back up the international program. At Montreal, the EBU-OIRT Operations Group carried out 296 unilaterals totaling 245 hours, while the multilateral program totaled 133 hours.[38]

Differing viewer tastes and interests can also limit the exchange of arts and culture. Light entertainment offers, for instance, tend not to be taken unless international artists are involved.[39] The successful television program is normally made with a specific domestic audience and a particular objective in mind. Thus, for a program to be of interest to all European viewers, careful planning is needed. But, even with careful planning, success is not guaranteed. The Eurovision transmission of Harold Pinter's play "Tea Party" in 1965, for example, was widely criticized by British viewers. Some felt the play was not worth showing all over Europe, while others felt, as one viewer wrote, that if "Tea Party" was "accepted as typical of the taste of (the United Kingdom), it would make (the British) a laughing stock in the eyes of the world."[40]

Another reason for a certain sluggishness in the Eurovision program exchange is that the prerogatives of national sovereignty remain strong. In Chapter One, it was suggested that because television programs can have important political implications, no government can afford the unrestricted flow of information. All states, to varying degrees, regulate the content of programs because they might contain material that is detrimental to the regime in power. Of course, political authorities do not want their national program content decisions reversed by programs originating outside their borders. Thus, Eurovision cannot be expected to transmit programs which may pose a threat to national security, to the integrity of the nation's culture or to the fulfillment of national goals. Marcel Bezençon, the father of Eurovision, recognized this limit when he wrote: "... the more (Eurovision) develops, the more dependent it becomes ... on a large number of nations whose policies it cannot oppose on its millions of screens. It is therefore condemned to the strictest silence in most of the fields where there is a clash of ideas and ideals."[41]

A clash of ideas and ideals occurred on July 10, 1963 when the French Government refused to relay a transatlantic television debate among leading statesmen to other Eurovision members because it feared the program was controversial and political. The program, "Town Meeting of the World," featured a discussion among former President Dwight D. Eisenhower from Denver; Jean Monnet, "the father" of the European Economic Community, from Brussels; former West German Foreign Minister, Dr. Heinrich von Brentano from Bonn; and former British Prime Minister, Anthony Eden from London. Organized by the Columbia Broadcasting System (CBS) in New York, the program was to honor the anniversary of the first transatlantic television transmission and was to be seen live in the United States and Western Europe. Pictures from the three European capitals were to be beamed to the United States via Telstar II from the British earth station on Goonhilly Downs. Then the American portion and the full program were to be picked up from the satellite by the French earth station at Pleumeur Bodou — the only one on the continent at the time — and sent over Eurovision to Britain, Ireland, West Germany, Belgium, the Netherlands, and Italy.

The program was seen live in the United States, but not in Western Europe because France refused to let its satellite station be used for such a relay. The reasons were twofold. First, the French felt that a scientific rather than a political discussion was better suited for Telstar's first anniversary. Second, the French Government feared giving Monnet a platform for views on European integration that differed from those of General de Gaulle. In the end, the program was taped in New York and flown to Europe for later showing.[42]

The recording of a Eurovision transmission for later broadcast is a convenient way for states to edit unwanted material. In 1982, for example, Swiss television taped the Eurovision feed of the annual Farnborough Air Show from the United Kingdom. But, when the program was later shown, the Swiss commentator admitted that several scenes were cut to avoid what they deemed to be excessive patriotic references by the British, particularly in light of their victory in the Falkland Islands.[43]

Limit television advertising is another important policy objective for many Western European countries. The majority of Eurovision members, like France and the United Kingdom, are state-subsidized companies; thus advertising on television is either banned or strictly limited. In some countries, laws exist against alcohol, tobacco, and pharmaceutical commercials as well as political statements and religious slogans. Apart from protecting the health of its own people, one reason political entities supervise advertising is that they fear overt commercialism will generate a demand for consumer goods among their own citizens that will harm national economic and social development plans.[44] Another fear is that ads for foreign goods will displace local goods and industries. Outdoor advertising at sports stadiums may not even be attractive to commercial broadcasters for fear of reducing the possibility of selling their advertising time.[45]

When receiving a Eurovision program offer, members always check to see what the advertising will be. If the advertising is offensive, the offer may be rejected. In September 1974, for example, West Germany's second national network, ZDF, decided, against much public discontent, to cancel a live transmission from Basel of a football match between Switzerland and West Germany because of excessive advertising within camera range.[46] During the same year, excessive advertising also prompted West Germany's first network, ARD, to cancel several major sporting events from Austria, Italy and Switzerland.[47]

To minimize the chances of program offers being rejected because they contain advertising, the EBU has drawn up a set of guidelines to unacceptable advertising — the so-called "nine principles of advertising." In 1976, the administrative council recommended that the broadcaster originating an international sports transmission ban advertising: *1)* that disturbs transmission quality and satisfactory viewing such as ads placed more than one tier around the stadium; *2)* that uses fluorescent color, luminous lights, or colors adversely affecting the television picture; *3)* that comes between the camera and the action; *4)* that uses mobile or occasional installations; *5)* that visually hampers the picture of the event from any angle; *6)* that produces sound during the transmission; *7)* that infringes on national rules of the originating country; *8)* that is not in the language of the country where the event takes place; *9)* that appears on equipment, uniforms and playing surfaces, especially when it is not customary for the type of event (e.g., advertising on officials).[48] These criteria of unacceptable advertising were unilaterally agreed to by the majority of Eurovision members partly because of the wide variety of sporting events and of sports organizers, and partly because of the difficulties which the EBU faced in signing contracts containing a "no advertising" clause. In addition to being an EBU doctrine, the "nine principles" have been adopted by many members in their national contracts with sports federations and other organizers.[49]

Underlying the EBU advertising guidelines is the belief of broadcasters that advertising at events should be for the spectators in the stadium. Broadly speaking, broadcasters recognize that ads can be an essential source of revenue to sports. They also recognize that the primary reason advertising is in the stadium is because of television. But, at the same time, broadcasters want to control it for fear that the screen might become flooded with advertisements and thus render the event secondary.[50]

But advertisers can be clever in getting around broadcasters' anti-ad restrictions, as the March 12, 1975 football game in London between the United Kingdom and West Germany shows. Before the game, West German broadcasters decided that they would not transmit the event because of excessive West German advertising — particularly Jägermeister ads. They argued that the ads should be in English because it was the language of the country where the game was being staged. To counter the broadcasters' actions, Jägermeister, a West German hard-liquor company, bought up the offending ad panels, thus emptying the stadium of all advertising. Then Jägermeister ran a press campaign highlighting the benevolent attitude it had taken to ensure that West German viewers could see the event. Not only was the game transmitted over Eurovision as scheduled, but Jägermeister gained publicity at home.[51]

Enforcing the EBU anti-advertising guidelines has often required coordinated actions among Eurovision members. A case in point was the World Nordic Championships from Lahti, Finland in February 1978. Although interest for coverage was widespread, Eurovision members told the Finnish television network, YLE, that they would refuse to take pictures of the event because of excessive advertising. Common to the complaints was that the size of many of the ads was larger than the skier. New talks started between the organizers and YLE executives — even Finnish President Urho Kaleva Kekkonen became involved — to reduce the advertising. Meanwhile, European viewers did not know whether the championships would be aired. But two days before the opening day, an agreement to considerably reduce advertising on the course was reached.[52]

Despite these difficulties — or maybe because of them — many broadcasters are attempting to broaden the scope and depth of television through international coproductions. Program production costs can be lowered in international coproductions. But coproductions can also offer broadcasters of different countries greater control over what viewers will see. By participating in a coproduction, a television service can have a say in the content of scripts, in the choice of actors and in film locations. In addition, coproductions offer a way of overcoming government quotas on program imports. They also solve problems caused by different foreign audiovisual standards. Despite the benefits, however, coproductions have largely been limited to countries sharing the same culture, language and religion.[53]

The strengths and weaknesses of commissioning a television drama transmitted live to all of Western Europe is illustrated by "The Largest Theater in the World." To encourage greater Eurovision drama exchanges, Jean Luc, program director of Radio-Tele-Luxembourg, proposed before the GTV/2 Working Party in March 1958 that the EBU become involved in managing a drama series called "The Largest Theater in the World." The first "Theater" exchange came in 1962 when EBU members jointly commissioned Sir Terence Rattigan to write "Heart to Heart." The program was rebroadcast by fourteen services in nine languages and was seen by an estimated 50 million viewers.[54]

Although details varied, a typical production for the "Theater" series went like this: any active member could nominate a European playwright to the EBU. The Union then notified all active members of the proposed play, checking their interest and inquiring if they would guarantee a copyright fee to be shared among the participating services. Once interest and fees were agreed upon, the director of the Legal Department drew up the contract. When the script was completed, each participating service could film the play as it wished. While some services made their own production, others relayed another service's production. But the productions were to be shown as simultaneously as possible. The original idea behind the "Theater" was that, at the same time, viewers throughout Europe could watch a play made for TV. Over the years, six scripts were commissioned by playwrights such as Fritz Hochwalder and Ingmar Bergman.[55]

But, in 1971, the "Theater" closed its doors. The decision to end the series is attributed partly to the difficulty of hiring an internationally known playwright. While members proposed names of playwrights, others rejected them because they were not well known in their countries.[56]

In addition, copyright and production costs became expensive. In 1966, for example, the EBU commissioned François Billetdoux's play "Pitchi Poi ou la parole donnée". This play differed from other co-productions in that the action took place in fifteen countries, requiring a central producer, national producers, a central laboratory, a central director of photography and an internal film team. The total budget came to about 200,000 dollars, including copyright fees. Also, as production was drawing to a close, legal and sales problems arose. Moreover, members were not free to make their own versions.[57]

Moreover the "Theater" ran into censorship problems as shown by Fritz Hochwalder's play "The Order," a script inspired by the life of Anne Frank. In 1967, Dutch broadcasters refused the Eurovision transmission of the play because they felt it treated Nazi war crimes such as persecution of the Jews too softly.[58] In West Germany, "The Order" was censored as too harsh on the Germans. In Austria, a reference to the enthusiastic acclaim given to Hitler on entering Vienna was cut as was a reference that Austrian war criminals were sentenced to an average of "three minutes in jail per murder committed."[59] The difficulties encountered by the "Theater" series led an EBU official to observe that joint commissions of drama performances had changed; developing more along the lines of bilateral rather than European-wide productions.[60]

5.3 Eurovision News Exchange

In looking at how members use the Eurovision news exchange, the first observation is that they rely greatly on the network for their daily foreign news. Of the thirty Eurovision members participating in the 1982 EVNs, an average of 24.2 services relayed each news item.[61] Moreover, the largest user of EVN in 1982 was Swiss television, with 96 percent of all the offered material.[62]

A glance at one day's EVNs not only shows the extent of member usage but also serves as a guide of what is "news."

On June 30, 1977, the EVNs carried the following stories:

> United Kingdom: (BBC)-presser by british p.m. james callaghan at the close of the european summit meeting. (BBC)-wimbledon mens quarter-final match: connors-mcenroe. (BBC/VIS)-film shows: mauritius delegate introducing resolution calling on member states to provide military support for mozambique. (BBC/VIS)-film shows: members of the opposition democratic and united parties arriving and meeting to merge and form new republic opposition party

(South Africa). (BBC/VIS)-b-1 bomber library film. (ITN/UPITN)-meeting in support of soviet dissidents + human rights attended by various personalities including jean-paul sartre. (ITN/UPITN)-film shows: lebanese f.m. fouad butros arriving for talks on lebanon + fouad presser. *Italy*: (RAI/VIS)-film report shot in gaza prison following report by london sunday times that israel is torturing arab prisoners (report includes interviews with three prisoners in english); note: visnews advises that the film was viewed by israeli authorities and heavily edited. (RAI)-film shows: departure of dutch lorries carrying chilean copper for holland; the lorries were stopped by milan crowd yesterday in demonstrations against pinochet regime. *Czechoslovakia*: (CST)-further coverage of international ideological conference. *Poland*, (TVP)-gierek-brandt meeting + brandt visiting former concentration camp in gdansk region. *Finland*: (YLE)-highlights of helsinki athletic games. *United States*: (CBS)-ebu summary of carter presser in which he is expected to discuss the b-1 bomber, mideast, human rights, detente and domestic affairs.[63]

As the Eurovision news telex shows, politics is the most frequently exchanged kind of news. Consider the Callaghan press conference, the most widely accepted item. Of thirty-six participating organizations (including ABU, ASBU, Intervision and the American networks), thirty took the story. The second most accepted item that day related to sports. Coverage of the Wimbledon men's tennis match was taken by twenty-three services. Participation in the remaining items — mostly political — was as follows: film of the UN Council meeting on Mozambique was taken by nineteen services; followed by the Helsinki games, with sixteen; the Carter press conference, by fourteen; the Gaza prison film, by twelve; the B-1 bomber library film, by eleven; the meeting in support of Soviet dissidents, by eight; Brandt's Polish visit, by eight; the South African opposition merger, by seven; and the attack on the Dutch trucks, by seven.[64] Press conferences by world leaders, major international political meetings and visits, and sport championships are among the items which interest most EVN members.

Finnish media researchers Tapio Varis and Renny Jokelin[65] collected information on the content of EVN transmissions. They showed over a long period how Eurovision was becoming the greatest source of international political news. In the first three months of 1973, 1974, and 1975, over 46 percent of total EVN transmissions concerned politics (Table 5-3). Second only to political news in international penetration were disaster items and sports — each averaging 16 percent — followed by stories dealing with security and war, with 13 percent; financial items, with four percent; and cultural, social and scientific news; with two percent. Varis and Jokelin grouped items such as New Year's festivities and the carnival in Rio under the heading "others," which averaged one percent of the transmissions.[66]

Table 5-3
Contents of the Eurovision News Exchange 1973-1975 (January-March)

	1973		1974		1975	
	Feeds	Percent	Feeds	Percent	Feeds	Percent
Politics	454	40	579	53	638	46
Sports	162	14	199	18	221	16
Disasters	223	20	168	15	186	13
Security/War	177	16	76	7	231	16
Economic	65	6	30	3	50	4
Cultural, Social, Scientific	34	3	15	1	36	3
Others	6	1	34	3	25	2
Total	1,121	100	1,101	100	1,387	100

Source: Tapio Varis and Renny Jokelin, *Television News in Europe, A Survey of the News-film Flow in Europe,* (Tampere, Finland: University of Tampere, 1976), p. 60.

Why do Eurovision members take what they do? In selecting and analyzing what is "news," most broadcasters seem to insist on recent events. The newer the event, the more likely that the editor will include it in the news bulletin. Material on an event that has taken place two or more days earlier is no longer of any use to most services. In October 1978, a film of a pilgrimage of an estimated 800,000 people in Argentina in tribute to the death of Pope John Paul I and a film of talks between Argentine and Chilean officials to solve the Beagle Channel dispute were not accepted into EVN mainly because the News Coordinator deemed the stories too old.[67] Of course, providing sameday news coverage is a major pillar supporting Eurovision. As already noted, EVN's history, as well as the profession of news provision in general, is a history of a series of human efforts to provide more information more quickly and more directly on the day's events.[68] During the winter months, for instance, news items from North America to Europe are being sent increasingly by satellite in time for injection into EVN-0, rather than risking tapes being delayed at airports due to foul weather.[69]

Another factor influencing the selection of EVN offers appears to be geography. Proximity to a news event may increase interest and, at the same time, increase the degree of distortion. Because the bulk of Eurovision's membership is West European, EVN may contain a bias against exchanging truly international news. Varis and Jokelin found that the most frequently exchanged EVN items are related to visits by politicians to other European and North American countries, while diplomatic exchanges between Asian, African, and South American countries tend to go unreported.[70] The geographic criterion also evokes a bias against foreign items, especially if they involve the national politics of another country.[71] Varis and Jokelin discovered that reporting of political news centered largely on events occurring in the big countries like France, Italy, the United Kingdom, and West Germany, while the internal politics of small European countries were generally overlooked.[72] As one example, film of the results of the Swiss Federal Parliament elections in October 1979 was relayed by eight members.[73] On the other hand, the October elections in Turkey drew the participation of fifteen EVN members.[74] If the news under preparation is destined for a national audience, then the events described must carry some meaning for that nation.[75]

In addition, most members seem to give priority to items, even if relatively unimportant, if they are part of an ongoing story which the news department has been covering thoroughly all along.[76] On December 14, 1978, nine EVN members took film of U.S. Secretary of State Cyrus Vance's trip to Egypt surely because it acted as a guide to Middle East peace developments.[77] Aftermath stories also tend to be attractive to most members.[78] On November 11, 1978, six EVN members relayed the San Francisco memorial service for the 913 Jonestown, Guyana suicide victims.[79] Certain events, however, may be forced into obscurity after a long-running story is deemed to be boring.[80] In October 1978, only seven members took film of the continuing arrival of Vietnamese "boat people" in Malaysia, while a bombing in Ireland drew thirteen members.[81]

Furthermore, EVN members take items which appeal to mass taste. The greatest interest of most editors seems confined to a few sports, particularly football and auto racing. For athletic contests, interest arises only when new world records have been set.[82] But EVN seems to exchange few human-interest stories. A survey of the EVN exchange from October 1-30, 1979, only revealed the story of a person trying to cross the United States in a hot-air balloon, which was taken by seven members. Incidentally, only two EVN members took the story of his crash which occurred the following day.[83] Perhaps one reason why so few stories of this nature are exchanged is that national editors would prefer using human-interest stories occurring in their own country.[84]

Moreover, most EVN editors will give priority to those items which are made for television. Most Western broadcasters agree that events such as disasters, plane crashes, earthquakes, and great fires satisfy perfectly the needs of television because they offer unpredictable human drama. As a result, disaster and sports stories will inevitably gain precedence over economic and educational stories, which are also more difficult to realize in visual terms (Table 5-3).[85]

Furthermore, the selection and analysis of what is "news" depends upon a particular nation's internal structure. Quite obviously, television news is distorted by outright manipulation in most authoritarian countries, and, even in such professed democracies as France, sensitive programs are sometimes taboo. In 1964, for example, French television allegedly threatened to cut its national circuits if a BBC interview with Georges Bidault, a former French prime minister who fled to the United Kingdom, was offered to EVN. Because the French Government accused Bidault of being a traitor for his membership in an anti-government organization, French broadcasters reportedly told the BBC, that if they offered the item to EVN, the circuit through France to the rest of Europe would be cut.[86] According to a study by Charles E. Sherman and John Ruby, the Bidault case is the only attempt ever made to exclude a story from the Eurovision news exchange.[87] Even countries with a strong tradition of television freedom — like the United Kingdom — can be reluctant to have their ills exposed on television all over the world. The United Kingdom's ITN, for example, withheld film of a soccer riot in Scotland in response to pressure from the football association who threatened to bar television coverage of all future games if the story was sent over Eurovision. Fearing grave economic consequences, ITN did not offer the item to Eurovision, although it was shown on British television.[88]

Finally, the acceptance or rejection of EVN items depends on a particular nation's news values. Of course, many well-intentioned reports from abroad reflect the values that are acceptable to the editors and viewers of the organizations the correspondents represent. Yet, despite the Western libertarian traditions of freedom of the press and the right of the people to know, these values may be totally repugnant to the people of another country. On December 5, 1977, for instance, Swiss television refused to broadcast an accepted EVN offer showing the crowning of Bokassa I as Emperor of the new Central African Empire for fear the pictures would fuel racial prejudice in regard to Africa.[89]

The diverse news beliefs and priorities existing in EVN member organizations can also color the judgment of the News Coordinator. Offers of public hangings and floggings have been made to EVN, but most, if not all, have not been transmitted over the network mainly because the News Coordinators tend to deem such items as repugnant to West European television ethics.[90]

Some EVN participants feared giving the News Coordinator power to make journalistic decisions for the whole of Europe. One complaint was that the News Coordinator's power to preselect and to determine satellite usage would result in greater costs. Because vision circuit costs for EVN-0 and EVN-1 are not shared on a per-item basis, but rather on a daily transmission basis

Eurovision Programming 155

between the services taking them, some EVN members did not want a news editor from another country committing them to greater costs for items which they might not use.[91]

But the point that other EVN members made to counter this criticism was that preselection was necessary for efficient news gathering. Prior to 1974, news was chosen entirely at an EVN editorial conference where each participant decided what to take.[92] A major problem with this system was that members had to pay for an offer which they did not use. This was primarily because the usual brief offer telex, upon which members had solely based their selection, poorly described the story or was misleading.[93] The start of "choice after viewing" for EVN-0 in 1974 and its extension to EVN-1 in 1977 solved such problems because each member was able to choose its item after viewing it. To prevent members from paying for sending useless offers over the expensive vision circuits, the News Coordinator was charged with preselecting items.

No rules of journalist conduct for the News Coordinator exist. But a study by the EBU Working Party for Television News in 1974 identified several principles that could guide the Coordinator's choice of events. The study called for the Coordinator to:

1) Beware of political news of an anecdotal character; there must be a definite news event;
2) Beware of enthusiasm for a piece of news that recurs at frequent and regular intervals;
3) Always place the item in the news context of the day;
4) Beware of press conferences or declarations. These items only seem to be acceptable when they are "hot" news. The language barrier and lack of visual interest should be kept in mind;
5) Watch for insufficient description of items and the absence of agency dispatches for commentary use;
6) Beware of horrific or over-violent general information pictures, and do not forget the use of moral discretion;
7) Beware of items whose visual content is not what the viewers will expect;
8) Beware of editing too complicated news for quick use of the item; and
9) When the EVN-0 is justified by one or more indispensable items, not to hesitate to add other items that could have a complementary effect.[94]

The News Coordinator's job can be a difficult one, since he selects items not only of definite general interest but also of limited interest likely to be used by a small number of members.

Besides preselecting news stories, the News Coordinator also determines satellite usage. In granting this power to the Coordinator, members believed that the Coordinator's judgment of an actual situation and the value of the material being offered would be better suited to members' needs than services booking satellite transmissions a week ahead without even knowing whether the material would be available. They also noted that no procedure, however legitimate, should prevent an item considered to be journalistically essential from being available.[95]

Still, despite the power of the News Coordinator, editorial control rests completely with each member. Every station connected to Eurovision is free to receive or reject any news item and program which the network sends out. Stations are free to reject requests made by other members. Also each member is free to determine how pictures should be edited and interpreted (see the Gaza prison report on the EVN offer telex). How members use EVN items is of no concern to the EBU, which only acts as an administrative and technical coordination center.

Nevertheless, checks and balances to ensure objective news flow do exist. Apart from cases where newsmen are prohibited from entering a country, nothing prevents a country from sending its own television newsmen to cover the trouble in another country, although it might have to send the film home by plane, rather than by Eurovision. In addition, competition by — and among — the news agencies makes the suppression or overlooking of a truly significant story improbable. Because French television, during the de Gaulle period, never covered any demonstrations against the General, the agencies provided the world with much of the newsfilm of the May 1968 revolts.[96] Even today, the agencies help get film of French strikes, particularly when French television itself is on strike.[97] Agency materials have never been barred by the EBU.[98] Finally, the performance of a News Coordinator can be gauged — like viewer ratings — by determining how many members take stories off of EVN. The higher the participation, the better the News Coordinator's decision meet the needs of EVN members.[99] Thus, the News Coordinator will be responding to the pressure of his colleagues, as news filters down into the processes of television making.

5.4 Conclusion

In closing, we looked for consensus and instead found contradictions. Eurovision program and news traffic continues to grow, with the small members taking the most transmissions. But members do not take all that the network sends out. In the Eurovision program exchange, members clearly take more sports than they do current affairs, light entertainment, religion, drama, and folklore programs. In the Eurovision news exchange, political, disaster, and sports stories are reported more frequently than are financial, social and scientific events. Moreover, the network only accounts for about 4 percent of all television air time in Western Europe.

Greater and more varied Eurovision programming is limited by many factors. The exchange of Eurovision programs often depends upon the price of television rights and upon whether a particular program warrants live transmission over the expensive circuits. Beyond economic factors, social and cultural limits exist. Language barriers limit the live exchange of operas, ballets, and drama. The popularity of a sport or of a particular performer may also heighten interest. In both the Eurovision program and news exchange, the greatest interest has been confined to a few sports. Most members will reject news items which are not new. Also, EVN news editors tend to reject items which have no meaning to national viewers. Because of the geographic similarity of EVN membership, European news often takes precedence over news of equal importance from Asia, Africa, and South America. Moreover, the prerogatives of national sovereignty remain strong. Because of different national program and news values, news in one country may be construed as propaganda in another. Members have not permitted Eurovision to exchange offensive advertising and stories of public hangings and floggings.

Eurovision brings the world and its events visually into the living rooms of many Europeans. But it seems that those who anticipated that Eurovision would make the greatest range of entertainment and information available in Europe and who forecast a "European village" — where everyone sees the same events — forgot one thing: television screens can be fitted with politically tinted glass.

Endnotes
Chapter 5

1. F. Pisseloup, "Technical Progress and the Growth of Eurovision," *EBU Review,* 175, (June 1979), pp. 114-119.
2. *Ibid.,* p. 115.
3. "Statistics of Cooperation," *TV World,* 2, (July 1978), pp. 18-19.
4. EBU, *Weekly Liaison Bulletin,* 24, (June 20, 1979).
5. Pisseloup, *op. cit.,* p. 118.
6. Calculated by author from EBU Doc. No. SPG 2279, June 1983.
7. Author's analysis from the Eurovision Program Summaries (1982) of the EBU.
8. *Ibid.* The final was also covered by the television services from Australia, Congo, Egypt, Ivory Coast, Kuwait, Malaysia, Mexico, Oman, Qatar, Saudi Arabia, and the United Arab Emirates as well as the SIN network.
9. *Ibid.*
10. *Ibid.*

11. Author's analysis from the Weekly Liaison Bulletins (1979) of the EBU.
12. Television set figures from UNESCO, *Yearbook of Statistics 1978-79*, (Paris: UNESCO, 1980).
    The television services from Lebanon and Malta occasionally take recorded Eurovision programs, but are not permanently linked to the network; thus, they are not considered Eurovision members.
13. EBU Doc. no. SPG 2279, *op. cit.*
14. *Ibid.*
15. Calculated by author from "Expansion of Television During 1981," *EBU Review*, 193, (June 1981), p. 145.
16. Konrad M. Kressley, "Eurovision: Distributing Costs and Benefits in an International Broadcasting Union," *Journal of Broadcasting*, 22:1, (Spring 1978), p. 181.
17. EBU Doc. no. SPG 2279, *op. cit.*
    Because the EBU calculates the participation of the three Swiss services separately, and because certain material is often used by more than one service, the average of the participation figures was used. The Swiss-Italian television service, the smallest of the three national organizations, tends to take the most Eurovision programs and news items.
18. Interview with Miroslav Vilcek, Director, Television Program Department, EBU, Geneva, October 1979.
19. EBU Doc. no. SPG 2279, *op. cit.*
20. EBU, "Statistics of Eurovision Programs and News Exchanges, 1.1.1981-31.12.1981," *EBU Review*, 33:3, (May 1982), p.39.
21. Interview with Horst Fischer, Administrative Officer, TV News Division, EBU, Geneva, October 1982. In addition to separate contributions, the news agencies pool their resources. In 1981, for example, the agency pool provided ten items to the EVNs. For more about the newsfilm agencies, see Richard Clark, "Purposes and Problems of Newsfilm Agency Coverage," *EBU Review*, 91B, (May 1965), pp. 38-39; Charles Curran, "Eurovision and the News Agencies: A Reply," *EBU Review*, 30: 6, (November 1979), pp. 30-32; Yrjö Länsipuro, "Newsfilm Agencies Out of Focus?" *Intermedia*, 5:6, (August 1977), pp. 10-11; John Mahoney, "The News Exchange: The Agency Dimension," *EBU Review*, 26:3, (May 1975), pp. 32-34; and "Western Television Agencies Hold Grip on International News," *BM/E's World Broadcast News*, 3:9, (May 1981), pp. 22-24.
22. EBU Doc. no. SPG 2279, *op. cit.*

23. Interview with Tony Dunn, Foreign News, BBC, London, October 1982, and with Heinz Schallenberger, Eurovision News Coordinator, SRG, Zurich, November 1982.
24. EBU Doc. no. SPG 2279, *op. cit.*
25. Eurovision programs can be divided into the following categories:
    Sports: This category refers to coverage of national and international sports events of all kinds, ranging from hockey to swimming.
    Current affairs: This category includes programs such as elections, space flights, royal weddings, and coronations. It does not include short daily news items.
    Light entertainment: This category includes programs such as variety shows, children's programs and song contests.
    Religion: This category includes church services.
    Drama/music: Programs in this category include plays, concerts, operas, and ballet.
    Folklore: This category refers to programs dealing with ethnic and racial traditions.
26. Author's analysis from the Eurovision Program Summaries (1982) of the EBU.
27. Interview with Richard Bunn, Head, Eurovision Program Division, EBU, Geneva, August 1982.
28. EBU, "Model Contract for the International Televising of a Sporting Event," Collection of Legal Recommendations and Decisions of the Administrative Council and the General Assembly.
29. Alex Frere, "Sports on European Television: The Viewer is Missing, Something," International Herald Tribune, November 10-11, 1979. See also "Soviet Spartakiade Touches Off Concern by Cost-Conscious Broadcasters," BM/E's World Broadcast News, 1:6, (July-August 1979), p. 4.
30. See "Olympians Reject $9.3 Million TV Bid," *New York Times*, August 13, 1975; "Europe TV Balks at Olympic Coverage," *New York Times*, December 15, 1974; and "TV Accord Reported," *New York Times*, September 10, 1975.
31. The offers which drew no Eurovision interest were: RAI's "Magic Flute" by Mozart; RTBF's "Cendrillon" opera by J. Massenet; ZDF's concert offer with Lorin Maazel; YLE's "Midsummer Night Concert," and RTBF's "Festival de la Chanson Française." While Eurovision members did not take these offers, Intervision members took the last two items. Author's analysis from the Eurovision Program Summaries (1982) of the EBU.

32. Miroslav Vilcek, "Twenty-five Years of TV Exchanges Via Eurovision," *Television*, 17, (July-August 1979), p. 10.
33. For a survey of international linguistic broadcasting associations, see Simone Courteix, *Télévisions sans frontières, un problème de coopération internationale,* (Paris: Ed. Economica, 1975), pp. 73-79. See also René Schenker, "French-language Television Broadcasting," *EBU Review,* 10B, (March 1968), pp. 13-15; Jacques Landry, "The Community of French-language Television Programs," *EBU Review,* 23:5, (September 1972), pp. 16-18; and T.S. Duckmanton, "INTERTEL — The International Television Federation," *EBU Review,* 114B, (March 1969), pp. 18-19.
34. See David Smith,"Where Soccer is King,"*TV World*, 3:12,(December 1979), p. 20.
35. Daniele Doglio, "The Ratings Winner Which Brings Balance," *TV World*, 3:1, (December, 1979), pp. 21-22; and Jim Hodgetts, "Moving into the World of 'Démocratisé'," *TV World*, 3:1, (December 1979), p. 21, respectively.
36. In descending order, they were: boxing, 18 (70 h); figure skating, 18 (56 h 30); track and field, 15 (39 h 20); Nordic skiing, 15 (24 h 25); equestrian/show jumping, 13 (42 h 10); speed ice skating, 12 (40 h 25); auto racing, 12 (21 h); rugby, 12, (15 h 05); ski jumping, 11 (20 h 35); basketball, 10 (20 h 35); bobsled, 6 (18 h 30); judo, 6 (16 h 10), table tennis, 4 (16 h 20); horse racing, 4 (5 h 45); badminton, 3 (11 h); biathlon, 3 (8 h); ski flying, 3 (6 h 15); motorcross, 3 (6 h 35); decathlon, 3 (2 h 30); motorcycle racing, 2 (14 h 40); field hockey, 2 (11 h); diving, 2 (7 h); gymnastics, 1 (2 h 05) and power boat racing, 1 (- h 50). Author's analysis from the Eurovision Program Summaries (1982) of the EBU. The transmission times are estimates.
37. Interview with Hugo Marty, former Head of Logistics, Administration and Financing for the EBU-OIRT Operations Group for the 1976 Summer Olympic Games, SSR, Bern, August 1977. One article dealing with some of the problems in organizing Olympic Games coverage has been written by a former head of an EBU-OIRT operations group, Jarle Hoysaeter, "The Games Must Go On! — But With What Kind of Radio and Television Coverage?" *EBU Review,* 27:6, (November 1976), pp. 6-10.
38. *Ibid.*
39. Interview with Richard Bunn, Head, Eurovision Program Division, EBU, Geneva, October 1979.
40. *Daily Telegraph*, April 6-7, 1965; and *Radio Times*, April 8, 1965, respectively.

41. Marcel Bezençon, "Eurovision or the Price of Fame," *EBU Review*, 85B, (May 1964), p. 9.
42. "France Refuses to Transmit Television Discussion," *The London Times*, July 11, 1963; " 'Telstar II' diffuse un colloque à quatre," *Journal de Genève*, July 11, 1963; "L'émission anniversaire de 'Telstar' n'a été vue que par des spectateurs américains," *Tribune de Genève*, July 12, 1963; "Eisenhower Hails Strong Europe in Telstar Talk," *New York Times*, July 11, 1963.
43. Observation by author, September 1982.
44. See Eduardo Contreras, James Larson, John K. Mayo and Peter Spain, *Cross-Cultural Broadcasting*, (Paris: UNESCO, 1976); and "Yugoslavs Fear Ads Undermine Ideology," *New York Times*, April 10, 1977.
45. Bunn, *op. cit.*, October 1979.
46. "Why Bargee Threw His TV Set into the Rhine," *The London Times*, September 7, 1974.
47. "Advertising," *1975 Britannica Book of the Year*, (Chicago: Encyclopedia Britannica, Inc., 1975), p. 45.
48. EBU, Principles on Advertising at Venues for Internationally Televised Sports Events, Administrative Council Decision, December 11, 1976.
49. For more about the principles and rules of conduct laid down over the years by the EBU in sports television, see Madeleine Larrue, "Sports Programs and International Television: The Legal Aspect," *EBU Review*, 110B, (July 1968), pp. 52-58; and Hans Brack, "Aspects of the Legal Committee's Work Within the Framework of the EBU, 1965-1972," *EBU Review*, 24:1, (January 1973), p. 40.
50. Bunn, *op. cit.*, October 1979.
51. *Ibid.*
52. "Lahti à la TV," *Tribune de Genève*, February 17, 1978.
53. Vincent Porter, "Television and Film Production Strategies in the European Community," *Entertainment: A Cross-Cultural Examination*, ed. Heinz-Dietrich Fischer and Stefan R. Melnik, (New York: Hastings House, Inc., 1979), p. 264. See also Hans Kimmel, "The ZDF's International Co-productions. A Medium-sized Television Organization's Experience With a Contentious Form,' *EBU Review*, 25:6, (November 1974), pp. 18-21; Robin Scott, "Going It Together. An Account of BBC Television's Experience with Co-production," *EBU Review*, 27:1, (January 1976), pp. 6-10; and Georg Kacher, "Co-producing: We Want a Share of the Action," *TV World*, 2:4, (March 1979), pp. 40-41.

54. Interview with Norma Hull, Senior Assistant, Television Program Department, EBU, Geneva, October 1977.
55. They were Terence Rattigan, (1962); Diego Fabbri, (1963); Harold Pinter, (1965); Fritz Hochwalder, (1966); Francois Billetdoux, (1967) and Ingmar Bergman, (1970).
56. Hull, *op. cit.*
57. Interview with Madeleine Larrue, Department of Legal Affairs, EBU, Geneva, August 1977.
58. "A Play on Anne Frank Theme Given Premiere on French TV," *New York Times*, January 18, 1967.
59. *Ibid.*
60. Larrue, *op. cit.*
61. EBU Doc. no. SPG 2279, *op. cit.*
62. *Ibid.*, p. 40.
63. EBU, Eurovision News Confirmation of Participation and Usage, June 30, 1977 (hereafter referred to as EVN participation sheets). Because that day's EVN-0 was canceled for lack of interest, these items were sent over EVN-1 and EVN-2.
    Up-to-date EVN confirmation and participation sheets are available from the EBU. But, with the start of the EVN-1, "choice after viewing" procedure (on a trial basis in September 1977), it is no longer possible to find out which members took what programs, particularly Intervision members.
64. *Ibid.*
65. Tapio Varis and Renny Jokelin, *Television News in Europe, A Survey of the News-film Flow in Europe,* (Tampere, Finland: University of Tampere, 1976). Tapio Varis has done some stimulating and pioneering work in Eurovision-Intervision news content analysis. See "Television News in Eurovision and Intervision," (Paper presented to the EBU Working Party on Television News, Lisbon, September 1974, O.A./5013-Com. Pro./1343). His findings are summarized in Yrjö Länsipuro, "Joint Eurovision/Intervision News Study," *EBU Review*, 26:3, (May 1975), pp. 37-40.
66. Varis and Jokelin divided the news according to the following definitions:
    Politics: This category refers to items such as elections, government crises, visits by foreign politicians, conferences and strikes.
    Disasters/social unrest: Items in this group include crimes, fires, bombings and riots.
    Sports: This category contains all kinds of sports news.
    Finance: Items in this group include monetary developments, stock exchange activities and EEC acts. In the Intervision countries, items

Eurovision Programming

like COMECON affairs, five-year plans and factory openings are classified as financial news.
Security/war: Includes police and military activities.
Social policy/science: Contains cultural events, new technical developments and inventions. Varis and Jokelin included cultural exchange activities and factory openings of a predominately non-economic nature in this group. *Ibid.,* p. 46.

67. EBU, *Weekly Liaison Bulletin,* 9, (February 27, 1979); EBU, *Weekly Liaison Bulletin,* 2, (January 10, 1979); and EVN Participation Sheets for October 1, 1978 and October 3, 1978, respectively.
68. For an account of how the presentation of news has changed with the arrival of new news gathering and distributing technologies, see Anthony Smith, *The Shadow in the Cave, A Study of the Relationship Between the Broadcaster, His Audience and the State,* (London: Quartet Books, 1976), pp. 158-164.
69. Doherty, *op. cit.*
70. Varis and Jokelin, *Television News in Europe,, op. cit.,* p. 61.
71. Smith, *The Shadow in the Cave, op. cit.,* pp. 171-172.
72. Varis and Jokelin, *Television News in Europe, op. cit.,* p. 62.
73. EVN Participation Sheets of October 20, 1979.
74. *Ibid.,* October 14, 1979.
75. See Smith, *The Shadow in the Cave, op. cit.,* pp. 171-172.
76. *Ibid.*
77. EVN Participation Sheets for December 14, 1978.
78. EBU, *Weekly Liaison Bulletin,* 9, *op. cit.*
79. EVN Participation Sheets for November 11, 1978.
80. Smith, *The Shadow in the Cave, op. cit.,* p. 172.
81. EVN Participation Sheets for October 28, 1978 and October 1, 1978, respectively.
82. Doherty, *op. cit.*
83. EVN Participation Sheets for October 2-3, 1979.
84. For an account of the importance of human-interest items in national news programs, see Smith, *The Shadow in the Cave, op. cit.,* p. 172.
85. *Ibid.*
86. John E. Ruby, "The Daily News Exchange Scheme of the European Broadcasting Union," (Master's thesis, Indiana University, May 1965), pp. 79-80.
87. Charles E. Sherman and John E. Ruby, "The Eurovision News Exchange," *Journalism Quarterly,* 51:4, (Autumn 1974), p. 485.
88. Ruby, "The Daily News Exchange Scheme of the European Broadcasting Union," *op. cit.,* p. 79.

89. "La TV romande et l'empereur Bokassa Ier, un faux pas," *Journal de Geneve*, December 6, 1977; and EVN Participation Sheets for December 5, 1977.
90. Doherty, *op. cit.*
91. EBU, Weekly Liaison Bulletin, 4, (August 12, 1974).
92. For a description of the old EVN news selection system, see Pierre Brunel-Lantenac, "Live from the Eurovision Newsroom in Geneva —A Day Like Any Other," *EBU Review*, 26:3, (May 1975), pp. 11-14.
93. On October 15, 1977, for example, Visnews offered pictures of a chimpanzee's heart being transplanted into a human with a statement by Dr. Christiaan Barnard. But the offer proved misleading because the film was library material showing a classic transplant. Visnews admitted the error, but only after the item had gone out over the network. EBU, Weekly Liaison Bulletin, 45, (December 15, 1977).
94. EBU, Weekly Liaison Bulletin, 4, *op. cit.*
95. *Ibid.*
96. *Ibid.*
97. See EBU, Weekly Liaison Bulletin, 45, (November 13, 1978).
98. Doherty, *op. cit.*
99. Interview with Miroslav Vilcek, Director, Television Program Department, EBU, Geneva, March 1980.

CHAPTER 6
INTERVISION PROGRAMMING

Like elsewhere in the world, Intervision members exchange programs to satisfy the need for program variety. But Intervision also satisfies the need for programs which show the development of Socialism. Indeed, supporting the policies of the party and the government is an important media objective for most Intervision countries. Showing Socialism's development, however, also requires preventing the reception of foreign programs which may disrupt social cohesion. The need for supporting Socialism plays at least as great a role as popular taste in explaining why members exchange what they do.

This chapter looks inside the Intervision program and news exchange. It is divided into the following sections: *1)* the rate of participation and exchange, *2)* the content of the Intervision program exchange, and *3)* the content of the Intervision news exchange.

6.1 Intervision Traffic

The younger, smaller Intervision network exchanges more programs than the older, larger Eurovision network. In 1982, the nine Intervision member states originated a greater number of programs (1,898 programs versus 874) and for a longer duration (1,910 hours compared with 1,179) than the 34 Eurovision members combined. The growth rate also has been significant in recent years. From 1972 to 1982, the volume of traffic increased over 11 percent a year (Fig. 6-1).

Intervision news traffic is smaller than its Eurovision counterpart (5,205 items versus 7,636 in 1982). Nevertheless, it is increasingly becoming an important part of Intervision. Figure 6-2 shows that the number of news items exchanged has been rapidly growing, at an average annual rate of more than seven percent in the ten years ending in 1982.

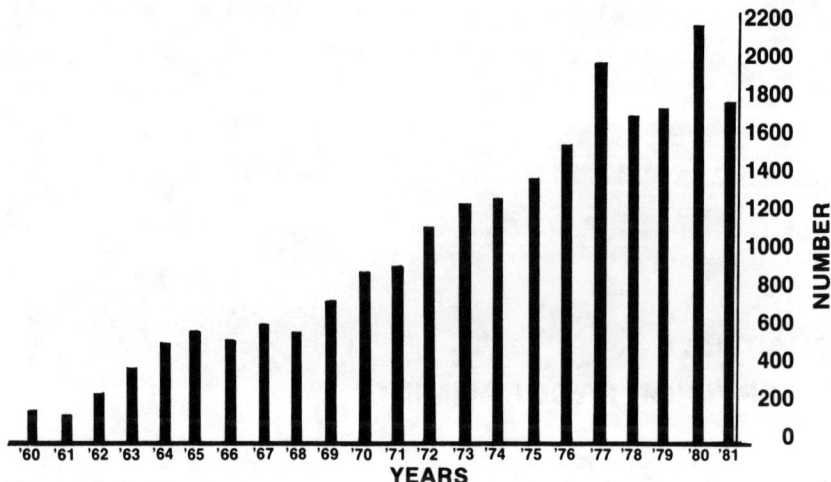

Figure 6-1
Growth of the Intervision Program Exchange 1960-1981
Source: OIRT

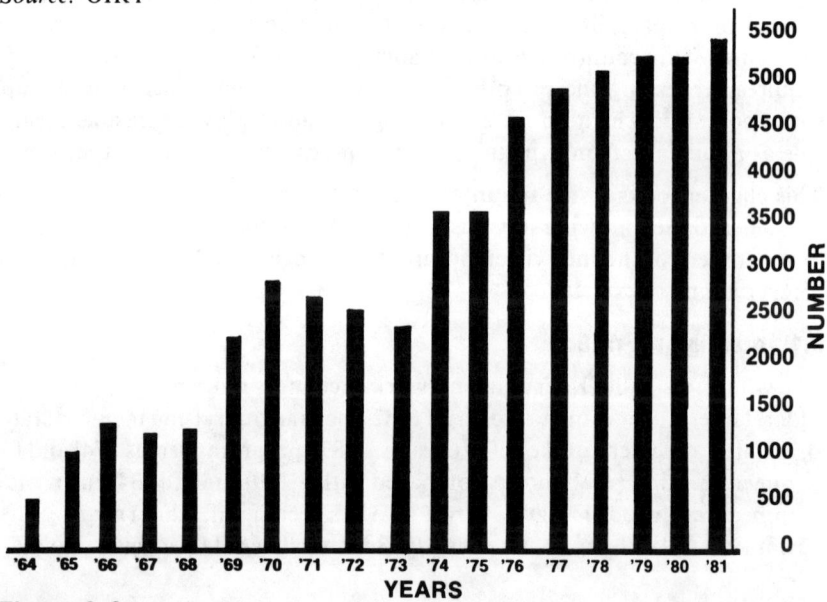

Figure 6-2
Growth of the Intervision News Exchange 1964-1981 *Source:* OIRT

The reasons for Intervision's rapid growth in traffic are numerous. The routing of Intervision transmissions still requires the participation of many members. Because of the traditional lack of international circuits, certain countries still must participate to relay an Intervision program over their national network so it may reach other members. By contrast, Eurovision circuits are permanently leased for international use.

Intervision's growth also owes much of its momentum to cost factors. Because transmission costs are usually covered in state budgets, Intervision members can send many programs — particularly cultural and artistic — which their West European counterparts would not exchange due to the high costs of Eurovision circuits. In addition, Intervision is a recourse for broadcasters who wish to produce more programming that is cost-effective. In July 1982, for example, the East German government decreed that while cuts would be made in television transmission times and production budgets, considerable cost savings should be achieved through a greater exchange of news, current affairs, and "similar ideological work to advance State goals" through Intervision.[1]

Eurovision also aids Intervision's growth. Intervision countries receive a great number of programs and news stories from Western Europe and elsewhere in the world through Eurovision. As we shall see in Chapter Seven, Intervision typically takes about 50 percent of the Eurovision and EVN transmissions. Moreover, Eurovision provides Intervision members access to news agency materials.

Furthermore, the volume of the program and news traffic depends upon the availability of events showing the development of Socialism. Without question, the marked increase in the number of Intervision exchanges in 1977 and 1980 is largely the result of important Soviet events including the sixtieth anniversary of the Russian Revolution in 1977 and the Moscow Olympics in 1980. The showing of events marking numerous economic, scientific, and cultural achievements, many of which are sent over Intervision, is an important policy of Socialist broadcasters.

Table 6-1 summarizes who gives the most Intervision program hours. Typically, about 35 percent of Intervision's programs come from the USSR. A survey of the Intervision program statistics from 1960 to 1982 shows that, with the exception of 1972-1974, the USSR originated the most programs (Appendix 0). East Germany and Czechoslovakia also make significant contributions.

The reasons most programs come from the Soviet Union are numerous. The USSR is the largest, most powerful and most important Socialist country in Europe. In addition, the media policies followed throughout the Socialist bloc were first applied in the USSR on a large scale. The large contribution of East Germany may be partly explained by the quality of its programs — ranked by many to be the best in Intervision countries. As Burton Paulu, in his study *Radio and Television Broadcasting in Eastern Europe*, remarked, the high quality of East German broadcasting owes much to the competition

Table 6-1
Origins of Intervision Programs
Rank order of members according to total hours of transmission

Rank Order	1971	Program Hours	Rank Order	1976	Program Hours	Rank Order	1982	Program Hours
1	USSR	205	1	USSR	664	1	USSR	719
2	East Germany	150	2	East Germany	395	2	Czechoslovakia	329
3	Czechoslovakia	144	3	Czechoslovakia	268	3	East Germany	311
4	Poland	127	4	Poland	232	4	Hungary	253
5	Bulgaria	116	5	Bulgaria	75	5	Bulgaria	103
6	Hungary	54	6	Hungary	74	6	Poland	82
7	Rumania	52	7	Rumania	48	7	Rumania	43
8	Finland	26	8	Finland	10	8	Finland	29
			9	Cuba	7	9	Cuba	21

Source: OIRT

Intervision Programming

with the West German networks.[2] Intervision's early years did see an attempt to balance members' contributions. In practice, however, it proved difficult, if not impossible, because events change sites frequently.[3]

Table 6-2 shows who takes the most Intervision programs. The big organizations surpass the small in program reception. Typically, Intervision contributes about 10 percent to national program output.[4]

The news exchange is becoming an important activity of Intervision. Figure 6-3 shows an upward trend in Intervision news origins. Of the 5,205 stories transmitted in the 1982 IVNs, Czechoslovak television originated the most, with 20 percent. The second largest contributions came from Soviet and

Table 6-2

Participation in the Intervision Program Exchange in 1974[5]

Rank Order		Total hours relayed
1	EAST GERMANY	877 hrs.
2	USSR	806
3	CZECHOSLOVAKIA	753
4	POLAND	623
5	HUNGARY	415
6	BULGARIA	404
7	RUMANIA	359
8	FINLAND	1

Source: OIRT

Polish television, each with 17 percent. The remaining items were supplied as follows: East Germany, 14 percent; Bulgaria, 11 percent; Hungary, 9 percent; Cuba, 5 percent; Rumania, 5 percent; and Vietnam, 1 percent. The countries which supplied the least were Algeria and Finland, each with less than 1 percent[6] Still, Soviet television is traditionally the largest supplier to IVN. In a ten-year period ending in 1982, the Soviets originated an average of 25 percent of the exchange. Largely because of a shortage of circuits, Vietnamese television can only offer, not receive IVN items today.

The gradual growth curves in Figure 6-4 show that East European and Soviet television significantly depend upon Intervision for their foreign news, particularly the small countries. Czechoslovakia traditionally takes the most IVN items. From 1972 to 1982, it took an average of 56 percent of the exchange. But recent years have seen a sharp increase in reception by the smallest IVN member, Cuba. In 1982, Cuba picked up the most offers, 3,682, or 71 percent of the offers. Czechoslovak television was second with 3,650, or 70 percent; followed by Poland with 3,161, or 61 percent; USSR with 2,556, or 49 percent; Bulgaria with 2,514, or 48 percent; Hungary with 2,223, or 43 percent; East Germany with 1,858, or 36 percent; and Rumania with 1,105, or

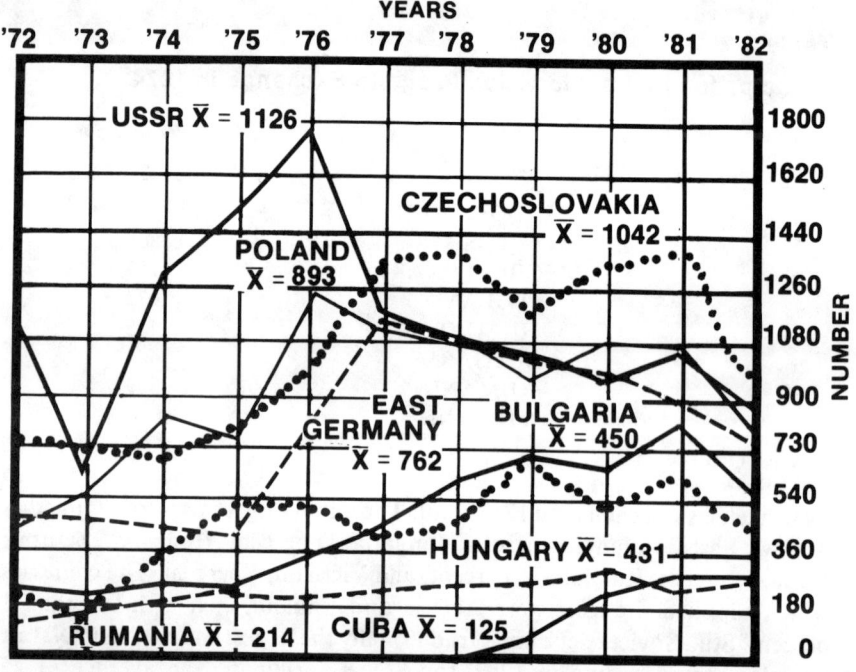

Figure 6-3
Average Number of News Items Originated in Intervision 1972-1982
Source: OIRT

Intervision Programming

21 percent. Algerian television also took 1,724 items, or 33 percent while Finnish television accepted 41 items from Intervision in 1982.[7] Although technically connected with IVN, YLE/Finland takes few items because the timing of IVN-1 is unsuitable for Finland. Moreover, YLE finds it more economical to take Intervision news via Vienna, which is Eurovision's coordination center for IVN.[8]

Interestingly, Japanese television also depends upon IVN. In 1981, Japan's second largest commercial station, TV Asahi, joined the OIRT to get IVN stories which are canceled by EVN for lack of interest. Because EVN requires the acceptance of a minimum of three members before an item is transmitted, TV Asahi can order an item from IVN which it receives by satellite through Western Europe. The item is transmitted from Prague to Vienna to an earth station in Raisting, West Germany, where the signal is linked up to an INTELSAT satellite and linked down to Tokyo. In 1981, TV Asahi accepted fifteen IVN items.[9]

Generally, the small nations use more exchanged material than the big

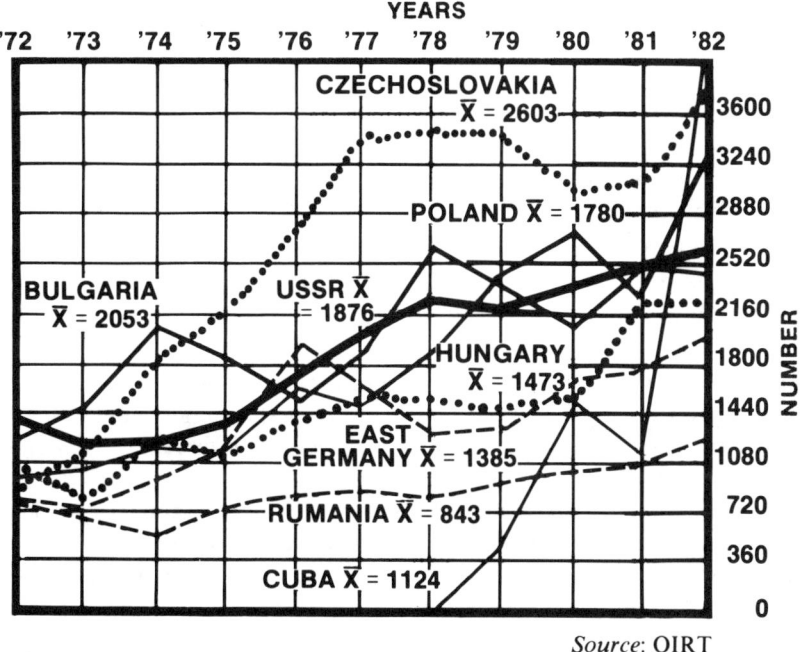

Source: OIRT

Figure 6-4
Average Number of Intervision News Items Received 1972-1982

countries. The big networks such as TSS/USSR and DDR-F/East Germany are able to produce video material by themselves with the aid of their own correspondents and film crews. In 1977, Moscow TV had more than fifty correspondents around the world, half of whom have their own film crews.[10] The heavy use of foreign material (mostly Soviet) in Bulgaria and Czechoslovakia may be partly explained by the fact that these countries are the Soviets' most dependent allies. Rumania, the only member of the Warsaw Pact to chart a foreign policy independent of Moscow's, takes the least amount of IVN items, although it devotes more air time to news than do Czechoslovak, Hungarian, and Polish television.[11] Another reason for the heavy use of Soviet material by Bulgaria is that on Fridays, Bulgarian television transmits the programs of Soviet television's Channel 1.[12]

6.2 Intervision Program Exchange

In addition to a higher volume of program traffic, Intervision exchanges far more varied kinds of programs than those of its West European counterpart. Unlike Eurovision, where sports account for over 80 percent of transmissions, Intervision members exchange nearly as many entertainment, cultural, and current affairs programs as sports. Indeed, Intervision can be pictured as a current affairs network (see Appendix K). In the ten years ending in 1982, the largest group of programs on Intervision was current affairs with 27 percent of the annual exchange. Sports programs were second, with 26 percent; followed by entertainment, with 22 percent; culture with 21 percent, and children's programs with 4 percent. A recent exception was in 1980 which was the year of the Moscow Olympic Games. Although most Western broadcasters surely would applaud the diverse and balanced exchange, they would disapprove of the political content of many Intervision programs. The consensus, prompted largely by Socialism, helps promote the exchange of Intervision programs.

Admittedly, obstacles to Intervision exchanges exist. All East European countries and the USSR serve substantial foreign-language populations.[13] Hungary and Rumania's unique languages complicate Intervision exchanges and increase costs.[14] Furthermore, the historical, social, and racial differences among Intervision countries are reflected in varying program tastes. The American television educational series "Sesame Street" was regularly shown on Polish and Yugoslav television, but banned on Soviet television as imperialistic.[15]

Despite the obstacles, sports, variety shows, series, operas, and children's television programs are as popular in Eastern Europe and the USSR as elsewhere in the world. According to a 1974 UNESCO study, nearly 10 percent of total television time in Eastern Europe is taken up by entertainment (about the same as in Western Europe) — except in Poland, where entertainment shows account for as much as 31 percent of the air time.[16] And like elsewhere in the world, the need for more entertainment programs has led most Socialist broadcasters to turn to imports largely because they cannot fulfill the demand themselves. Aside from other Socialist countries, Intervision members have come to rely on British, West German, and American programs.[17] One reason for the popularity of entertainment shows in Eastern Europe and the USSR is that they provide relief from the heavily didactic and propagandistic content of many programs.[18]

The enormous cultural traditions of Intervision countries also contribute to the high exchange of non-sports programs. East European and Soviet television are rich in cultural content, including theater, concerts, and opera. In Rumania and the USSR, music programs take up about 10 percent of the total — more than any West European country.[19] The reasons for the high priority which Socialist countries place on the performing arts — often lavish support despite low living standards — are partly traditional.[20] The USSR and its imperial predecessor have a good record in music with Russian composers, ballet, and opera winning widespread popularity.

Socialism, however, plays at least as big — if not even bigger — a role as mass taste and cultural heritage in explaining the large and varied Intervision program exchange. The direct state control of broadcasting — the practice in all East European countries and the USSR — implies that the government generally pays the expensive transmission circuits. Thus, being free of this financial burden, broadcasters can use Intervision to exchange kinds of television programs which their West European counterparts would likely send via the cheaper mail or air cargo service.

The similarly patterned social, economic, and political systems of Intervision countries also provide a compatibility of program values. The major belief and priority within a Socialist society, is that the primary job of television, as an instrument of government, is to support the policies of the party and the government.

Intervision programs frequently show the building up of Socialism in Eastern Europe and the USSR. Throughout much of 1982, for example, Intervision relayed numerous programs related to fulfilling the decisions of the twenty-sixth Congress of the CPSU, the sixty-fifth anniversary of the establishment of the USSR, and Salyut space flights. A year earlier, the OIRT General Assembly recommended that members give full coverage to:
> the implementation of decisions passed by the Party Congress of Communist and Workers parties in the Socialist countries and measures taken for the purpose of economic and cultural development and in favor the Socialist economic integration of the COMECON member countries. The OIRT will

cover the sixtieth anniversary of the existence of the USSR, the fortieth anniversary of the beginning of the USSR's Great Patriotic War, the twenty-fifth anniversary of the USSR Government Declaration Concerning the Foundations of Development and Further Consolidation of Friendship and Cooperation Between the USSR and Other Socialist Countries, the twentieth anniversary of the proclamation of the Cuban Revolution's Socialist character, the one hundredth anniversary of G. Dimotrov's birth, the thirty-fifth anniversary of the foundation of UNESCO and additional events.[21]

The frequent reporting of numerous economic, scientific, and cultural achievements is openly acknowledged as fulfilling various important political and social functions such as molding the Communist personality.[22] But such programs also appear to help offset the many shortages and limitations the public has to accept such as housing and consumer goods.[23] Similar ideas on education shared by East European countries and the USSR may also explain the significant exchange of children's programs — something that Eurovision has been unable to do. The Marxist-Leninist principles of education, chief of which is building a "new Communist man" who will work for the common good in restructuring economic and social institutions, are reflected in most Socialist children's educational programs.[24] In addition, the Socialist media policy of state control of both television and cinema production may also explain the high exchange of children's broadcasts.[25] Of all Intervision members, Bulgaria gives the most air time to children's television — 15 percent of its total air time — followed by the USSR with 12 percent.[26] Of the 1,898 Intervision programs exchanged in 1982, 54 were children's programs.[27] That same year, Eurovision did not exchange any children's programs. J.D. Halloran and P.R.C. Elliott, in their study of the exchange of children's television programs in Western Europe, concluded that one reason for the small exchange of children's and young people's programs is the "national" nature of so many programs. Further, they wrote that "much of the excitement and guts of television comes from its national basis and that European rivalries are more important and more attractive than European consciousness."[28] Although Eurovision is void of children's programs, we have already noted in Chapter Three that the EBU Television Program Committee is active in promoting the exchange of children's and young people's films.

Intervision programs also can be used to support governmental policies such as anti-dissident activities. In March 1976, Czechoslovak television originated a forty-five minute Intervision program which attacked Alexander Dubcek and his supporters and accused the CIA of being responsible for the 1968 "Prague Spring." Political observers interpreted the public attack on Dubcek as a warning against dissident activities.[29]

But Socialism also implies that Intervision members should not exchange programs apt to poorly reflect the policies of the party and of the government. Because organized religion is deemed as an enemy of the communist doctrine, Intervision does not transmit religious programs. Eurovision exchanged twenty-two religious programs in 1982.[30]

6.3 Intervision News Exchange

In every single society which broadcasts on any scale, news is under instruction to be objective. But the meanings given to the concept of objectivity can vary greatly in time and place.[31] In the Socialist countries of Europe, news reporters give priority to selecting and interpreting those stories which portray the development of Socialism, while deliberately omitting or delaying those items apt to embarrass the regime.

A guide to what is "news" in the Socialist countries of Europe is provided by the Intervision news story list which is telexed to participating members. On June 30, 1977, the following nineteen stories were transmitted.

> *Czechoslovakia*: — aftermath of derailment of international "meridian" express train. — further coverage of international ideological conference sponsored by the magazine "questions of peace and socialism" + speech by gdr delegate paul werner. — czechosl. president husak meeting soviet delegate at the prague conference ponomarev. — president husak receiving delegation of the baas party. — premier strougal meeting chairman of soviet committee for foreign trade relations shachkov. — strougal meeting member of yugoslav union committee markovich. — congress of national czechoslovak party. *Hungary*: — summer session of hungarian parliament. *Bulgaria*: bulgarian state council chairman zhivkov meeting chairman of czechosl. trade unions hoffman. — film shows: industrial plants built with soviet help. *Rumania*: — rumanian president ceausescu meeting zapu chairman nkomo. — session of rumanian national assembly. *USSR*: — tss correspondent commenting on pre-election campaigns in japan. — interview by gdr delegate at moscow conference on women's position in today's society. — conference on relations between ussr and mexico. — rally of solidarity with korean people. *Poland*: — edward gierek meeting willi brandt + brandt visiting the gdansk region and the former concentration camp at sztutowo. *East Germany*: — reporting on housing in the neubrandenburg district. — conference of artists' union on preparations for arts exhibition at leipzig.[32]

As can be seen, most Intervision offers concern politics. Tapio Varis and Renny Jokelin found, in their analysis of IVN offer telexes from 1973 to 1975 (January to March), that the most frequently exchanged subject was politics, with over 40 percent of transmissions (Table 6-3).[33] Closely following politics is the reporting of cultural, social and scientific achievements, with over 31 percent of transmissions. These included film reports on factory openings, fairs, art exhibits, space flights, and inventions. Economic stories were third, with over 13 percent. Typical features concerned summaries of five-year plans, reports on workers on their farms and in their fields, reports on the "heroes" of the year's harvest, public works projects and COMECON affairs. Sports reports took up less than 9 percent of IVN transmissions. Members took even fewer war and disaster stories.

Table 6-3
Contents of the Intervision News Exchange 1973-1975 (January-March)

	1973		1974		1975	
	Feeds	Percent	Feeds	Percent	Feeds	Percent
Politics	253	46	314	38	316	36
Sports	50	9	97	12	63	7
Disasters	8	2	17	2	7	1
Security, War	28	5	16	2	2	0
Economic	51	9	96	12	182	20
Cultural, Social, Scientific	153	28	249	31	306	35
Others	6	1	19	3	10	1
Total	549	100	808	100	886	100

Source: Tapio Varis and Renny Jokelin, *Television News in Europe, A Survey of the News-film Flow in Europe,* (Tampere, Finland: University of Tampere, 1976), p. 76.

Of course, members take news items because the network provides them with same-day news coverage, particularly of events from other Socialist countries. Like their counterparts elsewhere in the world, Socialist news editors realize that old events are less interesting and less useful. As early as 1960, four years before IVN was created, television news executives were studying ways to speed up the collection and dissemination of film about news in other Socialist countries. One scheme, submitted to the OIRT in 1963, called for the creation of a television newsfilm agency. Major aims of this proposed agency, which would be either attached to an existing agency such as TASS or run separately, included: *1)* supplying Intervision services with news from the Socialist countries; *2)* ensuring the distribution of film on Socialist states to non-Socialist countries; and *3)* preparing film from non-Socialist states according to Socialist requirements. The project, however, never came about partly because of its high costs and partly because the tasks of the proposed agency were fulfilled by the start of IVN.[34] Today, Intervision members are giving much attention to increasing the topicality and speed of IVN — among the basic problems of the exchange.[35]

Undoubtedly, members also give priority to events which are part of a long-running story, and which will tend to interest a "mass" audience.[36] Nevertheless, Socialism is clearly the global common denominator in explaining why members exchange what they do. Or, as the Head of the Intervision News Exchange put it: "IVN has become the first and most important source of pictorial material on the events of the day in the Socialist countries. IVN materials reflect the intensification of co-operation and integration among countries of the Socialist community."[37]

News reporting in any society involves political questions, but especially so in the Socialist bloc, since they provide opportunities for supporting Socialism.[38] Intervision news editors give priority to events which tend to mark the development of Socialist integration. As Varis and Jokelin documented, much of IVN's political items related to international visits and conferences, with particular attention to reporting visits of government and party leaders from other Socialist states.[39] There also are many stories about Socialist achievements. The volume of news of the thirtieth anniversary of the victory over "Hitlerite fascism" was so great that a second IVN had to be set up from April to May 1975 in order to ease the burden on the normal exchange.[40] Aside from fulfilling important social and political functions, covering events showing the strengthening of Socialism helps to offset the many shortages and limitations of everyday life.

Showing the building up of Socialism, however, also requires that news about events which tend to disrupt social cohesion be censored. The media are permitted and even encouraged to look into issues such as street repair, housing shortages, and garbage collection. But they invariably stop short of finding wrongdoing in government, the party, or basic political concepts.

Politically sensitive stories are often delayed or omitted. For example, the Czechoslovak press first denounced the dissident manifesto Charter 77 a week after it was published in the West.[41] In 1980, the extreme sensitivity of the Polish labor strikes and the threat they posed to the whole Socialist bloc were emphasized by the Soviet decision to jam Western broadcasts and by the almost total silence in the Soviet media about Poland which prevailed nearly a month.[42] East German media first reported the establishment of independent trade unions in Poland ten days after the Warsaw government had signed agreements with strikers allowing them to be set up.[43] The reporting of East European and Soviet airline crashes also are deemed taboo unless foreigners are aboard or unless too many rumors circulate.[44] A collision between two Czechoslovak airliners on the ground at Prague airport on January 2, 1974, went publicly unreported, coming to light only from diplomatic and local sources.[45]

The reluctance of Socialist newsmen to report negative events clearly reflects itself in IVN. Varis and Jokelin observed that, of the many political offers, few related to government policy.[46] They also found that military news and disaster stories were the kind of news least likely to be exchanged. Moreover, while Middle East and energy problems were among the top EVN stories in 1975, they did not make up a major category in Intervision news.[47]

Strikes, crashes, and other negative phenomena are rarely reported because they poorly portray Socialist society. Professor Burton Paulu puts it this way: "These are not regarded as sufficiently important, in any case, since the ultimate purpose of broadcasting is to build the Communist society, too much reporting of that kind might provide bad examples at the same time that it takes space and time from items of more basic and lasting importance."[48]

Marx and Lenin might well have commended Intervision's role in Socialist societies. Although Marx rarely addressed the role of mass media, Alex Inkles in his study *Public Opinion in Soviet Russia,* remarks that "the Marxist concept of unity and the sharp distinction between right and wrong would not permit the press to function as a fourth estate."[49] Also from what Marx wrote about material determinism suggests that the working class would have to own the means and facilities of mass communication in order to have fair access.[50]

Lenin defined the social role of the mass media in Socialist society in his popular description of the press as a "collective propagandist, agitator, and organizer." Lenin saw that the party could not be an effective teacher, guide and leader of the masses in building a Socialist society without control over the media. For Lenin, the media represented a "driving belt" between the party and the masses, preventing the party from being isolated from the masses, while facilitating the fulfillment of goals set by party and government. Intervision developed as a response as much to Marxist-Leninist belief as to the gradual arrival of television links among Socialist countries of Europe.

After nearly thirty years of experience with television, however, Socialist broadcasters are in the midst of attempting to broaden the scope and depth of television news, perhaps, because programming which amounts to nothing other than one long commercial for Marxist-Leninist ideology can result in turned-off sets. Within Intervision, television editors are attempting to widen the scope of IVN items.[51] News offers will surely continue to stress mainly ideological messages, but they are trying to present such material in a more interesting way to viewers. The head of Intervision News Exchange wrote that the Intervision Group of Experts in News Exchange in 1973 judged that better

IVN quality meant:

> Thematical as well as journalistic one-sidedness and stereotyped monotony of forms are regarded as negative features. The necessity was further stressed to replace the predominantly official and merely protocol items by thematically wider information on events and processes from all fields of social life. Materials dealing with protocol events on the highest level have to be presented. They should, however, be thoroughly prepared with due journalistic skill so that their influence on the viewer corresponds to the importance of the event concerned.[52]

6.4 Conclusion

Intervision's ability to exchange television programs across political borders is largely a matter of how closely they respond to the requirements of Socialism. The major belief and priority within a Socialist broadcasting station is that television's primary job is to support the policies of the party and the government. At the same time, however, there is a converse force operating within program judgment which forces into obscurity events which poorly reflect party and government policies. Viewers in Intervision countries will see many programs about factories fulfilling their five-year plans, although they will not see reports of plane crashes and labor strikes. Marx and Lenin might well have commended Intervision's role in supporting Socialism.

Endnotes
Chapter 6

1. Steve Smith, "East Germany: Different System, Similar Problems," *BM/E's World Broadcast News*, 5:2, (October 1982), p. 21.
2. Burton Paulu, *Radio and Television Broadcasting in Eastern Europe*, (Minneapolis: University of Minnesota Press, 1974), p. 222.
3. Interview with Jerzy Rutkowski, former chief-engineer of Polish Television, Geneva, November 1976.
4. Interview with Dr. Ales Poledne, Editor, OIRT, Prague, November 1975.
5. These are the latest figures made public.
6. "Statistik des Aktualitatenaustausches zwischen den Intervisionslandern 1966-1982," (unpublished OIRT document).
7. *Ibid.*
8. Correspondence with Marja Salusjarvi, International Relations, YLE, Helsinki, September 1975.
9. Interview with F. Benkö, Deputy Director of the Technical Center, OIRT, Prague, May 1982. Figure from "Statistik des Aktualitatenaustausches zwischen den Intervisionslandern 1966-1982," *op. cit.*
10. Frank Gillard, "TV Watching in Russia," *Atlas World Press Review*, 24:11, (November 1977), p. 46.
11. See Tapio Varis and Renny Jokelin, *Television News In Europe, A*

Survey of the News-film Flow in Europe, (Tampere, Finland: University of Tampere, 1976).
12. *Ibid.*, p. 25.
13. See *World Radio TV Handbook – 1982*, (Hvidovie: Billboard A.G., 1982).
14. Paulu, *Radio and Television Broadcasting in Eastern Europe, op. cit.*, p. 14.
15. "Red Lands to see 'Sesame Street'," *New York Times*, March 20, 1972; and "'Sesame Street' Denounced by Soviets as Imperialistic," *New York Times*, August 17, 1973.
16. Kaarle Nordenstreng and Tapio Varis, *Television Traffic – A One-Way Street? A Survey and Analysis of the International Flow of Television Program Material*, (Paris: UNESCO, 1974), pp. 17-18.
17. *Ibid.*, pp. 23-25. See Len Scott, "Culture Ranks High in Hungarian Broadcasting," *BM/E's World Broadcast News*, 4:7, (March 1982), pp. 55-62; and "Polish Broadcasting: Homegrown from the Start," *BM/E's World Broadcast News*, 3:2, (October 1980), pp. 14-17.
18. James Feron, "TV Fare Stirs Up Budapest Debate," *New York Times*, January 12, 1972. See also David E. Powell, "Television in the USSR," *The Public Opinion Quarterly*, 39:3, (Fall 1975), pp. 287-295.
19. Nordenstreng and Varis, *Television Traffic – A One-Way Street?, op. cit.*, pp. 22-25.
20. Paulu, *Radio and Television Broadcasting in Eastern Europe, op. cit.*, pp. 151-153.
21. "30th Session of the OIRT General Assembly," *OIRT Information*, no. 5, (1981), p. 3.
22. For more about Socialist media functions, see Nikolai S. Mansurov, "The Study of the Mass Communications and Cultural Establishments in the USSR. Some Results of Sociological Resesarch," *Entertainment: A Cross-Cultural Examination*, ed. Heinz-Dietrich Fischer and Stefan R. Melnik, (New York: Hastings House, 1979), pp. 153-178; "Sound and Picture from Moscow: Interview with S.G. Lapin," *OIRT Radio-Television*, 3, (1982), pp. 7-9; and M. Susha, "Stages of Process," *OIRT Radio-Television*, 4, (1978), pp. 2-5.
23. Paulu, *Radio and Television Broadcasting in Eastern Europe, op. cit.*, p. 111.
24. See "Ideologies — Political Principles of Preparing Educational and Instructional Radio Programs," *OIRT Radio-Television*, 2, (1978), pp. 13-18; and "La Television Sovietique — a l'education nationale," *OIRT Radio-Television*, 3, (1978). pp. 6-18.
25. See Bruno Edera, "An International Survey of the Animated Film in Television," *EBU Review*, 31:1, (January 1980), pp. 10-24.

26. Nordenstreng and Varis, *Television Traffic - A One-Way Street?, op. cit.*, pp. 24-25.
27. See Appendix K.
28. J.D. Halloran and P.R.C. Elliott, *Television for Children and Young People*, (Geneva: EBU, 1970), p. 6.
29. "Prague TV Attacks Dubcek, Hints of CIA Links Since '68," *International Herald Tribune*, March 12, 1976.
30. See Appendix H.
31. See Anthony Smith, *The Shadow in the Cave, A Study of the Relationship Between the Broadcaster, His Audience and the State*, (London: Quartet Books, 1976), pp. 164-177.
32. For the purpose of comparing EVN-IVN participation in Chapter Seven, a more recent IVN offer telex could not be used. With the start of EVN-1, "choice after viewing" in September 1977 it has become difficult to determine individual Intervision reception of EVN offers.
33. See Varis and Jokelin, *Television News in Europe, op. cit.*, pp. 75-80.
34. Waclaw Wygledowski, *Daily News Exchange on the Intervision Network 1964-1976*, (Prague: OIRT, 1977), pp. 12-13.
35. *Ibid.*, pp. 7-9.
36. *Ibid.*, pp. 13-14.
37. *Ibid.*, p. 13.
38. A short bibliography describing Socialist news values would include: R.A. Boretsky and A. Yurovsky, *Television Journalism*, (Prague: International Organization of Journalists, 1970); and Harry J. Skornia, *Television and News: A Critical Appraisal*, (Palo Alto: Pacific Books, 1973).
39. Varis and Jokelin, *Television News in Europe, op. cit.*, pp. 76-77.
40. Wygledowski, *Daily News Exchange on the Intervision Network 1964-1976, op. cit.*, p. 10.
41. "Dissidents Denounced in Czech Press," *International Herald Tribune*, January 13, 1977.
42. See David Tonge, "Moscow Jams BBC, Voice of America," *Financial Times*, August 21, 1980; David Satter, "Russians Given Only the Barest Details," *Financial Times*, August 26, 1980; and David Satter, "Russia Says Polish Crisis is 'Internal Matter'," *Financial Times*, August 27, 1980.
43. "Polish Press Hits Strikes As Worker Unrest Goes On," *International Herald Tribune*, September 10, 1980.
    One unexpected result of the 1980 Polish strikes was that a reformist zeal developed in the state-controlled media. Before the imposition of

marshal law in 1981, the Polish media gave considerable time to the views of the free trade unionists and of the Catholic Church. See "Moscow's Polish Crisis," *Newsweek*, December 8, 1980, p. 11; and "Polish Roman Catholic Primate, Cardinal Stefan Wyszynski, Given Air Time," *Financial Times*, August 26, 1980.

44. Paulu, *Radio and Television Broadcasting in Eastern Europe, op. cit.*, p. 115.
45. Malcolm W. Browne, "Prague Mishap Adds to Fears on East European Air Safety," *International Herald Tribune*, January 24, 1974.
46. Varis and Jokelin, *Television News in Europe, op. cit.*, p. 77.
47. *Ibid.*
48. Paulu, *Radio and Television Broadcasting in Eastern Europe, op. cit.*, p. 115.
49. Alex Inkeles, *Public Opinion in Soviet Russia: A Study in Mass Persuasion*, (Cambridge: Harvard University Press, 1958), p. 34.
50. *Ibid.*
51. See Gillard, "TV Watching in Russia," *op. cit.*, p. 46; and Paulu, *Radio and Television Broadcasting in Eastern Europe*, pp. 118-120.
52. Waclaw Wygledowski, "20,000 News Items Within 10 Years of IVN Exchange," *OIRT Radio-Television*, no. 4, (1974), p. 4.

CHAPTER 7
EUROVISION — INTERVISION PROGRAMMING

When the Eurovision and Intervision networks were formally linked together in 1960, West and East European television viewers were able to watch the same programs. The beginning of the formal exchange promised to bring free trading of programming. Unfortunately, that promise has not been borne out. A one-way street has developed where viewers in Intervision countries see far more Eurovision programs than vice versa.

This chapter looks at this imbalance in exchanging programs and examines why it developed. The chapter studies *1)* the rate of participation and exchange, *2)* the content of the Eurovision-Intervision program exchange, and *3)* the content of the Eurovision-Intervision news exchange.

7.1 Eurovision-Intervision Traffic

In the past ten years ending in 1982, Intervision members have taken an average of 51 percent of all Eurovision transmissions a year, while Eurovision has taken only 8 percent of all Intervision programs. Figure 7-1 shows this quite well. In addition to this lopsided exchange, the number of programs exchanged from year to year has fluctuated widely. Intervision reception of Eurovision programs peak in Olympic years and years when World Cup football finals are held. Eurovision reception of Intervision programs fell to its lowest point in 1968 — the year of the Warsaw Pact invasion of Czechoslovakia (see Appendix L).

Figure 7-2 shows that the one-way flow also extends to the Eurovision-Intervision news exchange. The number of television news stories traveling from Western to Socialist Europe far outnumber those going in the opposite direction. From 1972 to 1982, Intervision members took an average of 71 percent of all EVN items. In some years, as in 1980 and 1982, the number of EVN items taken by Intervision exceeded those originated by its own members. Meanwhile, the record of Eurovision reception of IVN items has been poor. In the ten years ending in 1982, an average of 7 percent of all IVN offers were accepted by Eurovision members (see Appendix M).

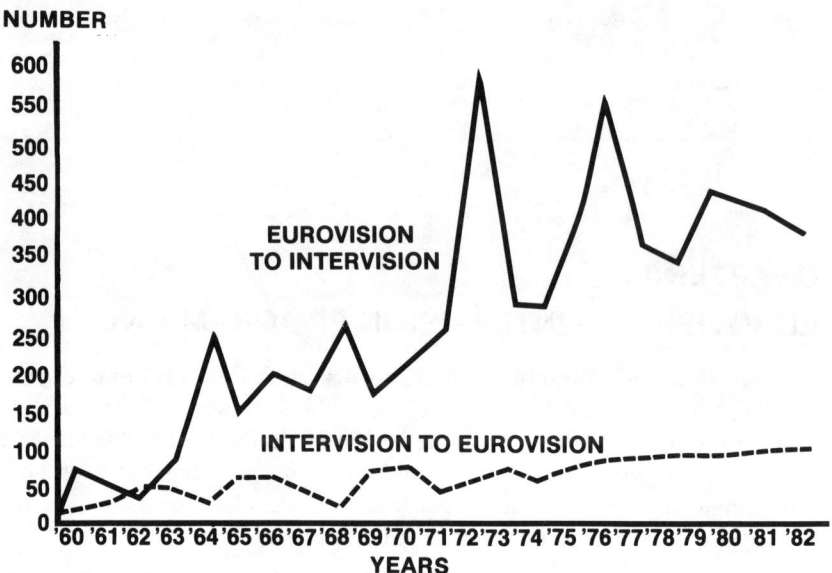

Figure 7-1
Growth of the Eurovision-Intervision Program Exchange 1960-1982
Source: EBU, OIRT

The imbalance in Eurovision-Intervision program and news traffic is but a small slice of the larger one-way flow of television programs between Western and Eastern Europe. Statistics on the one-way street in East-West television relations were collected by Kaarle Nordenstreng and Tapio Varis. They showed that in 1970, Socialist broadcasters imported more than 3,000 program hours from the West, while only about 1,000 program hours traveled to West European screens.[1] We will be better able to explain the reasons for the one-way exchange later in this chapter. In the EVN-IVN exchange, for example, the small Intervision organizations from Bulgaria, Czechoslovakia, and Poland tend to surpass the larger organizations in news reception because they do not have the resources to report news themselves (Table 7-1). The recent jump in Bulgarian reception largely reflects the increased availability of circuits to receive Eurovision items. The Soviet and East German services depend less upon Eurovision because of their large news-gathering capability.

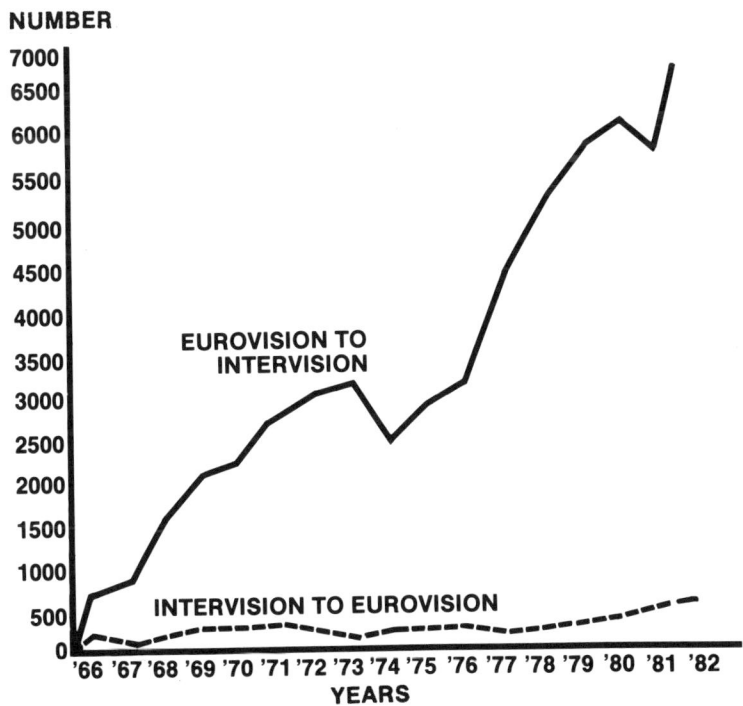

Figure 7-2
Growth of the Eurovision-Intervision News Exchange 1966-1982
Source: EBU, OIRT

Also, East Germany does not depend upon EVN because roughly 80 percent of the country can receive West German newscasts.

Eurovision members often limit their reception of IVN offers to Soviet news. Aside from the Soviet Union being a major world power, Soviet television is the biggest IVN originator. Although the reception of stories can vary widely due to the contents of items, Tapio Varis and Renny Jokelin found, in their three-year study of the Eurovision-Intervision news exchange, that Austria, Italy, Yugoslavia, Spain, Luxembourg, and Israel were the most avid takers of IVN transmissions.[2]

Table 7-1
Intervision Reception of Eurovision News
Rank order of members according to total number of items

Rank Order	1971	Program Hours	Rank Order	1976	Program Hours	Rank Order	1981	Program Hours
1	Czechoslovakia	1739	1	Czechoslovakia	2112	1	Bulgaria	5987
2	Poland	1653	2	Poland	2019	2	Poland	5726
3	Hungary	1449	3	Rumania	1922	3	USSR	5718
4	Rumania	1367	4	USSR	1412	4	Czechoslovakia	5682
5	USSR	493	5	East Germany	980	5	Rumania	5664
6	East Germany	113	6	Hungary	950	6	Hungary	5529
7	Bulgaria	1	7	Bulgaria	52	7	East Germany	5332
						8	Cuba	316

Source: OIRT

7.2 Eurovision-Intervision Program Exchange

From February 13 through 24, 1980, viewers in Western and Eastern Europe came together to watch the XIIIth Winter Olympics from Lake Placid. A potential audience of about 167 million European viewers saw Irena Rodnina and Aleksandr Zaitzer win the pairs skating and Eric Heiden receive his fifth gold medal.[3] Those television highlights were the result of a complex electronic operation. Although the television coverage was provided by the American network ABC, a joint EBU-OIRT operations group of 132 people routed 88 multilateral programs for 160 hours and 190 unilateral programs for 70 hours to Europe using three satellite channels.[4]

Coverage of the Lake Placid Olympics is only an example of how the Eurovision-Intervision link can literally unite the Western and Socialist countries of Europe. But not all kinds of programming travel well; the bulk of the Eurovision-Intervision traffic relates to sports (see Appendix N). In the 10 years ending in 1982, sports averaged 86 percent of the Eurovision programs taken from Intervision and 90 percent of the Eurovision programs taken by Intervision. In addition to taking more sports, Intervision members take all kinds of programs from Eurovision. Meanwhile, Eurovision members take few cultural and children's broadcasts from Intervision. Since 1968, Eurovision members have not taken any children's programs from Intervision largely because they do not warrant live transmission over the costly Eurovision circuits.[5]

Western and Socialist broadcasters take programs from one another for economic reasons. Apart from the almost universal dependence upon imported programs to satisfy television's ravenous appetite, collaboration is prompted by the often high cost of rights. Indeed, the buying of television rights to major sports events has become a major area of EBU-OIRT collaboration. The EBU and OIRT, for instance, jointly paid the Lake Placid Olympic Organizing Committee nearly four million dollars for television rights and certain facilities.[6]

Eurovision-Intervision collaboration also is prompted by technical needs. In August 1974, the Eurovision-Intervision link proved essential in getting pictures from Cuba to the United States. Program makers at ABC did not expect that the 140 km (87 miles) distance between Cuba and the United States would cause problems in providing live coverage of the world's boxing championships from Havana. But the project was nearly cancelled because no video circuit existed between the two countries. Intervision, to which Cuba belongs, solved the crisis by offering the use of INTERSPUTNIK satellites. Because of incompatible equipment, however, U.S. earth stations could not hook into the INTERSPUTNIK system. The Eurovision-Intervision link was used to overcome this obstacle. For two days, ABC's program from Havana was beamed by an INTERSPUTNIK satellite to East Germany, where it was sent by Intervision to Prague and relayed to Vienna. From Vienna, the program was relayed over Eurovision to a West German satellite uplink, picked up in West Virginia, where it was distributed over ABC's network. In the end, the distance for sending pictures was about 150,000 km. Interestingly, this program marked the first use of Soviet and U.S. satellites to overcome both distance and technical differences.[7]

Popular taste plays a big role in explaining the Eurovision-Intervision exchange. Sports programs are most frequently offered in the Eurovision program exchange and, to a lesser extent, in Intervision. Indeed, the hunger for live coverage of sports was largely responsible for first linking the two networks. Among the first programs transmitted under the Intervision emblem was the Eurovision feed of the 1960 Rome Summer Olympics.

Current affairs, entertainment, and cultural programs also may win wide popularity. The annual "Eurovision Song Contest," for example, is regularly taken by Intervision countries for recording, although they cannot enter songs. Other non-sports Eurovision program offers taken by Intervision in 1982 included ORF's "New Year's Concert from Vienna" and "Springtime in Vienna," as well as RAI's "Italian Song Festival from San Remo." In fact, Intervision frequently takes cultural programs which were not shown on Eurovision for lack of interest. In 1982, for example, Intervision took TRT's "4th International Festival of Children's Folk Dances and Songs," YLE's "Midsummer Night Concert," and RTBF's "Festival de la Chanson Française."[8] As already noted, Eurovision members are reluctant to accept cultural programs because of high circuit costs involved.

But differences in taste between Western and Socialist Europe can limit the exchange. In 1982, Eurovision members did not take any children's program and took only one entertainment program from Intervision (see Appendix N). In addition, Eurovision acceptance of Intervision offers tend to be limited to those in which Eurovision member countries are involved. No Eurovision member, for example, took coverage of the ice hockey match between Poland and Rumania at the World Championships from Austria in March 1982.[9] Also, most Eurovision members will ignore big sporting events in which only Socialist countries take part. Only French, Greek, and Yugoslav television regularly took daily summaries of Spartakiade from Moscow in 1979.[10]

Perhaps it is inevitable that the kind of program that best slips behind the Iron Curtain does not reflect controversial political issues. One reason sports dominate the Eurovision-Intervision program exchange is that they are generally a neutral subject. Sports can have political implications and thus may be censored or overlooked. A classic example is the Western television blackout of the 1980 Moscow Olympics imposed after the Soviets invaded

Afghanistan in December 1979.[11] In deference to the widely divergent program values of Western and Socialist countries of Europe, Eurovision-Intervision programming tends to avoid controversial political, social, and cultural issues.

Because showing the development of the Communist society is an important priority within a Socialist broadcasting organization, Intervision will tend to reject Eurovision offers which contradict Socialist goals. One example of this occurred on October 12, 1976, when French President Valéry Giscard d'Estaing used the Eurovision-Intervision link to address Soviet viewers during a week of Franco-Soviet friendship organized by French television. But Giscard's remarks about French living standards were excised during that evening's taped broadcast. Before the program was shown, a Russian translation omitted the conversion to roubles of the minimum guaranteed Frenchman's salary of 324 roubles (441 dollars) versus the minimum Soviet salary of 70 roubles. Also, after listening to the speech, Soviet authorities showed the program at 7 P.M. — pre-empting a children's show — though they had privately said that it would be shown on the 9 P.M. "Vremya," the most widely watched news show on Soviet television.[12] The Soviets apparently feared that the figures could lead to the impression that the French worker is better off than his Soviet counterpart.

In another example, none of the Intervision countries except Rumania took the feed of the 1979 "Eurovision Song Contest," perhaps because it was held in Jerusalem. Not only did this break a tradition (most Intervision members have recorded the contest since 1975), but several members, including the USSR, resumed their participation in 1980 when the "Eurovision Song Contest" was staged in the Hague.[13] Interestingly, the 1980 contest was not shown in its entirety in most Intervision countries. The recording and edited transmission of the contest is a breach of the contest rules.[14] Similarly, Intervision members, with the exception of Rumania, did not take live coverage of Egyptian President Anwar Sadat's visit to Jerusalem on November 19, 1977, an event covered by many countries in the world.[15] While much of the world regarded his visit as a historic peace initiative, Soviet media labeled Sadat as a traitor to the Arab liberation movement.[16] These two examples also show that Rumania's media policy can be as nationalistic as its foreign policy.

Moreover, Intervision members will surely never take religious programs from Eurovision because Socialist media policies call for the banning of religious programs. Some Eurovision religious programs can have almost universal participation. In 1979, for example, the "Midnight Mass from St. Peter's Basilica" was taken by seven Eurovision members and by twenty-three television stations from countries including Argentina, Brazil, Chile, Mexico, and the United States. But Intervision did not take part.[17] Also, Intervision countries did not take part in the "Easter Mass from Rome" in 1982, although the program was taken by fifteen Eurovision members.[18]

On the other side of the exchange, Eurovision members will tend to reject those Intervision offers which they consider to be full of Socialist propaganda. In 1982, for example, no Eurovision member took Intervision offers of the thirty-seventh anniversary of the defeat of Nazi Germany and the sixty-fifth anniversary of the founding of the USSR, two of the top offers of the Intervision program exchange that year.[19] A look at the kinds of Intervision programs shown over the years which drew no Eurovision interest included "The Visit of Mr. Brezhnev to Rumania" in 1976; "Military Parade and Procession of the Workers" from Moscow in 1976 (only YLE/Finland took coverage); "The 25th Congress of the Soviet Communist Party" in 1976; "Concert on the Occasion of the 50th Anniversary of Polish Radio from Warsaw" in 1975; and the "Women's World Conference from East Berlin" in 1975.[20] Eurovision members tend to reject those Intervision programs which mainly aim to promote Socialist policies.

7.3 Eurovision-Intervision News Exchange

That more news flows from West to East than *vice versa* should be no surprise. Intervision's dependence on news from Eurovision becomes evident by looking at one day's EVN-IVN exchange. On June 30, 1977, Intervision members took six of the eleven EVN offers listed in Chapter Five. The two most widely accepted items were the Callaghan press conference and the UN meeting on Mozambique. The Callaghan offer was taken by Czechoslovakia, East Germany, Poland, Hungary, and Rumania.[21] Five IVN members also took the UN story — Czechoslovakia, East Germany, Hungary, Rumania, and the USSR.[22] The third most popular item was film of the Wimbledon match which was taken by the following four members: Czechoslovakia, Poland, Rumania, and the USSR.[23] Another EVN sports item — the Helsinki games — was taken by Czechoslovakia, Poland, and the USSR.[24] The Gaza prison film report was taken by Czechoslovakia, East Germany, and Hungary.[25] The last EVN item concerned the South African opposition merger which was taken by Czechoslovakia and East Germany.[26]

While Intervision took half of the day's EVN offers, the EVN News Coordinator selected only two of the 19 IVN offers listed in Chapter Six. Of the twenty-nine EVN members, only six took film of the ideological conference in Prague. They were ORF/Austria, DR/Denmark, SRG/Switzerland, ERT/Greece, TVE/Spain, and JTV/Jordan.[27] The second IVN offer taken by Eurovision members related to Willy Brandt's visit to Poland. Again, only six members accepted the item — RTL/Luxembourg, ARD/West Germany,

ORF/Austria, SRG/Switzerland, JRT/Yugoslavia, and JTV/Jordan.[28]

What are the forces at work in a one-way flow? Eurovision enjoys a great advantage over Intervision in delivering the news. In Chapter Five, we saw that the international newsfilm services contribute substantially to EVN —sometimes offering more stories than EVN member services. In addition, Eurovision's position is strengthened by its membership which is more than three times as large as that of Intervision. Also EBU associate members, chiefly the American networks, often make large contributions. What's more, unlike Eurovision, Intervision does not exchange news directly with other regional program exchange networks. Thus, Intervision cannot get news from other parts of the world without having the stories first going over Eurovision.

More fundamental is the different hierarchy between the networks for selecting and defining "news." Finnish media researchers Tapio Varis and Renny Jokelin report that their content analysis of 2,766 EVN-IVN offers shows that, aside from the usual imbalance, IVN countries are interested in all kinds of news reported through Eurovision, while EVN countries are mainly interested in politics and sports.[29] As Table 7-2 shows, the contents of EVN-IVN traffic differ in many ways. Varis and Jokelin found that the reception of EVN offers by Intervision closely mirrored the subject breakdown of EVN itself (see Table 5-3). Of the 2,636 items taken by Intervision from 1973 to 1975 (January-March), about 46 percent concerned politics. Second to political news were sports, with an average of 16 percent; followed by disasters, 16 percent; war, 14 percent; financial, 4 percent; and cultural, social, and scientific news, 2 percent.

It was the Eurovision reception of IVN offers, however, which was narrow and unrepresentative. Eurovision members are generally interested in political items and sports from IVN. Varis and Jokelin counted that, of the 130 IVN items taken by Eurovision, over 59 percent concerned politics. Of the political items that EVN received from IVN, over 90 percent dealt with political visits and conferences. The second most recurrent kind of news was sports, 19 percent; followed by cultural, social, and scientific affairs, 11 percent; disasters 5 percent; war, 1 percent; and financial items, 0.9 percent. In certain years, EVN did not accept any war, econonic, or disaster stories from Intervision. The common ground for receiving EVN-IVN news is smaller for Eurovision than it is for Intervision.[30]

Imbalance in news flow and the question of differing news priorities between Eurovision and Intervision have long been matters of yearly EBU-OIRT meetings of news experts. The first meeting of the EBU Working Party for Television News, with representatives of its OIRT counterpart, took place in Vienna in September 1969. Since then, they have been held on a yearly basis.

Table 7-2
Contents of the Eurovision-Intervision News Exchange
1973-1975 (January-March)

EVN to IVN

	1973		1974		1975	
	Feeds	Percent	Feeds	Percent	Feeds	Percent
Politics	315	40	379	52	518	47
Sports	120	15	136	18	167	15
Disasters	155	19	107	14	151	14
Security, War	132	17	56	8	192	17
Economic	49	6	23	3	37	3
Cultural, Social Scientific	17	2	14	2	23	2
Others	5	1	19	3	21	2
Total	793	100	734	100	1109	100

IVN to EVN

	1973		1974		1975	
Politics	28	61	30	60	20	59
Sports	6	13	16	32	5	15
Disasters	4	9	3	6	0	0
Security, War	1	2	0	0	1	3
Economic	0	0	0	0	1	3
Cultural, Social Scientific	7	15	1	2	6	17
Others	0	0	0	0	1	3
Total	46	100	50	100	34	100

Source: Tapio Varis and Renny Jokelin, *Television News in Europe, A Survey of the News-film Flow in Europe,* (Tampere, Finland: University of Tampere, 1976), pp. 82-88.

The meetings did not try to persuade any television organization to change its sense of news priorities or context. But they did try to explore the technical and journalistic causes of the imbalance problem to enable newsmen of both unions to take full advantage of the exchange.[31]

Agreement on technical problems, such as Intervision's slowness in going to color, was quickly reached largely because the merits of quick news collection, distribution and good quality were recognized regardless of the social system.[32] For example, Intervision is increasingly offering items shot outside its territory. Admittedly, Eurovision members generally do not take Intervision offers such as strikes at French factories, or inflation in Portugal, because they can rely on their own members. Still, Intervision offers are appreciated when reporting on events in places like Afghanistan, Cambodia, and Vietnam, where Western journalists are forbidden. During the Chinese-Vietnam war in 1979, Eurovision received satellite pictures from Peking television, and the other side to the Chinese version of events in Vietnam was given in almost daily Intervision offers of reports from Czechoslovak, East German, and Soviet news teams.[33] Thus, the EVN-IVN link can provide Europe with a more complete and perhaps a more balanced view of events.

EBU-OIRT news experts realized that the EVN-IVN exchange could provide greater access to events, but only if the contrasting political and journalistic policies prevailing in the two unions were not insuperable obstacles. The journalistic complaints of the imbalance became evident during the discussions. On the one hand, Eurovision members complained that while they were offering Intervision wide coverage of the day's events around the world, they were getting nothing in return. They also complained that Western newsmen often had difficulties getting pictures out of Intervision countries, as in the 1974 case when the USSR halted American telecasts from Moscow on Soviet Jewish dissidents.[34]

On the other hand, Intervision critics felt that Western journalists should stop propagating anti-Communist ideas, such as looking for dissident stories and trying to impose their values upon the East. They have also accused Eurovision members of not implementing the Final Act of the 1975 Helsinki Human Rights Accords because Western news managers purposefully keep their reception of Intervision items low despite the growing number of Intervision offers.[35]

The fourteen years of discussions, complemented by screening sessions, allowed for developing professional journalistic contracts and for more studied approaches about newsfilm exchanges within and between Eurovision and Intervision.[36] The imbalance issue has not been solved, and can be expected to be a subject of further discussions. Indeed, the issue of printed and electronic newsflow has made a greater impact on world attention in UNESCO meetings, where many Socialist and Third World nations are calling for a "new world information order" that is less influenced by Western values.[37] What basically is the argument in Europe all about?

One of the first complaints by Eurovision has already been noted — that it is offering Intervision good coverage of the world's events without getting much beyond offers which are generally packaged as pro-Socialist propaganda. As Varis and Jokelin showed, EVN members take few, if any, cultural, social and scientific stories from Intervision. To Western critics, Intervision offers generally do not correspond to the Western news ethic of pure truthfulness. News from Intervision countries does not objectively report events to give the public the basic knowledge that will allow it to be informed and arrive at its own opinions.[38] Most Western televiewers would certainly complain if much of their evening news covered visits of foreign politicians whose arrivals are praised, but the purpose of their visits left unexplained.[39]

A complaint of many Intervision members is not that Eurovision newsmen report the truth — however troubling it may be — but that their reporting is intended for anti-Communist propaganda and for ideological diversion. This charge is the ostensible reason for ignoring or politely saying "no" to Eurovision requests for fires, crimes, and other negative phenomena. In February 1977, Soviet authorities barred Western correspondents from filming a hotel fire in Moscow which killed more than twenty persons. If a fire had swept through New York's largest hotel, television news stories would have been full of dramatic film. But the Moscow fire was largely ignored by the Soviet media because it was a national disaster which might blemish the Soviet's reputation and would also take space and time away from items of more lasting importance to Socialism. Some television films made of the fire by Western reporters were confiscated.[40]

Western journalists are often prevented from transmitting "anti-Socialist" news. In 1978, for example, Soviet television authorities refused to transmit American and West German television network film of the trial of two Soviet dissidents because they feared the news would be used for anti-Soviet propaganda.[41] In an equally unsuccessful effort to get news to the West, the Soviets refused to relay a West German television report on final preparations for the 1980 Moscow Olympics which they believed had political contents.[42]

The fear of having events which reflect poorly on Socialism shown all over the world prompted breaking the Eurovision-Intervision link during the 1968 Warsaw Pact invasion of Czechoslovakia. On August 21, 1968, Austrian television monitored Czechoslovak television coverage of the invasion for about 45 minutes — or until the Prague station was closed down by Soviet troops. The EBU recorded the pictures and transmitted them to the rest of the world.[43] The Eurovision-Intervision link between Vienna and Prague was reopened several days later.

In addition to preventing the transmission of politically sensitive programs to the West, Intervision members will tend to reject those Eurovision offers which are deemed to be harmful to the society's interests. As already noted, much of IVN news is selected and defined to support Socialism while deliberately omitting or delaying items that would embarrass the party and the government. In the previously discussed EVN-IVN exchange of June 30, 1977, we saw that the Paris meeting in support of Soviet dissidents aroused EVN interest, but no Intervision interest. Of course, Intervision countries, particularly the USSR, perceive dissidents as enemies of the State. Similarly, Czechoslovak television turned down the opportunity to transmit British newsfilm sent over EVN showing Martina Navratilova, who defected from Czechoslovakia to the United States in 1975, defeating Chris Evert at the 1978 Wimbledon women's single tennis finals. Czechoslovak television officials explained that the cost of the film was simply too high. But it seems that price did not prevent Czechoslovak television from showing Bjorn Borg defeating Jimmy Connors in the men's singles finals on the following day.[44]

EVN offers whose subjects contradict Socialist politics are particularly susceptible to censorship. For example, on June 20, 1979, Israeli television news showed highlights of a basketball game held in Turin, Italy, in which the USSR had defeated Israel for the European Basketball Championship. That same evening, Soviet television news chose to show highlights of a runner-up contest between the Czechoslovak and Yugoslav teams instead. It appears that Soviet television could not show a Russian all-star team beating all-stars from a country that officially does not exist in the Soviet government's eyes.[45] Another story — the Vietnamese "boat people" — aroused much international interest, but no interest at all in most Intervision countries. The USSR, Vietnam's ally, apparently felt the story was anti-Vietnamese, and thus anti-Soviet, and did not cover it on television news.[46]

While minimizing or ignoring civil strife, violence, and domestic disasters, Socialist news policy plays up similar stories in the West. Intervision plays up news from Eurovision such as unemployment in the United Kingdom, shootings in Italy, and inflation in the United States in part to ease concern over domestic shortcomings.[47]

Western news also may be taken to show the superiority of "Socialism over Capitalism" and to counter Western political propaganda. The head of the Editorial Department for Documentary Broadcasts of East German television reviewed the aims of filmed reports from the West:

> By our films (from the West), we wish to provide a contribution to the ideological controversy with the imperialist opponent. We strive to expose the unchangeable anti-human essence of imperialism as manifested in the events of the day, in the class struggles of our present time. We report directly from the fronts of class struggles in capitalist countries and observe ...how the world, in spite of many setbacks in the liberation movement, is being transformed in favor of Socialism. By our films, we foster the policy of peaceful co-existence.[48]

The Socialist practice of painting Western democracies in undemocratic hues and depicting countries such as the USSR as an open society seems to increase during times of East-West tension.[49] After the signing of the Helsinki Human Rights Accords in 1975, the Soviet media increased their anti-Western coverage to counter Western criticism that Moscow was not easing restrictions on the movement of people and ideas between East and West. To Soviet propagandists, the campaign was largely designed to show that Moscow can also take the offensive in the "struggle of ideas" and that despite the Helsinki Accords, Soviet society will not be opened to Western values and beliefs. Also, the anti-Western criticism was an effort to show that genuine human rights are guaranteed only by Socialist countries.[50]

Stationing international newsfilm crews in Intervision countries can overcome the limits of EVN-IVN exchanges. Western agencies active in Intervision countries have often delivered items that Intervision could not prepare in time for EVN news transmissions, or items that were not covered at all by Intervision services. In 1979, EVN got the first material sent by the new Phnom Penh government which was offered via East Germany by the agencies. Interestingly, East German television did not offer the film to Intervision, but the West got the film via the agencies.[51] In another example, with the inauguration of Pope John Paul II, Polish television listened to agency requests and provided film which might never have found its way to Western Europe via normal EVN procedures.[52]

Stationing news teams from Eurovision countries can also help. The first film of the 1980 Polish strikes were made by British, Swedish, and West German film crews already stationed in Poland. These crews continued to film events, although Polish authorities refused to allow other Western news teams into the country. In addition, the resident Western crews were not allowed to send their film back via Intervision, but had to send film or videotape out of the country by plane.[53]

At first glance, agency and Eurovision member activity in Intervision countries offers the advantages of faster coverage and of making more offers available from the East. But stories can be blocked if the coverage is anti-Socialist. Moreover, items from Intervision may not be accepted by Eurovision if they are deemed to be full of Socialist propaganda.

7.4 Conclusion

The heavy one-way flow of programs from Eurovision to Intervision will persist for a long time. One cause is the difference in popular taste between Western and Socialist Europe. Beyond that, Intervision's dependence upon Eurovision's supremacy in gathering and transmitting programs and news from around the world proves to be a disadvantage. In addition, Eurovision members do not take many non-sports programs from Intervision because they do not warrant transmission over the expensive network.

The principal cause of the imbalance problem is the desire of most Eurovision and Intervision members to protect their own people from programs they do not want. On the one hand, Eurovision members often reject Intervision offers because they consider them to be full of propaganda. On the other hand, Intervision members will not only fail to select and interpret those events that pose a threat to Socialist policies but also prevent the transmission of such events to Eurovision for fear they will be used for anti-Communist propaganda and for ideological diversion.

Endnotes
Chapter 7

1. See Kaarle Nordenstreng and Tapio Varis, *Television Traffic – A One-Way Street? A Survey and Analysis of the International Flow of Television Program Material*, (Paris: UNESCO, 1974), p. 41. In addition to this basic work, see the following: Glen Fisher, *American Communication in a Global Society*, (Norwood, N.J.: Ablex Publishing Corporation, 1979); Kaarle Nordenstreng and Herbert I. Schiller, eds., *National Sovereignty and International Communication*, (Norwood, N.J.: Ablex Publishing Corporation, 1979); and Tapio Varis, Raquel Salinas and Renny Jokelin, *International News and the New Information Order*, (Tampere: University of Tampere, 1977). Jeffrey Johnson also has made important contributions. See his *International Television Flows Project*, (Cambridge: University of Cambridge, June 1979).
2. Tapio Varis and Renny Jokelin, *Television News in Europe, A Survey of the News-film Flow in Europe*, (Tampere: University of Tampere, 1976), p. 110.
   Tapio Varis did a pioneering study for the EBU and OIRT on the news flow between Eurovision and Intervision entitled "Television News in Eurovision and Intervision" (unpublished EBU document O.A./5013 — Com. Pro/1343, September 1974). This work is summarized in an article by Yrjö Länsipuro, "Joint Eurovision/Intervision News Study," *EBU Review*, 26:3, (May 1975), pp. 37-40.
3. Interview with Richard Bunn, Head of Eurovision Program Division, EBU, Geneva, May 1982.
4. Interview with Miroslav Vilcek, Director, Television Program Department, EBU, Geneva, March 1980.
   For more about televising the Lake Placid games, see "Winter Olympics, U.S. Network Coordinates Coverage," *BM/E's World Broadcast News*, 2:5, (January 1980), pp. 10-13.
5. *Ibid.*
6. "EBU Set for Winter Olympics; Will Cover Moscow Games Regardless of Boycotts," *BM/E's World Broadcast News*, 2:6, (February 1980), p. 26.

7. Interview with F. Benkö, Deputy Director of the Technical Center, OIRT, Prague, November 1975.
   For accounts of the logistics in coordinating live international coverage, see "Winter Olympics, U.S. Network Coordinates Coverage," *BM/E's World Broadcast News*, op. cit., pp. 10-13. "Pope's Irish, U.S. Visit Sets Off Extensive Radio and TV Coverage," *BM/E's World Broadcast News*, 2:3, (November 1979), p. 4: "Spartakiade Provides Broadcasters a Taste of Olympic Games Coverage," *BM/E's World Broadcast News*, 2:1, (September 1979), pp. 1, 10-11; Nathan Cohen, "President Sadat's Visit to Jerusalem, Broadcasting Aspects," *EBU Review*, 29:1, (January 1978), pp. 8-12; and "Arrangements for Exchanges of News Items During the European Elections," *EBU Review*, 176, pp. 196-198.
8. Author's analysis from the Eurovision Program Summaries (1974-1982) of the EBU.
9. *Ibid.*
10. *Ibid.*
11. "Olympics Coverage Treated As News," *BM/E's World Broadcast News*, 2:12, (August 1980), p. 2.
12. "Les dirigeants soviétiques ont été embarrassés par l'éloge qu'a fait M. Giscard d'Estaing de la société libérale," *Le Monde*, October 14, 1976; and "Giscard Praises Détente in a TV Talk to Russians," *International Herald Tribune*, October 13, 1976.
    For more about the "Vremya" ("Time") news program, see V. Korolev, "Events of the Day on the TV Screen," *OIRT Radio-Television*, 6, (1978), pp. 3-5.
13. Eurovision Program Summaries (1974-1982), *op. cit.* The following Intervision member countries recorded the 1980 contest: Cuba, Rumania, and the USSR.
14. Vilcek, *op. cit.*.
15. Eurovision Program Summaries (1974-1982), *op. cit.*
    For more about television coverage of Sadat's visit, see "TV's Role in Mideast: Almost Diplomacy?" *New York Times*, November 18, 1977; and "Israelis Say Sadat Visit Surprised Soviet Radio-Jamming System," *New York Times*, November 20, 1977.
16. Alexander Laviengier, "Sadat Visit to Jerusalem," *Atlas World Press Review*, 25:1, (January 1978), p. 9.
17. Eurovision Program Summaries (1974-1982), *op. cit.*
18. *Ibid.*
19. *Ibid.*
20. *Ibid.*

21. EVN Participation Sheets for June 30, 1977.
22. *Ibid.*
23. *Ibid.*
24. *Ibid.*
25. *Ibid.*
26. *Ibid.*
27. *Ibid.*
28. *Ibid.*
29. Varis and Jokelin, *Television News in Europe, op. cit.*, pp. 80-93.
30. Lansipuro, "Joint Eurovision/Intervision News Study," *op. cit.*, p. 40.
31. *Ibid.*, p. 38.
32. *Ibid.*
33. EBU, *Weekly Liaison Bulletin*, no. 14, April 4, 1979.
34. See "Television and Radio," *1979 Britannica Book of the Year* (Chicago: Encyclopedia Britannica, Inc., 1979). pp. 661-662.
35. International Organization of Journalists, "30 Years of the OIRT," *Journalists' Affairs*, no. 22-24, (1976), p. 27.
    Surprisingly, negotiations of Basket Three of the "Final Act" — which deals with increased human contacts between East and West, including the flow of information — ignored the Eurovision-Intervision exchange. Indeed, Helsinki does not appear to have corrected the imbalance. For example, the large jump in Intervision reception of Eurovision programs in 1976 was largely the result of the 1976 Winter and Summer Olympics (see Figure 7-1). Also no marked jump in EVN-IVN exchanges can be seen.
36. *Ibid.*, pp. 25-28.
37. Studies on the nature of the "new world information order" are growing. The following, however, are of particular value: Dieter Bielenstein, *Towards A New World Information Order: Consequences for Development Policy* (Bonn: Institut für Internationale Begegnungen, 1979); and Kaarle Nordenstreng and Herbert I. Schiller, eds., *National Sovereignty and International Communication, op. cit.* The work of UNESCO's MacBride Commission has attracted worldwide attention. Apart from numerous documents prepared for the Commission, see International Commission for Communication Problems, *Interim Report on Communication Problems in Modern Society*, (Paris: UNESCO, 1978). For a collection of essays of Socialist views, see Oldrich Bures, ed., *Current Views on the World Information Order*, (Prague: International Organization of Journalists, 1977). For the Western point of view, see Academy for Educational Development, *The United States and the Debate on the World Information Order*, (Washington, D.C.: Academy for Educational Development, 1978).

38. A classic work on the contrasting social functions of news institutions, see Fred S. Siebert, Theodore Peterson, and Wilbur Schramm, *Four Theories of the Press*, (Urbana: University of Illinois Press, 1956).
39. Interview with Pierre Brunel-Lantenac, Head of the TV News Division, EBU, Geneva, March 1980.
40. "News of Hotel Fire in Moscow is Minimized by the Authorities," *New York Times*, March 1, 1977.
41. "Freeze Frame," *TV World*, 1:8 (August 1978), p. 4.
42. David Satter, "Row Over Olympics Reporting Develops," *Financial Times*, July 15, 1980.
43. "TV: Czech Staff Defies Soviet Troops," *New York Times*, August 22, 1968.
44. "Freeze Frame," *op. cit.*
45. Don Kowet, "Whose 'Truth' Can You Believe?" *TV Guide*, (September 22, 1979), p. 8.
46. *Ibid.*
47. Burton Paulu, *Radio and Television Broadcasting in Eastern Europe*, (Minneapolis: University of Minnesota Press, 1974), pp. 108-109.
48. Sabine Katins, "Peaceful Co-existence and Journalistic Responsibility Ideas Concerning Reportages from the Capitalist World," *OIRT Radio-Television*, 1, (1977), p. 3.
49. "The War of Words," *Newsweek* (Atlantic edition), December 8, 1975, pp. 10-11.
50. *Ibid.* See also Paul Hofmann, "Soviet Bloc Steps Up Ideology Drive," *New York Times*, April 14, 1977.
51. EBU, *Weekly Liaison Bulletin*, no. 9, February 27, 1979.
52. *Ibid.*, no. 2, January 10, 1979.
53. Interview with Mike Doherty, Head of Eurovision News Exchange Service, EBU, Geneva, January 1982. See "Summer Strikes: Cooperation and Scandal," *BM/E's World Broadcast News*, 3:2, (October 1980), p. 16.

CHAPTER 8
PROBLEMS AND PROSPECTS

The preceding chapters have tried to provide the reader with an insight into what is involved when television programs cross national boundaries. This closing chapter shall examine problems of international television networks and which direction European collaboration may take in the future.

8.1 Problems

International television networks have a great potential for increasing world understanding and providing program variety. Unfortunately, political boundaries can become insurmountable obstacles which inhibit communication. Large-scale transmissions require a measure of agreement on standardizing equipment, on linking stations, and on administrative procedures including sharing circuit costs. Moreover, programs cannot cross boundaries without mechanisms for preventing the reception of harmful propaganda. Because of different values, the news, entertainment, and advertising in one country may be construed as propaganda in another. While cooperation on technical and administrative details is imperative, international networks must require the preservation of national rights to reject material which is deemed harmful.

The major problem of television concerns the methods of program control. In the early years of television, the issues were expressed more technically, such as frequency interference and equipment compatibility. But as the medium matured, problems such as how much news, entertainment, and advertising should appear in programs became increasingly important. The fear that cigarette commercials may harm public health, for instance, lead many governments to ban tobacco advertising on television.

Today's world broadcasting community contains nations of widely different cultural backgrounds with great variations in television systems, each claiming sovereign control over its programming decisions. Under such conditions, collaboration not only becomes difficult, but can also limit the number and kinds of exchanges.

Perhaps no other international arrangement so dramatically shows the difficulties and limits of international television transmissions than the networks of the EBU and OIRT. Although the exchanges have increased in number and variety, members do not accept all the offers Eurovision and Intervision send out. Eurovision only accounts for about 4 percent of all air time in Western Europe. Intervision makes up a larger share, typically about 10 percent of national program output. Also, in looking at the kinds of programs exchanged over Eurovision, we find that members take more sports than current affairs, entertainment, religion, drama, and folklore programs combined. More political, disaster, and sports items are exchanged than financial, social, and scientific news in the EVNs.

Intervision, by contrast, has a more balanced exchange where members take nearly as many entertainment and cultural programs as sports. Still, in the Intervision news exchange, political, cultural, and economic news offers are accepted more frequently than sports and, in particular, disaster stories.

Many factors work against greater and more varied Eurovision and Intervision program exchanges. The exchange of Eurovision programs often depends upon the price of television rights and upon whether a program warrants live transmission over the expensive circuits. Intervision members lack hard currency for buying Western programs. In addition, numerous social and cultural limits exist. Language barriers limit the live exchange of operas, ballets, and drama. The popularity of a sport or of a performer will also heighten interest.

Viewers in the Socialist countries of Europe see far more Western programs than vice versa. The primary reasons are political. On the one hand, Eurovision members often reject Intervision offers because they regard them as being full of Socialist propaganda. On the other hand, Intervision members will not only fail to select and interpret those events that pose a threat to Socialism, but also prevent the transmission of such events to Eurovision. Running through all this is the general recognition that controlling the reception of foreign programs is an important element of sovereignty; the supreme power over citizens.

Obviously, a big distinction exists between program control in Eurovision and Intervision countries. Governments in both the Socialist and Western countries of Europe have the final say in broadcasting. But, unlike the direct control in the Socialist countries, Western media are generally free and responsible for what they televise. Indeed, EBU members often oppose politicians to defend their own (legally) guaranteed autonomy. Criticism of the BBC's coverage of the Falklands/Malvinas crisis by Margaret Thatcher's Tory government offers a relevant example.

Problems and Prospects

These differences also extend to the other television activities of the EBU and OIRT. The OIRT is not as active as the EBU in preparing for ITU conferences, often turning down EBU invitations to collaborate on common frequency problems. The main reason for the lack of concern is that OIRT views the drawing up of frequency plans as a matter for governments — not for broadcasters. In the legal field, the EBU has been able to protect its members from paying high rights fees by concluding various agreements with different international rights-holding bodies. The legalities of Intervision are generally handled on a program-by-program basis — not by the OIRT — but by the originating organization. The limited commitment of OIRT members in the legal field is also reflected by the absence of a permanent legal organ.

European television exchanges could only develop by finding ways to permit governments to protect their own people from programs they do not want. As pointed out in Chapter One, each country has decided for itself, at least in a general way, who may televise what programs, and each regards it as essential that the integrity of these decisions be protected.

Eurovision and Intervision are well designed to recognize this objective and to deal with it. The various editorial powers are vested in their members, not in their viewers. Viewers can only suspect subtle manipulation by government bureaucrats when major events are not shown. Every station connected to the networks may receive or reject any program which the networks send out.

The success of Eurovision and Intervision is based, among other factors, on mechanisms to prevent the transmission of harmful programs. Eurovision is not governed by any written rules such as a constitution. Still, EBU members have adopted an agreement recommending that members require sports organizers to list the advertising that will appear. Although this agreement primarily aims to ensure that sports programs sent over Eurovision are negotiated on a uniform basis, it also serves to prevent offensive advertising. EBU members will even threaten to boycott events if harmful advertising is not removed.

The importance which members give to retaining the national right to reject material which may be deemed harmful is reflected in the refusal to give the EBU and OIRT power to make programs. Neither Eurovision nor Intervision have a central program production studio or staff. Rather, all programs and news items sent over the networks are made by members or by newsfilm agencies. The EBU and OIRT only act as administrative and technical coordination centers.

There are other indications of the reluctance of members to create an organ affecting their television programs that would be beyond and possibly above governments. EBU members were initially unwilling to create a program committee which would mainly concern itself with international television transmissions. Eurovision is not an organization but rather an activity that has been internalized into much of the EBU's work. No Eurovision *ad hoc* working parties, study groups or committees exist. Intervision members have institutionalized their network. It has members and a constitution, but the constitution does not function as an instrument for regulating programs. The ultimate validity of Intervision programming is largely found in the requirements of Socialism — a doctrine common to all Intervision members.

Control of programming is a prerequisite to large-scale international television transmissions. Broadcasters cannot get one another's programs without an international institution capable of coordinating the exchanges. Television programming across national boundaries is impossible without at least a measure of agreement on linking stations to a coordinated network and on administrative procedures for making offers and requests. The EBU and OIRT have performed these functions admirably. But international exchanges will not succeed without mechanisms to prevent transmissions that give rise to program controls in the first place.

8.2 Prospects for the Future

The EBU and OIRT have maintained European television collaboration for nearly 40 years. Whether or not this collaboration will survive the sweeping changes of the future is uncertain. The consequences of this uncertainty are far greater than at any other time since the birth of broadcasting because television has become a more critical element in every society and has become subject to greater technological, economic, and political pressures. Let us look at three factors which will have major effects on the future of the EBU and OIRT.

First, Europe is witnessing the arrival of private broadcasters. Historically, EBU membership has consisted of public organizations which have been given a monopoly to provide all national programming. This generally meant that only viewers along borders were able to turn their sets to a different channel. Today, however, European broadcasting is increasingly being decentralized. Recent years have seen established broadcasters providing greater local and regional programming and the start of private local stations — often commercial. Some of these private stations represent social and cultural groups, while others are backed by business interests such as newspaper publishers.

Indeed, private broadcasting is making its return to Europe. Private stations existed in many countries during the early years of radio, but government control increased with the start of World War I. After the war, politicians came to the conclusion that broadcasting was too important to be left to private interests.

The advent of local and regional stations does not necessarily signal a loss of government control over television. Politicians in most countries will still prohibit commercial interests from making programming decisions. But the decentralization will surely continue as frequencies become available and as technological advances such as satellites and cable television (CATV) offer more channels. Above all, the decentralization will take place as political systems become more liberal. Private broadcasters now operate in countries which once had strong central governments such as in Italy and Spain.

The arrival of new broadcasters signals increased competition for the EBU. Private over-the-air and CATV stations may form their own networks to share the high costs of television programming. Politicians may not allow such networks to develop for fear of increased competition with the state-owned network. Still, private stations in various countries can be linked together by a satellite. A private London-based satellite company moved recently to link several CATV systems in countries like Finland and Switzerland with an international satellite. Continued growth of such networks could lead to increased competition with the EBU in transmitting news and sports.

To win this battle, the EBU must integrate these new broadcasters into the organization. The task will not be easy. It will involve important changes in the functions and structure of the EBU. Although long hostile to cablecasters, the EBU must make cablecasting part of its activities and open its membership to cable operators. Failure to do so will result in cases where private media interests outbid EBU members for programs.

The second threat to the ability of the EBU and OIRT to exchange programs will come from the anemic economic standing of members. Today, many broadcasters are in a precarious financial position. On the one hand, the costs of television technology, of programs, and of talent have grown rapidly over the years and continue to increase rapidly. Also, the advent of private broadcasters is cutting into the budgets of established broadcasters. On the other hand, revenues are not growing as fast. Many established broadcasters can no longer entirely depend upon license fees. Not only has the growth in the number of television sets leveled off, but raising license fees is politically unpopular in many countries. In addition, the money supplied by governments in some countries may decrease if the global recession continues. The sale of advertising will become compelling, if not inevitable. But advertisers will turn away from the established television networks as CATV and home video fragments viewers. New sources of income will have to be found.

If the financial state of members does not improve, the economic crisis could become a major crisis for the EBU. The agency has established many cost-sharing procedures. But the continuing economic weakness of members will undermine the EBU's ability to buy television rights for important events such as Olympic Games, the costs of which continue to mount. The financial weakness of the EBU will also restrict the implementation of sophisticated equipment and practices to efficiently route programs.

OIRT members are not immune from the current weak economic situation. Although subsidized directly from government budgets, the ability of Socialist broadcasters to buy Western programs and technology is limited by the lack of hard currency.

A third danger comes from the start of satellite systems. The ability of satellites to "see" an entire continent prompted the EBU and OIRT to incorporate satellites into their networks. The advantages of satellites to the OIRT are important. OIRT officials see the benefits of a geostationary satellite for Intervision as a way not only to provide greater coverage but also to relay programs and news items when land circuits are occupied. The benefits to the EBU are also immense. In 1981, the EBU agreed to use ESA's European Communications Satellite (ECS) for point-to-point transmission of Eurovision programs. ECS will permit stations on the periphery of Europe to receive Eurovision. It also permits Eurovision to expand into Africa and to lessen its dependence on INTELSAT. Above all, ECS will relieve the heavy traffic on the land network. But the likelihood of one satellite covering Eastern and Western Europe is doubtful. Satellite projects continue to emphasize incompatible transmitting and receiving facilities in order to limit overspill between the Western and Socialist countries of Europe.

But the start of direct broadcasting satellites (DBS) troubles EBU members. For years, they were able to reject any program which Eurovision sent out. But the blanket of DBS projects such as the Franco-German satellites and ESA's L-SAT will cover all of Europe. Thus, anyone will be able to receive Eurovision programs through individual dishes or CATV systems. Even language barriers will be eroded as new digital sound equipment will permit viewers to hear foreign programs in their own language. At the very least, satellites can dilute program control.

Steps have been taken to control unauthorized satellite broadcasts. National sovereignty over satellite programming has been recognized internationally. At the 1977 World Administrative Radio Conference (WARC-BS), governments allocated satellite channels on the basis of national coverage. It also agreed to limit the overspill of one country's programs into others.

In addition, cable television will help prevent unwanted broadcasts. Although cable can help strengthen a country's high-tech industry, an important motive for building cable systems is the fact that they permit controlling the reception of foreign programs.

Despite increased control, the new DBS satellites can result in program piracy. Short of signal scrambling, little prevents a station or CATV system from picking up a Eurovision transmission through overspill without payment. Signal piracy will prompt organizers and performers to demand higher fees, not to mention lost revenues to the EBU.

In addition, the growth in satellite channels will fragment Eurovision viewers. Satellites as well as CATV may offer as many as twenty programs at one time to people who now have no more than two to choose from. Opportunities may also exist for pan-European programming. But increased viewer choice will divide the audience for Eurovision programs. Viewers may no longer be interested in watching the best of another Eurovision station.

Actions related to satellite broadcasting taken by other international organizations will challenge the jurisdiction of the agencies. UNESCO has already taken actions such as sponsoring North-South news exchanges and holding communications conferences. The EBU will have to take a lead in asserting the union's expertise in the field of program exchanges.

The flow of programs between Eurovision and Intervision will surely continue, although it will decrease during times of East-West crisis. The need to fill the new television channels in the West can result in greater imports of non-political programs from the East. But because of differing program values, more Western programs will continue to be shown in Intervision countries than Socialist programs on the networks of Western Europe. As long as different criteria for selecting and interpreting events continue to exist between the Western and Socialist countries of Europe, the possibility of public misunderstanding will remain.

Such differing journalistic decisions, among other factors, might prevent the grouping of existing regional broadcasting unions into a global organization. The IBU Experiment showed the difficulties of housing European broadcasters under one roof.

Still, extending existing exchanges around the world will be impossible without international collaboration. Broadcasters may, for pragmatic reasons, join in creating a universal organization to facilitate television exchanges among regional broadcasting unions. This organization would enable broadcasters to get pictures from around the world. Its primary task would be coordinating and routing offers and requests. But each regional union would have to be free to offer and reject programs. This would permit countries, particularly those who fear the invasion of foreign programs, to guard against any loss of their decision-making power.

It seems clear that great battles are pending in the field of European television. The stakes are high, and the changes needed are large. When the battles are over, television will look very different from today. Viewers will have access to a multitude of channels. But the danger exists that politics, economics, and technology will harm the survival of the EBU's and OIRT's television networks. Established public broadcasters and policymakers must understand the potential future developments in television. A failure to adapt to changes will prevent them from taking full advantage of developments to better send television programs across national boundaries.

Appendix A

Members of the IBU

(with the date of their admission to the Union)

	Active Members	
Albania	Enti Shqiptare Audicijoni Radiofonike	1941
Algeria	Gouvernement Général de l'Algérie Service Central des PTT	1933
Austria	*Oesterreichische Radio-Verkehrs-AG.	1925
Belgium	*Radio-Belgique S.A.	1925
	N.V. Radio-Louvain	1929
	Institut National Belge de Radiodiffusion (INR)	1931
Bulgaria	Radio Sofia	1937
Croatia	Hrvatski Krugoval	1942
Czechoslovakia	*Radiojournal	1925
	Cesky Rozhlas	1939
Danzig	Danziger Rundfunk-Sendebetrieb der Post-und Telegraphenverwaltung	1931
Denmark	Radioraadet	1926
	Statsradiofonien	1941
Egypt	Egyptian State Telegraphs and Telephones	1933
Estonia	S.A. Raadio Ringääling	1932
	Riigi Ringhääling	1934
Finland	Osakeyhtio Suomen Yleisradio	1927
	Oy Suomen Yleisradio Ab	1934
	Oy Yleisradio Ab	1944
France	*Le Petit Parisien	1925
	*Compagnie Française de Radiophonie Radio-Paris	1925
	Service de la Radiodiffusion de l'Administration Française des Postes et des Télégraphes	1933
	Radiodiffusion Nationale	1939
	Radiodiffusion Française	1944

	Radio-Toulouse, La Radiophonie du Midi	1926
	S.A. La Radiophonie du Midi	1943
	Syndicat de la Radiophonie Lyonnaise	1926
	S.A. Radio-Lyon	1943
	S.A. Radio-Meditérranée	1943
	Société Méridionale de Radiodiffusion	1943
Germany	*Reichsrundfunk gesellschaft	1925
Greece	Greek Broadcasting Service	1938
Hungary	Magyar Telefonhirmondo es Radio R.T.	1926
Ireland	Broadcasting Service, Department of Posts and Telegraphs	1928
	Direction of Broadcasting, General Post Office	1937
Italy	Unione Radiofonica Italiana	1926
	EIAR	1927
	Radio Audizioni Italiano (RAI)	1944
Latvia	Department of Posts and Telegraphs	1933
	Latvijas Radiofons	1937
Lithuania	General Direction of Posts and Telegraphs	1935
Morocco	Office Chérifien des Postes, Télégraphes et Téléphones	1941
Netherlands	*Nederlandsche Seintoestellen Fabriek (NSF)	1925
	N.V. Nederlandsche Draadlooze Omroep	1927
	Algemeene Vereeniging Radio-Omroep (AVRO)	1929
	Katholieke Radio Omroep (KRO)	1929
	Nederlandsche Christelijke Radio Vereeniging (NCRV)	1929
	Vereeninging van Arbeiders Radio Amateurs (VARA)	1929
	Vrijzinnig Protestantsche Radio Omroep (VPRO)	1929
	Rijksradio Omroep de Nederlandsche Omroep	1940
Norway	*Kringkastingselskapet A.S.	1925
	Norsk Rikskringkasting	1933
Palestine	Palestine Broadcasting Service	1936

Appendix A

Poland	Polskie Radjo S.A.	1927
Portugal	Administração Geral dos Correios, Telegrafos e Telefones	1930
	Emissora Nacional de Radiodifusão	1940
Rumania	Societatea de Difuziune Radiotelefonica	1928
	Societatea Româna de Radiodifuziune	1937
Slovakia	Slovensky Rozhlas	1940
Spain	*Asociación Nacional de Radiodifusión	1925
	Unión Radio S.A.	1926
	Servicio de Radiodifusión de la Republica Española	1938
	Dirección de Telégrafos, Comisión de Obras Públicas y Comunicaciones	1938
	Departamento Radio del Servicio Nacional de Propaganda	1939
	Departamento Radio, Servicio de Telecommunicación — Ingeniería — Ministerio de la Gobernación	
Sweden	Aktiebolaget Radiotjänst	1926
Switzerland	*Société des Emissions "Radio-Genève"	1925
	Radiogenossenschaft Bern	1925
	Société Romande de Radiophonie (Radio-Lausanne)	1927
	Société Suisse de Radiodiffusion (SSR)	1931
	Service de la Radiodiffusion Suisse	1939
Tunisia	Office des Postes, Télégraphes et Téléphones	1940
Turkey	Turkish Wireless Telephony Company	1927
	Broadcasting Service of the Department of Posts and Telegraphs	1939
	Radio-Ankara	1940
United Kingdom	*British Broadcasting Company	1925
	British Broadcasting Corporation	1927
Yugoslavia	Wireless Telegraphy Company	1926
	Radio A.D. Beograd	1929
	Radiostanica Zagreb	1928
	Radio Oddajna	1930
	Special Member	
Vatican State	Vatican Broadcasting Service	1936

	Associate Members	
Argentina	Estación de Radiodifusión del Estado, Dirección General de Correos y Telégrafos (Servicio de Radiocomunicaciones)	1938
	Asociacion de Broadcasters Argentinos (ADEBA)	1936
Australia	Amalgamated Wireless, Ltd.	1927
	Central Broadcaster, Ltd.	1927
	National Broadcasting Service	1929
	Australian Broadcasting Company	1929
	Australian Broadcasting Commission	1933
Burma	Burma State Broadcasting Service	1939
Canada	James Richardson and Sons, Ltd.	1931
	Canadian Broadcasting Corporation	1937
China	The Central Broadcasting Station (XGOA)	1936
Cuba	Telephone Company, Havana	1927
Haiti	Radio-Haiti	1939
India (British)	The Indian Broadcasting Service	1927
	All-India Radio, New Delhi	1937
Indies (Dutch)	N.V. Nederlandsch-Indische Radio Omroep Maatschappij (NIROM)	1939
Iran	Wireless Telegraphy Department, Pahlevi, at the Ministry of Posts, Telegraphs and Telephones	1939
Japan	Nihon Hoso Kyokai (JOCK Broadcasting Station)	1927
	Nippon Hoso Kyokai (Broadcasting Corporation of Japan)	1927
Kenya	British East Africa Broadcasting Company	1928
Manchukuo	Manshu Denshin Denwa Kabushiki Kaisha	1943
Mexico	Departamento Autónomo de Prensa y Publicidad	1938
Netherlands	N.V. Philip's Omroep Holland-Indie (PHOHI)	1934

Appendix A

New Zealand	New Zealand Broadcasting Board	1934
	New Zealand Broadcasting Service	1936
Peru	Administration of Posts and Telegraphs of Peru	1927
Puerto Rico	Radio Corporation of Puerto Rico	1935
South Africa	African Broadcasting Company	1929
	South African Broadcasting Corporation	1936
United States	Columbia Broadcasting System	1930
	Mutual Broadcasting System	1938
	National Association of Broadcasters	1937
	National Broadcasting Company	1927
	The Tribune Company, Chicago	1931
	World-Wide Broadcasting Foundation	1939
	Northwestern Broadcasting	1931
	Head of the Lakes Broadcasting Company	1931
Uruguay	Servicio Oficial de Difusion Radio-Eléctrica	1939

Source: IBU

Appendix B

Members of the EBU

(with the date of their admission to the Union)

(as of February 1983)

	Active Members	
Algeria	Radiodiffusion-Télévision Algérienne	1970
Austria	Österreichischer Rundfunk	1953
Belgium[1]	Belgische Radio en Televisie (BRT) Radio-Télévision Belge de la Communauté Française (RTBF)	1950
Cyprus	Cyprus Broadcasting Corporation	1969
Denmark[2]	Danmarks-Radio	1950
Federal Republic of Germany	Arbeitsgemeinschaft der öffentlichrechtlichen Rundfunkanstalten der Bundesrepublik Deutschland (ARD)	1952
	Zweites Deutsches Fernsehen	1963
Finland	Oy Yleisradio Ab	1950
France[3]	Antenne 2 France	1950
	Europe No. 1 Télécompagnie	1958
	France Regions 3	1950
	TéléDiffusion de France	1950
	Télévision Française 1	1950
Greece	Elliniki Radiophonia-Tileorassis	1950
Iceland	Rikisútvarpid	1956
Ireland	Radio Telefis Eireann	1950
Israel	Israel Broadcasting Authority	1957
Italy	RAI-Radiotelevisione Italiana	1950
Jordan	Jordan Television	1970
Lebanon	Radiodiffusion Libanaise/	1950
	Télé-Liban	1980
Libya	Libyan Jamaherya Broadcasting	1974
Luxembourg	Radio-Télé-Luxembourg	1950
Malta	Broadcasting Authority-Malta/	1950
	Xandir Malta	1982
Monaco	Radio-Télé Monte-Carlo	1950

Appendix B

Morocco	Radiodiffusion-Télévision Marocaine[4]	1950
Netherlands	Nederlandse Omroep Stichting[5]	1950
Norway	Norsk Rikskringkasting	1950
Portugal[6]	Radiodifusão Portuguesa EP	1950
	Radiotelevisão Portuguesa EP	1960
Spain	Radiotelevisión Española	1955
	Sociedad Española de Radiodifusión	1981
Sweden[7]	Sveriges Radio Ab	1950
Switzerland	Société Suisse de Radiodiffusion et Télévision	1950
Tunisia	Radiodiffusion-Télévision Tunisienne	1950
Turkey	Türkiye Radyo-Televizyon Kurumu	1950
United Kingdom	British Broadcasting Corporation	1950
	Independent Broadcasting Authority and Independent Television Companies	1960
Vatican State	Radio Vaticana	1950
Yugoslavia	Jugoslovenska Radiotelevizija	1950
Algeria	Radiodiffusion-Television Algerienne	1970
	Associate Members	
Argentina	Dirección General de Radio y Televisión	1971
Australia	Australian Broadcasting Commission	1950
	Federation of Australian Commercial Television Stations	1962
	Special Broadcasting Service	1980
Bangladesh	Bangladesh Television	1974
Barbados	Caribbean Broadcasting Corporation	1971
Brazil	Associacão Brasileira de Emissoras de Rádio e Televisão	1964
	Empresa Brasileira de Radiofusão-Radiobrás	1977
	TV Globo Ltda	1969
Canada	Agency for Tele-Education in Canada	1975
	Canadian Broadcasting Corporation	1950
	CTV Television Network Ltd.	1970
Chile	Corporación de Televisión	1970
	Universidad Católica de Chile (Canal 13)	1971
Congo	Radiodiffusion-Télévision Congolaise	1972

Djibouti	Radiodiffusion-Télévision de Djibouti	1980
Egypt[8]	Egyptian Radio and Television Corporation	1975
Gabon	Radiodiffusion-Télévision Gabonaise	1980
Ghana	Ghana Broadcasting Corporation	1958
Greenland	Grønlands Radio	1978
Guyana	Guyana Broadcasting Service	1976
Hong Kong	Rediffusion Television Ltd.	1976
	Television Broadcasts Ltd.	1981
India	All India Radio	1979
Indonesia	Radio Republik Indonesia	1972
	Televisi Republik Indonesia	1972
Iran	Islamic Republic of Iran Broadcasting	1969
Iraq	Iraqi Broadcasting and Television Establishment	1976
Ivory Coast	Radiodiffusion-Télévision Ivoirienne	1963
Jamaica	Jamaica Broadcasting Corporation	1971
Japan	Asahi National Broadcasting Company	1967
	Fuji Telecasting Company Ltd.	1969
	Mainichi Broadcasting System Inc.	1969
	National Association of Commercial Broadcasters in Japan	1967
	Nippon Hoso Kyokai	1951
	Nippon Television Network Corporation	1968
	Tokyo Broadcasting System Inc.	1967
Kenya	Voice of Kenya	1963
Kuwait	Kuwait Broadcasting and Television Service	1968
Malawi	Malawi Broadcasting Corporation	1962
Malaysia	Radio Television Malaysia	1970
Mauritius	Mauritius Broadcasting Corporation	1980
Mexico	Corporación Mexicana de Radio y Televisión SA de CV	1973
	Televisa SA	1973
New Zealand	Broadcasting Corporation of New Zealand	1950
Niger	Office de Radiodiffusion-Télévision du Niger	1963

Appendix B

Nigeria	Federal Radio Corporation of Nigeria	1962
Oman	Oman Directorate General of Radio and Television	1976
Pakistan	Pakistan Television Corporation	1969
Papua New Guinea	National Broadcasting Commission	1974
Peru	Compania Peruana de Radiodifusion	1982
Qatar	Qatar Television and Broadcasting Service	1973
Republic of Korea	Korean Broadcasting System	1974
Saudi Arabia	Saudi Arabian Broadcasting and Television Service	1970
Sénégal	Office de Radiodiffusion Télévision du Sénégal	1972
Sri Lanka	Sri Lanka Broadcasting Corporation	1951
Syria	Organisme de la Radio-Télévision Arabe Syrienne	1978
Tanzania	Radio Tanzania — Dar es Salaam	1963
United Arab Emirates	Dubai Radio and Colour Television	1975
United States	American Broadcasting Companies Inc.	1959
	CBS Inc.	1956
	Corporation for Public Broadcasting/Public Broadcasting Service/National Public Radio	1971
	National Broadcasting Company Inc.	1953
	United States Information Agency	1951
	WFMT Inc.	1981
Venezuela	Corporación Venezolana de Televisión CA	1972
	Proyecciones Orinoco CA	1977
Zaire	La Voix du Zaïre	1951
Zimbabwe	Zimbabwe Broadcasting Corporation	1981

[1] Founding member was INR, which was reorganized into BRT and RTBF in 1960.
[2] Founding member was Statsradiofonien, which became DR in 1959.
[3] Founding member was Radiodiffusion Française, which became l'Office de Radiodiffusion-Télévision Française (ORTF) in 1964. In 1975, ORTF was replaced by seven independent organizations. French broadcasting underwent another reform in 1982.
[4] Originally broadcasters from Morocco and Tunisia signed the Torquay document as a single member. Tunisia became an active member in 1957.

[5] Founding member was Stichting Nederlandsche Radio-Unie (NRU). In 1956, NRU was joined by NTS. In 1965, NRU and NTS were merged into a single supervisory body, the NOS.
[6] Founding member was Emissora Nacional de Radiodifusão.
[7] Founding member was Radiotjänst.
[8] Was an EBU founding member. Resigned in 1958 as a result of Israel's admittance. Egypt was readmitted as an associate member in 1975. Syria rejoined the EBU in 1978.

Source: EBU

Appendix C

Members of the OIRT

(with the date of their admission to the Organization)

(as of February 1983)

	Active Members	
Afghanistan	People's Radio and Television Afghanistan	1982
Algeria	Radiodiffusion-Télévision Algérienne	1982
Bulgaria	Bolgarskoe Radio i Televidenie	1946
Byelorussia	Televidenie Sovietskoio Bielorossy	1946
Cuba	Instituto Cubano de Radiodifusion	1961
Czechoslovakia	Ceskoslovenska Radio i Televize	1946
Democratic People's Republic of Korea	Radiodiffusion Coréenne	1955
Egypt	Egyptian Radio and Television Corporation	1959
Estonian SSR	Televidenie Sovietskoio Estony	1946
Finland	Oy Yleisradio Ab	1946
German Democratic Republic	Deutscher Demokratischer Rundfunk und Fernsehfunk	1951
Hungary	Magyar Radio es Televizio	1946
Kampuchea	Voice of the People of Kampuchea	1981
Latvian SSR	Latvia Televidenie	1946
Lithuanian SSR	Lietuvos Televidenie	1946
Moldavian SSR	Televidenie Sovietskoio Moldavy	1946
Mongolia	Radiodiffusion Mongole	1953
Nicaragua	Dirección de Medios de Communicación	1982
People's Democratic Republic of Yemen	PDR of Yemen Broadcasting Service	1982
Poland	Polskie Radio i Telewizja	1946
Rumania	Radiodifuziunea si Televiziunea Romana	1946

Ukrainian SSR	Televidenie Sovietskoio Ukrainy	1946
USSR	Televidenie Sovietskoio Soyuza	1946
Vietnam	La Voix du Vietnam	1956
	Associate Members	
Japan	Asahi National Broadcasting Company	1981

Source: OIRT

Appendix D

Members of Eurovision

(with the date in which they were linked to the network)

(as of February 1983)

	Members	
Belgium	Belgische Radio en Televisie (BRT)	1954
	Radio-Télévision Belge de la Communauté Français (RTBF)	1954
Denmark	Danmarks-Radio	1954
Federal Republic of Germany	Arbeitsgemeinschaft der öffentlichrechtlichen Rundfunkanstalten der Bundesrepublik Deutschland	1954
France	Télévision Française 1 Antenne 2 France Régions 3	1954
Italy	Radiotelevisione Italiana	1954
Netherlands	Nederlandse Omroep Stichting	1954
Switzerland	Schweizerische Radio und Fernsehgesellschaft Société Suisse de Radiodiffusion et Télévision Società Svizzera Radiotelevisione	1954
United Kingdom	British Broadcasting Corporation	1954
Austria	Osterreichischer Rundfunk GmbH	1956
Luxembourg	Radio-Télé-Luxembourg	1956
Monaco	Radio-Télé Monte-Carlo	1956
Sweden	Sveriges Radio	1958
Norway	Norsk Rikskringkasting	1959
United Kingdom	Independent Broadcasting Authority/Independent Television Companies	1959
Portugal	Radiotelevisão Portuguesã	1960
Spain	Televisión Española	1960
Yugoslavia	Jugoslovenska Radiotelevizija	1960

Finland	Oy Yleisradio Ab	1961
Federal Republic of Germany	Zweites Deutsches Fernsehen	1963
Ireland	Radio Telefis Eireann	1963
Algeria	Radiodiffusion-Télévision Algeriénne	1966
Tunisia	Radiodiffusion-Télévision Tunisienne	1966
Morocco	Radiodiffusion-Télévision Marocaine	
Greece	Elliniki Radiophonia Tileorassis	1969
Israel	Israel Broadcasting Authority	1972
Jordan	Jordan Television	1972
Turkey	Türkiye Radyo-Televizyon Kurumu	1974
Libya	Libyan Jamaherya Broadcasting	1976
Cyprus	Cyprus Broadcasting Corporation	1982
Iceland	Rikisutvarpid	1983

Source: EBU

Appendix E

Members of Intervision

(with the date in which they were linked to the network)

(as of February 1983)

	Members	
Czechoslovakia	Ceskoslovenska Televize	1960
German Democratic Republic	Deutscher Fernsehfunk	1960
Hungary	Magyar Televizio	1960
Poland	Polskie Telewizya	1960
USSR	Televidenie Sovietskoio Soyuza	1961
Bulgaria	Bolgarskoe Radio i Televidenie	1962
Rumania	Radiodifuziunea si Televiziunea Romana	1962
Finland	Oy Yleisradio Ab	1965
Mongolia	Radiodiffusion Mongole	1972
Cuba	Instituto Cubano de Radiodifusión	1979
Democratic People's Republic of Korea	Radiodiffusion Coréenne	1980
Vietnam	La Voix du Vietnam	1980
Afghanistan	People's Radio and Television Afghanistan	1982

Source: OIRT

Appendix F

Growth of the Eurovision Program Exchange

1954 — 1982

Year	Total Number of Programs Transmitted	Total Number of Hours Transmitted
1954	55	73 h
1955	91	115 h
1956	250	273 h
1957	207	261 h
1958	203	259 h
1959	292	339 h
1960	498	440 h
1961	679	606 h
1962	476	586 h
1963	602	762 h
1964	480	664 h
1965	541	743 h
1966	563	813 h
1967	617	812 h
1968	636	898 h
1969	668	951 h
1970	645	986 h
1971	662	1097 h
1972	709	1138 h
1973	663	1164 h
1974	758	1102 h
1975	763	1237 h
1976	756	1235 h
1977	791	1109 h
1978	824	1488 h
1979	833	1460 h
1980	894	1689 h
1981	926	1842 h
1982	963	1942 h

Source: EBU

Appendix G

Growth of the Eurovision News Exchange

1960 — 1982

Year	Total Number of News Items Transmitted
1960	150
1961	450
1962	951
1963	1246
1964	1134
1965	1267
1966	1540
1967	2009
1968	2419
1969	3087
1970	3800
1971	4278
1972	4564
1973	5423
1974	5085
1975	6018
1976	6353
1977	5410
1978	5934
1979	6696
1980	6803
1981	6820
1982	7636

Source: EBU

Appendix H

Type of Eurovision Programs: Number and Percentage

(excludes the Eurovision news exchange)

Year	Sports	Current Affairs	Light Entertainment	Religion	Drama/ Music	Folklore
1954	28 50.9%	4 7.2%	9 16.3%	4 7.2%	2 3.6%	8 14.5%
1955	53 58.2	8 8.7	13 14.2	7 7.6	5 5.4	5 5.4
1956	178 71.2	26 10.4	17 6.8	11 4.4	12 4.8	6 2.4
1957	121 58.4	39 18.8	26 12.5	6 2.8	14 6.7	1 0.4
1958	125 61.5	24 11.8	25 12.3	8 3.9	18 8.8	3 1.4
1959	145 49.6	86 29.4	19 6.5	11 3.7	21 7.1	10 3.4
1960	276 55.4	148 29.7	18 3.6	13 2.6	32 6.4	11 2.2
1961	293 43.1	314 46.2[a]	20 2.9	22 3.2	27 3.9	3 0.4
1962	323 67.8	73 15.3	27 5.6	24 5.0	24 5.0	5 1.0
1963	400 66.4	131 21.7	22 3.6	22 3.6	23 3.8	4 0.6
1964	342 71.2	84 17.5	14 2.9	15 3.1	20 4.1	5 1.0
1965	381 70.4	84 15.5	29 5.3	25 4.6	7 1.2	15 2.7
1966	418 74.2	77 13.6	45 7.9	18 3.1	2 0.3	3 0.5
1967	463 75.0	86 13.9	24 3.8	30 4.8	13 2.1	1 0.1
1968	471 74.0	97 15.2	38 5.9	21 3.3	8 1.2	1 0.1
1969	423 63.3	115 23.2	52 7.7	22 3.2	14 2.0	2 0.2
1970	518 80.3	55 8.5	48 7.4	14 2.1	10 1.5	0 0.0
1971	515 77.7	81 12.2	38 5.7	17 2.5	6 0.9	5 0.7
1972	553 77.9	92 12.9	36 5.0	17 2.3	9 1.2	2 0.2
1973	535 80.6	67 10.1	36 5.4	15 2.2	7 1.0	3 0.4
1974	660 87.0	51 6.7	27 3.5	11 1.4	4 0.5	5 0.6
1975	634 83.0	76 9.9	17 2.2	18 2.3	9 1.1	9 1.1
1976	634 83.8	67 8.8	24 3.1	20 2.6	6 0.7	5 0.6
1977	664 83.9	61 7.7	26 3.2	20 2.5	18 2.2	2 0.2
1978	703 85.3	34 4.1	41 4.9	18 2.1	18 2.1	10 1.2
1979	641 76.9	75 9.0	43 5.1	43 5.1	26 3.1	5 0.6
1980	744 83.2	72 8.0	31 3.4	18 2.0	21 2.3	8 0.8
1981	774 83.6	68 7.4	42 4.5	15 1.6	23 2.5	4 0.4
1982	775 80.4	100 10.4	37 3.8	22 2.3	27 2.8	2 0.2

Source: EBU
[a] Includes news items.

Appendix I

Growth of the Intervision Program Exchange

1960 — 1982

Year	Total Number of Programs Transmitted	Total Number of Hours Transmitted
1960	153	170 h
1961	131	213 h
1962	214	300 h
1963	338	392 h
1964	519	498 h
1965	556	552 h
1966	543	496 h
1967	612	641 h
1968	543	529 h
1969	711	877 h
1970	825	943 h
1971	841	873 h
1972	1105	1124 h
1973	1212	1342 h
1974	1218	1351 h
1975	1389	1587 h
1976	1524	1773 h
1977	1964	2009 h
1978	1769	1869 h
1979	1709	1843 h
1980	2188	2759 h
1981	1764	1826 h
1982	1898	1910 h

Source: OIRT

Appendix J

Growth of the Intervision News Exchange

1964 — 1982

Year	Total Number of News Items Transmitted
1964	500[a]
1965	1000[a]
1966	1441
1967	1326
1968	1430
1969	2380
1970	2815
1971	2792
1972	2634
1973	2411
1974	3366
1975	3612
1976	4672
1977	4984
1978	5162
1979	5257
1980	5260
1981	5461
1982	5205

Source: OIRT

[a] Estimated

Appendix K

Type of Intervision Programs: Number and Percentage

(excludes the Intervision news exchange)

Year	Sports	Current Affairs	Culture	Entertainment	Children's Programs
1960	99 64.7%	7 4.5%	19 12.4%	17 11.1%	11 7.1%
1961	64 48.8	15 11.4	25 19.0	15 11.4	12 9.1
1962	105 40.0	30 14.0	32 14.9	22 10.2	25 11.6
1963	93 27.5	117 34.6	56 16.5	31 9.1	41 12.1
1964	97 18.7	212 40.9	91 17.5	63 12.1	55 10.6
1965	127 22.8	205 36.8	103 18.5	62 11.1	59 10.6
1966	147 27.0	166 30.5	107 19.7	53 9.7	70 12.8
1967	161 26.3	165 26.9	99 16.1	88 14.3	99 16.1
1968	100 18.4	121 22.2	129 23.7	89 16.3	104 19.1
1969	201 28.2	132 18.5	137 19.2	163 22.9	78 10.9
1970	180 21.8	187 22.6	206 24.9	129 15.6	123 14.9
1971	232 27.5	140 16.6	185 21.9	182 21.6	102 12.1
1972	259 23.4	159 14.3	288 26.0	305 27.6	94 8.5
1973	321 26.4	138 11.3	300 24.7	367 30.2	86 7.0
1974	359 29.4	225 18.4	285 23.3	279 22.9	70 5.7
1975	375 26.9	421 30.3	269 19.3	275 19.7	49 3.5
1976	376 24.6	487 31.9	274 17.9	333 21.8	54 3.5
1977	499 25.4	665 33.8	326 16.5	369 18.7	105 5.3
1978	437 24.7	521 29.4	356 20.1	394 22.2	61 3.4
1979	441 25.8	531 31.0	347 20.3	324 18.9	66 3.8
1980	708 32.3	611 27.9	402 18.3	385 17.5	82 3.7
1981	426 24.1	605 34.3	333 18.8	355 20.1	45 2.5
1982	343 18.0	685 36.0	413 21.7	403 21.2	54 2.8

Source: OIRT

Appendix L

Growth of the Eurovision-Intervision Program Exchange

1960 — 1982

Year	Eurovision Programs to Intervision[a]	Eurovision Programs from Intervision[b]
1960	74	22
1961	54	30
1962	38	49
1963	87	48
1964	246	34
1965	148	59
1966	199	62
1967	174	47
1968	265	20
1969	171	68
1970	204	73
1971	253	40
1972	595	58
1973	285	72
1974	413	57
1975	323	79
1976	555	83
1977	377	83
1978	352	90
1979	423	87
1980	414	93
1981	402	97
1982	384	46

Source: [a]Figures from the OIRT. No figures on total transmission hours available.
[b]Figures from the EBU.

Appendix M

Growth of the Eurovision-Intervision News Exchange

1966 — 1982

Year	Eurovision Programs to Intervision[a]	Eurovision Programs from Intervision[b]
1966	709	167
1967	832	93
1968	1590	206
1969	2111	272
1970	2464	275
1971	2911	291
1972	3060	222
1973	3115	175
1974	2486	215
1975	2853	251
1976	3103	257
1977	4324	241
1978	5106	273
1979	5812	319
1980	6121	356
1981	5830	512
1982	6797	384

Source: [a]Figures from the OIRT.
[b]Figures from the EBU.

Appendix N

Type of Eurovision-Intervision Programs: Number of Transmissions
(excludes the EVN-IVN news exchange)
1972-1982

			Eurovision Programs to Intervision			
Year	Total	Sports	Current Affairs	Entertainment	Culture	Children
1972	595	564	8	10	12	1
1973	285	240	22	17	5	1
1974	413	383	12	11	7	0
1975	323	302	3	10	7	1
1976	555	519	11	16	6	3
1977	377	342	15	7	12	1
1978	352	316	2	19	14	1
1979	423	368	21	22	10	2
1980	414	368	22	15	9	0
1981	402	366	10	10	15	1
1982	384	352	3	13	15	1

			Eurovision Programs from Intervision			
Year	Total	Sports	Current Affairs	Entertainment	Culture	Children
1972	111	94	13	3	1	0
1973	128	113	12	3	0	0
1974	104	93	10	1	0	0
1975	136	124	10	2	0	0
1976	122	113	7	1	1	0
1977	121	111	4	2	4	0
1978	115	112	2	1	0	0
1979	154	123	27	1	3	0
1980	93	84	7	1	1	0
1981	179	166	9	0	4	0
1982	111	103	5	1	2	0

Source: OIRT

Appendix O

Origins of Intervision Programs 1960-1982

	Bulgaria		Cuba		Czecho-slovakia		East Germany		Finland		Hungary		Poland		Rumania		USSR	
	No.	Hrs.	No.	Hrs.	No.	Hrs.	No.	Hrs.	No.	Hrs.	No.	Hrs.	No.	Hrs.	No.	Hrs.	No.	Hrs.
1960	–	–	–	–	43	59	79	80	–	–	16	25	15	6	–	–	–	–
1961	–	–	–	–	44	75	54	100	–	–	13	16	20	22	–	–	–	–
1962	–	–	–	–	62	119	49	67	–	–	21	27	37	39	–	–	–	–
1963	10	2	–	–	52	80	60	75	–	–	29	37	52	51	16	9	45	48
1964	21	22	–	–	70	81	50	54	–	–	67	63	79	78	40	37	119	138
1965	27	24	–	–	61	94	80	80	1	1	55	66	83	61	24	24	192	163
1966	19	16	–	–	70	87	78	82	9	4	53	61	61	70	20	17	225	202
1967	39	41	–	–	68	87	69	72	20	29	42	52	83	77	41	34	233	159
1968	55	54	–	–	68	85	80	94	4	2	39	36	74	73	40	36	250	249
1969	40	51	–	–	68	95	125	184	8	4	65	63	112	133	60	77	183	149
1970	71	100	–	–	120	128	143	158	2	2	74	85	88	103	49	59	233	270
1971	86	116	–	–	167	144	161	150	7	26	75	54	109	127	39	52	278	308
1972	85	94	–	–	257	261	174	191	2	1	78	75	173	161	89	84	197	205
1973	63	66	–	–	248	284	300	354	1	1	59	55	202	164	55	50	247	257
1974	80	128	30	73	210	225	277	309	5	6	80	74	235	220	34	35	284	370
1975	57	47	15	24	226	275	318	337	21	24	94	102	177	164	38	36	267	282
1976	78	75	3	7	224	268	347	395	6	10	93	74	189	232	42	48	443	577
1977	161	209	3	8	213	251	395	407	34	65	184	142	147	155	63	49	542	664
1978	91	95	50	70	323	418	331	317	28	42	131	89	171	163	28	25	764	723
1979	150	139	26	22	201	270	395	395	8	16	129	114	201	194	63	67	577	572
1980	164	130	19	49	286	313	386	388	2	2	166	143	196	176	55	50	536	626
1981[a]	152	149	16	21	274	324	315	300	17	43	202	178	119	111	50	47	603	600
1982[b]	103	88	21	20	329	299	311	310	29	61	253	269	82	71	43	37	613	642
																	719	752

[a] In 1981, Mongolian television originated 6 programs (11 hours).
[b] In 1982, Laos television originated 2 programs (1 hour) and Vietnamese television originated 6 programs (2 hours).

Source: OIRT

LIST OF ACRONYMS

ABC	American Broadcasting Companies, United States
ABU	Asia-Pacific Broadcasting Union
AIR	Asociación Inter-Americana de Radiodifusión
ARD	Arbeitsgemeinschaft der öffentlichrechtlichen Rundfunkanstalten der Bundesrepublik Deutschland (Working Committee of the Public Broadcasting Corporations of Federal Republic of Germany), Federal Republic of Germany
ASBU	Arab States Broadcasting Union
BBC	British Broadcasting Corporation, United Kingdom
BIEM	Bureau International de l'Edition Mécanique (International Bureau of the Societies Administering the Rights of Mechanical Recording and Reproduction)
BRT	Belgische Radio en Televisie, Belgium
BT	Bolgarskoe Radio i Televidenie, Bulgaria
BUs	Basic Units
CATV	Cable Television
CBA	Commonwealth Broadcasting Association
CBS	Columbia Broadcasting System, United States
CBU	Caribbean Broadcasting Union
CCIR	Comité Consultatif International des Radiocommunications (International Radio Consultative Committee), International Telecommunication Union
CCITT	Comité Consultatif International Télégraphique et Téléphonique (International Telegraph and Telephone Consultative Committee), International Telecommunication Union
CDU/CSU	Christian Democratic Union, Federal Republic of Germany
CEM	Centre d'Ecoutes et de Mesures (Receiving and Measuring Station), European Broadcasting Union
CEPT	Conférence Européenne des Postes et Télécommunications (European Conference of Postal and Telecommunications Administrations)
CLT	Compagnie Luxembourgeoise de Télédiffusion, Luxembourg
COMECON	Council of Mutual Economic Assistance
COMSAT	Communications Satellite Corporation
CST	Ceskoslovenska Radio i Televize, Czechoslovakia
DDR-F	Deutscher Demokratischer Rundfunk und Fernsehfunk, German Democratic Republic
DR	Danmarks Radio, Denmark
EBU	European Broadcasting Union
ECOSOC	Economic and Social Council, United Nations
ECS	European Communications Satellite
EIAR	Ente Italiano per le Audizioni Radiofoniche, Italy
ENG	Electronic News Gathering
ERT	Elliniki RadiophoniaTileorassis, Greece

ESA	European Space Agency
EVC	Eurovision Control Center, European Broadcasting Union
EVN	Eurovision News Exchange
FIA	Fédération Internationale des Acteurs (International Federation of Actors)
FIAV	Fédération Internationale des Artistes de Variétés (International Federation of Variety Artists)
FIM	Fédération Internationale des Musiciens (International Federation of Musicians)
IBA	Independent Broadcasting Authority, United Kingdom
IBU	International Broadcasting Union (also known as UIR)
ICR	Instituto Cubano de Radiodifusión, Cuba
IEC	International Electrotechnical Commission
IFPI	International Federation of Phonographic Industry
IFRB	International Frequency Registration Board, International Telecommunication Union
ILO	International Labor Organization or International Labor Office
INCA	National Audiovisual Communications Institute, France
INR	Institut National Belge de Radiodiffusion, Belgium
INTELSAT	International Telecommunications Satellite Organization
IOC	International Olympic Committee
IPCC	Intervision Program Coordination Center, International Radio and Television Organization
IRI	Istituto per la Ricostruzione Industriale, Italy
ISO	International Organization for Standardization
ITCC	Intervision Technical Coordination Center, International Radio and Television Organization
ITN	Independent Television News, United Kingdom
ITU	International Telecommunication Union
ITV	Independent Television, United Kingdom
IVN	Intervision News Exchange
JRT	Jugoslovenska Radiotelevizija, Yugoslavia
LF	Low Frequency
MF	Medium Frequency
MTV	Magyar Radio es Telvizio, Hungary
NANBA	North American National Broadcasters Association
NBC	National Broadcasting Company, United States
NDR	Norddeutscher Rundfunk, Federal Republic of Germany
NHK	Nippon Hoso Kyokai, Japan
NOS	Nederlandse Omroep Stichting, Netherlands
NRK	Norsk Rikskringkasting, Norway
NRU	Stichting Nederlandsche Radio-Unie, Netherlands
NSF	Nederlandsche Seintoestellen Fabriek, Netherlands
NTS	Nederlandse Televisie Stichting, Netherlands

List of Acronyms

NTSC		National Television System Committee
OIR		Organisation Internationale de Radiodiffusion (International Broadcasting Organization)
OIRT		Organisation Internationale de Radiodiffusion et Télévision (International Radio and Television Organization)
ORF		Österreichischer Rundfunk, Austria
ORTF		Office de Radiodiffusion-Télévision Française, France
OTI		Organización de la Televisión Iberoamericana
PAL		Phase Alternating Line
PBS		Public Broadcasting System, United States
PCC		Production Coordination Circuits, Eurovision
PKN		Program Conference Network, Intervision
PNS		Permanent Sound Network, Eurovision
PNV		Permanent Vision Network, Eurovision
PTT		Posts, Telegraph and Telephone Administration
RAI		Radiotelevisione Italiana, Italy
RIAS		Rundfunk in American Sector, West Berlin
RMC		Radio-Télé Monte-Carlo
RRG		Reichsrundfunkgesellschaft, Germany
RTBF		Radio-Télévision Belge de la Communauté Française, Belgium
RTE		Radio Telefis Eireann, Ireland
RTF		Radiodiffusion-Télévision Française, France
RTL		Radio-Télé-Luxembourg, Luxembourg
RTP		Radiotelevisão Portuguesa EP, Portugal
RTVE		Radiotelevisión Española, Spain
SACD		Société des Auteurs et Compositeurs Dramatiques (Society of Dramatic Authors and Composers)
SECAM		Séquentiel à Mémorie
SICUIR		Société Immobilière du Centre de Controle de l'Union Internationale de Radiodiffusion
SIN		Servicio Iberoamericano de Noticias
SOFIRAD		Société Financière de Radiodiffusion, France
SPD		Social Democratic Party, Federal Republic of Germany
SR		Sveriges Radio AB, Sweden
SRF		Société Nationale de Radiodiffusion (Radio France), France
SSR		Société Suisse de Radiodiffusion et Télévision, Switzerland
SVT		Sveriges Television Ab, Sweden
TCC		Technical Coordination Circuits, Eurovision
TDF		Télédiffusion de France, France
TF 1		Télévision Française 1, France
TSS		Televidenie Sovietskoio Soyuza, USSR
TV		Television
TVE		Televisión Española, Spain
TVP		Polskie Telewizja, Poland

TVR	Radiodifuziunea si Televiziunea Romiana, Rumania
UIE	Union Internationale des Editeurs (International Union of Editors)
UIR	Union Internationale de Radiodiffusion (International Broadcasting Union)
UNESCO	United Nations Educational, Scientific, and Cultural Organization
UPITN	United Press International Television News
URI	Unione Radiofonica Italiana, Italy
URTNA	Union des Radiodiffusions et Télévisions Nationales d'Afrique (Union of National Radio and Television Organizations of Africa)
VIS	Visnews
VTR	Videotape Recorders
VUs	Vision Units
WARC-BS	World Administrative Radio Conference on Broadcasting-Satellites
WIPO	World Intellectual Property Organization
YLE	Oy Yleisradio Ab, Finland
ZDF	Zweites Deutsches Fernsehen (Second German Television), Federal Republic of Germany

BIBLIOGRAPHY

SOURCES

Documents of International Organizations

European Broadcasting Union

Collection of Legal Recommendations and Decisions of the Administrative Council and the General Assembly.

EBU Statutes Revision, Presentation Report. Geneva: EBU, 1982.

Eurovision, EBU Administrative Council Ruling on Cost-Sharing. September 1975.

Eurovision News Confirmation of Participation and Usage.

Eurovision Program Summaries.

Principles on Advertising at Venues for Internationally Televised Sports Events. Administrative Council Decision, December 11, 1976.

Statutes of the European Broadcasting Union. Geneva: EBU, 1982.

Television News in Eurovision and Intervision. Report by Tapio Varis, EBU Doc. no. O.A./5013-Com. Pro/1343, September 1974.

Weekly Liaison Bulletins.

International Broadcasting Union

Activities of the International Broadcasting Union and Its Post-War Plan. Geneva: IBU, 1945.

Memorandum on the Activities of the International Broadcasting Union for the Use of Broadcasting in the Cause of Peace. IBU Doc., Serial no. 5970, August 1936.

The Problems of Broadcasting. Geneva: IBU, 1930.

Statutes of the International Broadcasting Union. Geneva: IBU, 1925.

Twenty Years of Activity of the International Broadcasting Union. Geneva, IBU, 1945.

International Radio and Television Organization

International Radio and Television Organization, General Information. OIRT Doc. no. 17878 M/E.

Information über den Austausch zwischen der Eurovision und Intervision. Prague: OIRT, (no date).

Intervision Regeln für den Aktualitätenaustausch zwischen den Intervisionsländern. Prague: PKCI, May 1971.

Intervision Rules Governing the International Television Program Exchange Among OIRT Member Countries. Prague: OIRT, 1960.

Intervisionsstatistik des Programmaustausches zwischen Intervisionsmitgliedern und zwischen Intervision und Eurovision 1960-1982.

Reglement der Intervision. Prague: OIRT, 1964.

Statistik des Aktualitätenaustausches zwischen den Intervisionslandern 1966-1982.

Statuts de l'Organisation Internationale de Radiodiffusion et Télévision. Tampere, 1969.

United Nations

The International Convention Concerning the Use of Broadcasting in the Cause of Peace, Geneva, 1936. Doc. E/CN. 4/Sub. 1/104.

WORKS

Books

Unpublished

Barber, Russell B. "Eurovision as an Expression of International Cooperation in Western Europe." Ph.D. dissertation, Northwestern University, 1963.

Bellac, Paul. "L'Origine de l'Eurovision." Bern, 1962.

Bombardier, Denise. "The Conception of News in Western Countries." Paper submitted to the Symposium on the Nature, Content, and Values of News in Diverse European Social Systems, organized by the Polish Institute of International Affairs and the Graduate Institute of International Studies, held in Krakow, Poland, 6-8 May, 1976.

Dickinson, J. Treeby. "News Exchanges in Eurovision." Paper presented to the 2nd International Television Symposium, 30 April-4 May, 1962, Montreux, Switzerland.

European Cooperation Research Organization. "Broadcasting, East and West." Report no. 6, London, 1975.

Larrue, Madeleine. "Talk by Mrs. Larrue on the Legal Aspects of Eurovision." Briefing for Eurovision Program Staff on December 11, 1967.

Ruby, John E. "The Daily News Exchange Scheme of the European Broadcasting Union." Master's Thesis, Indiana University, May 1965.

Sherman, Charles E. "The Structure and Functions of the European Broadcasting Union." Ph.D. dissertation, Wayne State University, May 1967.

Smith, Anthony. "News Values and the Ethic of Journalism — A View of the Western Tradition." Paper submitted to the Symposium on the Nature, Content, and Values of News in Diverse European Social Systems, organized by the Polish Institute of International Affairs and the Graduate Institute of International Studies, held in Krakow, Poland, 6-8 May 1976.

Szecsko, Tamas. "Broken Mirror or Magnifying Glass? Notes on the Concept of News Values." Paper submitted to the Symposium on the Nature, Content, and Values of News in Diverse European Social Systems, organized by the Polish Institute of International Affairs and the Graduate Institute of International Studies, held in Krakow, Poland, 6-8 May 1976.

Published

Academy for Educational Development. *The United States and the Debate on the World Information Order*. Washington DC: Academy for Educational Development, 1978.

Bielenstein, Dieter. *Towards A New World Information Order: Consequences for Development Policy*. Bonn: Institut für Internationale Begegnungen, 1979.

Brack, Hans. *The Evolution of the EBU Through Its Statutes from 1950 to 1976*. Geneva: EBU, 1976.

Bures, Oldrich, ed. *Current Views on the World Information Order*. Prague: International Organization of Journalists, 1977.

Carnegie Endowment for International Peace and the Twentieth Century Fund. *Planning for a Planet: An International Discussion on the Structure of Satellite Communications*. New York: Carnegie Endowment for International Peace and the Twentieth Century Fund, 1971.

Chayes, Abram; Fawcett, James; Ito, Masami; Kiss, Alexandre-Charles, et al. *Satellite Broadcasting*. London: Oxford University Press, 1973.

Codding, George A. Jr. *Broadcasting Without Barriers*. Paris: UNESCO, 1959.

─────── . *The International Telecommunication Union: An Experiment in International Cooperation*. Leiden: Brill, 1952.

Conteras, Eduardo; Larson, James; Mayo, John K.; and Spain, Peter. *Cross-Cultural Broadcasting*. Paris: UNESCO, 1976.

Courteix, Simone. *Télévisions sans frontières; un problème de coopération internationale*. Paris: Economica, 1975.

da Costa, Alcino Louis; Aboubakr, Yehia; Chopra, Pran, and Matta, Fernando Reyes Matta. *News Values and Principles of Cross-Cultural Communication*. Paris: UNESCO, 1980.

Debbasch, Charles. *Traité du droit de la radiodiffusion*. Paris: R. Vancon, 1967.

Emery, Walter B. *National and International Systems of Broadcasting: Their History, Operation and Control.* East Lansing, MI: Michigan State University Press, 1969.

Fisher, Glen. *American Communication in a Global Society.* Norwood, NJ: Ablex Publishing Corporation, 1979.

Green, Timothy. *The Universal Eye: World Television in the Seventies.* London: The Bodley Head, 1972.

International Commission for the Study of Communication Problems. *Interim Report on Communication Problems in Modern Society.* Paris: UNESCO, 1978.

Martin, L. John. *International Propaganda: Its Legal and Diplomatic Control.* Minneapolis: University of Minneosta Press, 1958.

Namurois, Albert. *Structures and Organization of Broadcasting in the Framework of Radiocommunications.* Geneva: EBU, 1972.

Nordenstreng, Kaarle, and Schiller, Herbert I., eds. *National Sovereignty and International Communication.* Norwood, NJ: Ablex Publishing Corporation, 1979.

Nordenstreng, Kaarle and Varis, Tapio. *Television Traffic – A One-Way Street? A Survey and Analysis of the International Flow of Television Program Material.* Paris: UNESCO, 1974.

Paulu, Burton. *Radio and Television Broadcasting in Eastern Europe.* Minneapolis: University of Minnesota Press, 1974.

_____.*Radio and Television Broadcasting on the European Continent.* Minneapolis: University of Minnesota Press, 1967.

Siebert, Fred. S.; Peterson, Theodore; and Schramm, Wilbur L. *Four Theories of the Press: The Authoritarian, Libertarian, Social Responsibility and Soviet Communist Concepts of What the Press Should Be and Do.* Urbana: University of Illinois Press, 1956.

Signitzer, Benno. *Regulation of Direct Broadcasting from Satellites. The U.N. Involvement.* New York: Praeger Publishers, 1976.

Smith, Anthony. *The Shadow in the Cave: A Study of the Relationship Between the Broadcaster, His Audience and the State.* London: Quartet Books Ltd., 1976.

Smith, Delbert D. *International Telecommunication Control; International Law and the Ordering of Satellite and Other Forms of International Broadcasting.* Leiden: A.W. Sijthoff, 1969.

Sommeriad, E. Lloyd. *National Communication Systems: Some Policy Issues and Options.* Paris: UNESCO, 1975.

Tomlinson, John D. *The International Control of Radiocommunications.* Geneva: Imprimerie des "Journal de Genève," 1938.

Varis, Tapio and Jokelin, Renny. *Television News in Europe, A Survey of the News-film Flow in Europe.* Tampere, Finland: University of Tampere, 1976.

Varis, Tapio; Salinas, Raquel; and Jokelin, Renny. *International News and the New Information Order*. Tampere, Finland: University of Tampere, 1977.

Vasari, Bruno. *Financial Aspects of Broadcasting*. Geneva: EBU, 1965.

Wetting, Gerhard. *Broadcasting and Détente, Eastern Policies and Their Implications for East-West Relations*. New York: St. Martin's Press, 1977.

Wygledowski, Waclaw. *Daily News Exchange on the Intervision Network 1964-1976*. Prague: OIRT, 1977.

Wykes, James. *Echanges internationaux de programmes de télévision scolaire: problèmes juridiques et économiques: une étude européenne*. Strasbourg: Council of Europe, 1966.

Articles

"A propos de la création de l'Intervision." *OIRT Radiodiffusion-Television* no. 8, 1960, pp. 71-75.

Bellac, Paul. "Origin and First Steps of the EBU Program Committee, Start of Eurovision." *EBU Review*, no. 85B, May 1964, pp. 21-24.

Bezençon, Marcel. "The Birth of Eurovision." *EBU Review*, 30:3, May 1979, pp. 20-24.

_____."Eurovision Under Examination." *EBU Bulletin*, no. 37, May-June 1956, pp. 349-352.

Borodich, S.V.; Kantor, L.Y.; and Kurilov, S.P. "The Intersputnik International Communications Satellite System." *Telecommunication Journal*, 45:3, March 1978, pp. 116-123.

Bourely, Michel. "L'Eurovision et les satellites européennes de télécommunications." *L'utilisation des satellites de diffusion directe*, Paris: PUF, 1970, pp. 31-36.

Buckalew, James. "News Elements and Selection by TV News Editors." *Journal of Broadcasting*, 14:4, Winter 1969, pp. 47-54.

Caze, Marcel. "Eurovision: The Legal Aspects." *EBU Review*, 30:3, May 1979, pp. 50-54.

"Creation of European Broadcasting Union (EBU)." *IBU Monthly Bulletin*, no. 290, April 1950, pp. 268-274.

Curran, Charles. "Eurovision and the News Agencies: A Reply." *EBU Review*, 30:6, November 1979, pp. 30-32.

de Sola Pool, Ithiel. "Direct-Broadcast Satellites and Cultural Integrity." *Trans-Action*, 12:5, September-October 1975, pp. 47-56.

_____."The Functions of Mass Media in International Exchange." *UNESCO Handbook of International Exchanges*, Paris: UNESCO, 1965, pp. 63-72.

Dickinson, J. Treeby. "Birth and Growth of Eurovision." *EBU Review*, no. 175A, June 1979, pp. 107-113.

Douglas, J.N. "Quality Control of the Eurovision Permanent Vision Network." *EBU Review*, no. 175A, June 1979, pp. 120-127.

Edera, Bruno. "An International Survey of the Animated Film in Television." *EBU Review*, 31:1, January 1980, pp. 10-24.

"Europe's Twin News Exchanges Keep the World Posted." *BM/E's World Broadcast News*, 5:5, January 1983, pp. 17-19.

Fernandez-Shaw, Felix. "Television Relations Between Europe and Latin America, (Part I)." *EBU Review*, 22:4, July 1971, pp. 43-45.

_____."Television Relations Between Europe and Latin America, (Part II)." *EBU Review*, 22:5, September 1971, pp. 22-25.

Fischer, Heinz-Dietrich. "The Contribution of Eurovision and Intervision to Global Television." *International and Intercultural Communication*, ed. by Heinz-Dietrich Fischer and John C. Merrill, New York: Hastings House Publishers, 1976. pp. 350-371.

Greco, P. "Monopoly in Television Broadcasting Services and Freedom of Expression." *EBU Review*, no. 64B, November 1960, pp. 29-34.

Hansen, Georges. "Evolution of the Activities of the EBU Since Its Establishment." *ASBU Technical Review*, 1:1, January 1974, pp. 9-15.

_____."The Technical Adventure of Eurovision." *EBU Review*, no. 143A, February 1974, pp. 2-3.

_____."Some Technical Aspects of Eurovision." *Telecommunication Journal*, 28:7, July 1961, pp. 441-448.

Hansen, Georges and Griffiths, Eric. "World-Wide Television." *Journal of the SMPTE*, 80:6, June 1971, pp. 459-464.

Harwood, Kenneth. "The International Radio and Television Organization." *Journal of Broadcasting*, 5:4, Winter 1960-61, pp. 61-72.

Hondius, Fritz W. "International Control of Broadcasting Programs in Western Europe." *The International Law of Communications*, 1971, pp. 69-84.

"International Sales of Children's Programming Subject to Varied National Perspectives." *Television/Radio Age International*, 3:6, June 1980, pp. A-23-A-32.

Jancik, Horst G. "The Exchange of News Between Eurovision and Intervision." *EBU Review*, 26:3, May 1975, pp. 26-27.

Kressley, Konrad M. "Eurovision: Distributing Costs and Benefits in an International Broadcasting Union." *Journal of Broadcasting*, 22:1, Spring 1978, pp. 179-193.

Kries, William von. "Intersputnik-Socialistisches Gegenstück zu Intelsat." *Zeitschrift für Luftrecht und Weltraumrechtsfragen*, 1:1, January 1973, pp. 12-20.

Länsipuro, Yrjö. "Joint Eurovision/Intervision News Study." *EBU Review*, 26:3, May 1975, pp. 37-40.

———."Newsfilm Agencies Out of Focus?" *Intermedia*, 5:8, August 1977, pp. 10-11.

Nichols, Josef C. "Some Aspects of Direct Satellite Broadcasting." *EBU Review*, 25:3, May 1974, pp. 10-19.

O'Brien, Richard S.; Monroe, Robert B.; and Anderson, Charles E.; "101 Years of Television Technology." *SMPTE Journal*, 85:7, July 1976, pp. 457-480.

Rengelink, J.W. "Eurovision News — A First Step to Worldwide News." *EBU Review*, no. 91B, May 1965, pp. 10-13.

———."The Eurovision News Transmissions." *EBU Review*, no. 85B, May 1964, pp. 12-13.

———."Operation Eurojournal." *EBU Review*, no. 10B, July 1959, pp. 15-17.

———."Origin and Development of the News Exchange." *EBU Review*, 30:3, May 1979, pp. 25-28.

Romantsov, V.P. "Intersputnik — Taking Part in the Olympiad — 80 Coverage." *OIRT Radio-Television*, no. 1, 1979, pp. 15-20.

Sherman, Charles E. "The International Broadcasting Union: A Study in Practical Internationalism." *EBU Review*, 25:3, May 1974, pp. 32-36.

———."OIRT." *International Broadcasting*, Washington, DC: Association for Professional Broadcasting Education, 1971, pp. 13-21.

———."Turmoil and Transition in International Broadcasting Organizations: 1938-1950." *Journal of Broadcasting*, Summer 1971, pp. 265-273.

Sherman, Charles E. and Ruby, John. "The Eurovision News Exchange." *Journalism Quarterly*, 51:3, Autumn 1974, pp. 478-485.

van Larebeke, Gaston. "Technical Side of Television News Exchanges." *EBU Review*, 26:3, May 1975, pp. 15-20.

Varis, Tapio. "European Broadcasting and the New International Information Order." *International News and the New Information Order*, ed. by Tapio Varis, Raquel Salinas, and Renny Jokelin, Tampere: University of Tampere, 1977, pp. 101-133.

———."European Television Exchanges and Connections with the Rest of the World." *Instant Research on Peace and Violence*, 1:1, 1973, pp. 27-44.

Vilcek, Miroslav. "Twenty-Five Years of TV Exchanges Via Eurovision." *Television*, 17:4, July-August 1979, pp. 7-10.

Von Plato, Heinz. "Eurovision and Youth Programs." *EBU Review*, no. 84B, March 1964, pp. 6-7.

Wallenborn, Léo. "From IBU to EBU: The Great European Broadcasting Crisis." *EBU Review*, 29:1, Part I, January 1978, pp. 25-34, Part 2, March 1978, pp. 22-30.

Wygledowski, Waclaw. "Intervision: The Growth of an Exchange." *Intermedia*, 11:6, June 1978, pp. 24-27.

———. "IVN-Daily News Exchanges on the Intervision Network." *OIRT Radio-Television*, no. 1, 1971, pp. 3-10.

———. "Television News Broadcasts in Intervision Countries." *EBU Review*, 26:3, May 1975, pp. 55-57.